Perceiving the Future through New Communication Technologies

James Katz • Juliet Floyd • Katie Schiepers
Editors

Perceiving the Future through New Communication Technologies

Robots, AI and Everyday Life

palgrave
macmillan

Editors
James Katz
Division of Emerging Media Studies
Boston University
Boston, MA, USA

Juliet Floyd
Department of Philosophy
Boston University
Boston, MA, USA

Katie Schiepers
Division of Emerging Media Studies
Boston University
Boston, MA, USA

ISBN 978-3-030-84882-8 ISBN 978-3-030-84883-5 (eBook)
https://doi.org/10.1007/978-3-030-84883-5

Cover illustration: Busakorn Pongparnit / Getty Images

This Palgrave Macmillan imprint is published by the registered company Springer Nature Switzerland AG.
The registered company address is: Gewerbestrasse 11, 6330 Cham, Switzerland

Acknowledgments

We the editors express our deep gratitude to our contributors and reviewers. Without their efforts the book would of course not be possible. Yet beyond the chapter contributions themselves, they have entered with us in probing conversations to understand the issues at hand. In that sense, they went above and beyond the call of duty to help provide a rich, contextualized approach to the subject.

The editors also sincerely thank the following people who supported the creation of this volume:

- Co-sponsors of the conference *Should Robots Be Our Friends?*—The Mellon Foundation Sawyer Seminar, Michaël Vallée and the Consulate General of France in Boston, and Margrit Betke and the Artificial Intelligence Research (AIR) Initiative of Boston University.
- Kenneth Feld and the Feld Family for their creation of the Feld Professorship at Boston University under whose auspices the catalyzing conference of this publication was held.
- Dean Mariette DiChristina and former Dean Tom Fiedler, Boston University College of Communication.
- Lauriane Piette, Associate Editor, Palgrave Macmillan, and Asma Azeezullah, Project Coordinator, Springer Nature.

We gratefully acknowledge your support.

James Katz and Juliet Floyd also owe thanks to the generosity of the Andrew W. Mellon Foundation, which funded their work with colleague Russell Powell on the Boston University Mellon Sawyer Seminar 2016–2019 on the topic of everyday life in a computational world.

About the Book

From tea leaf-reading to complex super-computer modeling, people have always sought to use available technology to know what lies ahead. This is true equally for figuring out how one will be spending one's leisurely weekend to deciding whether war is imminent. It is by use of these technologies that people learn about the world around them, make meaning out of it, and on occasion exercise influence over that world.

While there's always uncertainty in making predictions, and a persistent fog about how to make meaning of what is happening, today's technologies have thrown into sharp relief people's efforts to understand what is happening to them as new waves of communication technology embrace the spectrum of everyday life. This process is the focus of this book. It is organized on the principle that people use communication technology to come to grips with the ever-unfolding future which quickly becomes their present.

To understand these processes better, and shed new insight on them, the chapters in this volume are organized along three major axes. The first axis is contemporary views on the way in which new communication technologies are introduced and reconfigured for human interests. The second axis examines emerging technologies, particularly robotics and artificial intelligence, and how people react to them initially and then incorporate them into their regimes. The third axis is the philosophical and ethical dimensions of the changes brought about by these technologies. Here a special focus is the theory of Apparatgeist, which provides an interpretive framework for the understanding of human behavior related to new devices and operational regimes. In sum, this book takes a novel approach to understanding the way people create meaning through indication technology and the consequences of their lived experiences.

Contents

Notes on Contributors

Mark Aakhus is Professor of Communication and Associate Dean for Research in the School of Communication and Information at Rutgers University, New Brunswick, New Jersey. He investigates the relationship between communication and design, especially the uses of technological and organizational design, to augment human interaction and reasoning for decision-making and conflict management. He uses multiple methods from discourse analysis and computational social science to examine language, argumentation, and social interaction in professional practice, organizational processes, and information infrastructures. The aim in these streams of research is to improve understanding of the intentional, and emergent, design of institutions for communication and the consequences for the co-creation of health, wellness, and democracy.

Petra Aczél is Full Professor of Communication and Rhetoric at Corvinus University of Budapest and Head of the Institute of Communication and Sociology, as well as member of the Sociology and Communication Science Doctoral School. Born in Budapest, she studied at Eötvös Loránd University, where she was awarded her PhD degree in 2003, and she gave her habilitation lecture in 2011. Her research interests are focused on the theory and practice of rhetoric, science communication, new media, and future skills. She is the author of four books and co-author of another four books and has published more than 200 publications on verbal and visual communication, rhetoric, (new) media communication, and media literacy. She is Vice Chair of the Communication and Media Committee of the Hungarian Academy of Sciences, Chair and member in five editorial boards of Hungarian and international periodicals, and holds memberships in Hungarian and International Communication Associations. She is also known as a science communicator, giving talks at professional, corporate, and media events.

Pierre Cassou-Noguès is a full professor in the Philosophy Department of University of Vincennes-Saint Denis Paris 8. His work is concerned with the history of French philosophy and, in a perspective indebted to Bachelard, the role of fiction in recent scientific and technological investigations. His books, in French, include *Les cauchemars cybernétiques de Nobert Wiener* (The Cybernetic Nightmares of Norbert Wiener), which focuses on an unpublished short story by Wiener, and more recently *Technofictions*, a collection of short stories investigating the social potentialities of several technological apparatus. He has also co-authored a film *Welcome to Erewhon* based on Samuel Butler's novel *Erewhon*.

Pauline Cheong (Ph.D., University of Southern California) is a professor and director of Engagement and Innovation at the Hugh Downs School of Human Communication, Arizona State University. She studies the complex interactions between communication technologies and different cultural communities around the world. Her recent projects related to changing knowledge and authority practices examine the socio-cultural implications of Big Data, including user skills, perceptions, and practices of privacy and security within the Internet of Things. She is also examining how religious organizations use artificial intelligence and digital platforms to interact and form both local and global communities. Her past projects have investigated how social media facilitate and constrain relations within cyber-vigilante groups and rumor-mongers. She has also documented how underserved and youth populations experience multiple digital divides. Cheong has published more than 100 articles and books and has received research awards by the National Communication Association, Western Communication Association, and the International Communication Association. She is often invited to speak in Asia, North America, and Europe. She is the recipient of multiple teaching awards, including the Zebulon Pearce Distinguished Teaching Award in the Social Sciences, the highest teaching honor in the College of Liberal Arts & Sciences at the ASU.

Juliet Floyd is Professor of Philosophy at Boston University. Her research focuses on the interplay between logic, mathematics, and philosophy of language and emerging media. She has published widely in the history of

American philosophy and pragmatism in relation to European twentieth-century analytic philosophy (Vienna Circle, Carnap, Quine, Putnam, Rawls, Cavell). Her most recent books are (with Felix Muehlhoelzer) *Wittgenstein's Annotations to Hardy's Course of Pure Mathematics: An Investigation of Wittgenstein's Non-extensionalist Understanding of the Real Numbers* (Springer, 2020) and *Wittgensein's Philosophy of Mathematics* (Cambridge University Press, forthcoming). She has co-edited two volumes for Oxford University Press: with S. Shieh *Future Pasts: The Analytic Tradition in Twentieth Century Philosophy* (2001) and with J. Katz *Philosophy of Emerging Media* (2016). She has also co-edited with A. Bokulich *Philosophical Explorations of the Legacy of Alan Turing: Turing 100* (Boston Studies in the Philosophy of Science, Springer, 2017) and with G. Chase and S. Laugier *Stanley Cavell's Must We Mean What We Say? at Fifty* (Cambridge University Press, forthcoming).

Gang (Kevin) Han is an associate professor at the Greenlee School of Journalism and Communication, Iowa State University. His research interests include health communication, social media and social networking, public relations, and strategic communication.

Jukka Jouhki, PhD is Senior Lecturer in Anthropology at the University of Jyväskylä, Finland. Among his main research interests are human-technology relations and cultural meanings of technology. He has conducted ethnographic research on gender and mobile communication in rural India and has investigated media and new media culture, technonationalism, and information society visions in urban South Korea. He has also conducted anthropological research on online gambling and social media ethics. Jouhki often applies anthropological approaches to study media contents. He is the founding member of the Social Media Research Institute at the University of Jyväskylä, and the Editor-in-Chief of *Human Technology* journal. He thinks there should definitely be a discipline called cross-cultural anthropology of robotics.

James Katz, PhD, Dr.h.c. is Feld Professor of Emerging Media at Boston University's College of Communication, where he directs its Division of Emerging Media Studies. He recently concluded service as a distinguished professor at Peking University's New Media School. His publications on the effects of artificial intelligence (AI), social media, mobile communication, and robot-human interaction have been internationally recognized and translated into many languages. His two most recent books, *Journalism and the Search for Truth in an Age of Social Media*, co-edited with Kate Mays, and *Philosophy of Emerging Media*, co-edited with Juliet Floyd, were published by Oxford University Press in 2019 and 2016, respectively. An earlier book, *The Social Media President: Barack Obama and the Politics of Citizen Engagement*, was published in 2013 by Macmillan. Other volumes include *Social Consequences of Internet Use: Access, Involvement, Expression* (with Ronald E. Rice) and *Handbook of Mobile Communication Studies*, both of which were published by MIT Press. According to Google Scholar, his work has been cited more than 16,000 times. His work is promoted through Boston University and the Division of Emerging Media Studies' website and social media channels.

Kate K. Mays recently completed her PhD in Emerging Media Studies at Boston University's College of Communication, where she studied the influence of emerging technologies on social life with a particular focus on robots and artificial intelligence. She has presented her research findings at a variety of international conferences and in several journals. Most recently she co-edited a volume published by Oxford University Press, *Journalism & Truth in an Age of Social Media*. She was also a Graduate Student Fellow for computational and data-driven research at BU's Rafik B. Hariri Institute for Computing and Computational Science & Engineering.

Karen Mossberger is the Frank and June Sackton Professor at the School of Public Affairs at Arizona State University, and Director of ASU's Center on Technology, Data and Society. Her research interests include digital inequality, digital government, the impacts of technology use, and local governance. She is the author or co-author of five books, including *Digital Cities: The Internet and the Geography of Opportunity* (2012), *Digital Citizenship: The Internet, Participation and Society* (2008), and *Virtual Inequality: Beyond the Digital Divide* (2003). "The Effects of E-Government on Trust and Confidence in Government" was honored as one of the 75 most influential articles in the first 75 years of *Public Administration Review*. Her work has been supported by the National Science Foundation, the John D. and Catherine T. MacArthur Foundation, US Department of Housing and Urban Development, Smith Richardson Foundation, and the Chicago Community Trust, among others. In 2019 she was selected by the UK nonprofit Apolitical as one of the World's 100 most influential people in digital government. She is also a fellow of the National Academy of Public Administration.

Vanessa Nurock is Associate Professor of Political Theory and Ethics at Paris 8 University (France) and the holder of the UNESCO EVA Chair for the Ethics of the Living and Artificial (Ethique du Vivant et de l'Artificiel). Initially trained in philosophy and cognitive science, her research stands at the interface between ethics, politics, and science. More specifically, her work deals with bioethics understood as two complementary issues—the biological constraints of our moral valuation and our moral valuation of biology. Her books and articles address issues concerning bioethics, neuroethics, environmental and animal ethics, robots ethics, as well as ethics and politics of care and justice. She works on the ethics of emerging technologies such as nanotechnologies, cybergenetics, and artificial intelligence.

Katie Schiepers is the Division Administrator for Emerging Media Studies at Boston University. She holds a Master of Philosophy in Classics and Master of Science in World Heritage Conservation.

Philipp Stoellger is Full Chair for Systematic Theology (Dogmatics and Philosophy of Religion) at Heidelberg University, Germany. He was formerly the Director of the Institute of Iconicity at Rostock University, Germany (2013–2015), Full Chair of Systematic Theology at the same institution (2007–2015), and was speaker of the DFG-Graduiertenkolleg: Deutungsmacht: Religion und belief systems in Deutungsmachtkoflikten. His recent publications include *Figurationen des Menschen. Studien zur Medienanthropologie*, Würzburg: Königshausen & Neumann, 2019, 503 S. [Reihe: Interpretation Interdisziplinär, Bd. 18]; Bildmacht—Machtbild. *Deutungsmacht des Bildes: Wie Bilder glauben machen*, Würzburg: Königshausen & Neumann, 2018, 488 S. [Reihe: Interpretation Interdisziplinär, Bd. 17]; Wortmacht—Machtwort. *Deutungsmachtkonflikte in und um Religion*, Würzburg: Königshausen & Neumann, 2017, 450 S. [Reihe: Interpretation Interdisziplinär, Bd. 16], "As Turns Go By: New Challenges After the Iconic Turn", in the edited volume *Perspectives on Visual Learning: Vision Fulfilled, The Victory of the Pictorial Turn* (2019).

Satomi Sugiyama (PhD, Communication Studies, Rutgers University) is Professor of Communication and Media Studies at Franklin University Switzerland. Her research and teaching interests focus on emerging communication technologies and how they intersect with personal relationships, identity, and fashion. She has given numerous presentations of her work at academic conferences and other professional events. Her work has appeared in such journals as *New Media and Society* (with J. Katz), *First*

Monday, *International Journal of Social Robotics* (with N. Barile), *and Fashion Theory* (with N. Barile), as well as in edited books published by Springer, Peter Lang, Transaction, and Mimesis International.

Bing Wang and **Hao Zhang** are graduate students at the School of New Media, Peking University.

Xiuli Wang is an associate professor at the School of New Media, Peking University. Her research focuses on social media, health communication, and international public relations.

Xinzhou Xie is a professor at the School of New Media, Peking University. His research focuses on media convergence, Internet governance, and new media management.

Alexandra Weilenmann has over 20 years of experience of studying the use of mobile information and communication technology, and has undertaken fieldwork in many situations involving mobile technology and, in recent years, social media. In conducting this work, she draws upon and develops different methodological approaches to capture mobile situated practices and users' engagement with their technologies and services. These methods often combine data collected during ethnographic fieldwork "in the wild" with data from digital and social platforms to be able to study how everyday ordinary activities are increasingly played out across sites and platforms. Museum visitors, teenagers, news reporters, deer hunters, digital seniors, and selfie photographers are some of the groups she has examined, focusing on their interactions with and through digital technology and services. An overall ambition with her work is to contribute to a society where technology is supporting and enhancing our everyday interactions, in ways that can be both enabling and enjoyable. She participates and publishes in the field of human-computer interaction (e.g. CHI, MobileHCI) as well as in communication studies (e.g. *Mobile Media & Communication* and *Journal of Pragmatics*).Weilenmann is Full Professor in Interaction Design and Head of the Division of Human Computer Interaction at the Department of Applied Information Technology, University of Gothenburg, Sweden.

List of Figures

Likable and Competent, Fictional and Real: Impression Management of a Social Robot

PART I

Conceptual Framework

Introduction

James Katz, Katie Schiepers, and Juliet Floyd

Perceiving the Future through New Communication Technologies offers multiple perspectives on the way in which people encounter and think about the future. Drawing on perspectives of history, literature, philosophy, and communication studies, an international ensemble of experts offer kaleidoscopic views on these topics to provoke and enlighten the reader.

Trying to understand and affect the future is one of humanity's most long-standing interests, as reflected by the 15,000-year-old cave paintings in Lascaux and the "merely" 5000-year-old megaliths of Europe. Of course these old technologies have been replaced by their digital successors, including modeling with supercomputers and scenario analysis with artificial intelligence (AI) (Nah et al. 2021). By looking both backward and forward, we set out to take our own tack to add insight to the current

J. Katz (✉) • K. Schiepers
Division of Emerging Media Studies, Boston University, Boston, MA, USA
e-mail: katz2020@bu.edu; kschiep@bu.edu

J. Floyd
Department of Philosophy, Boston University, Boston, MA, USA
e-mail: jfloyd@bu.edu

J. Katz et al. (eds.), *Perceiving the Future through New Communication Technologies*,
https://doi.org/10.1007/978-3-030-84883-5_1

understandings about how people encounter the future and how they respond both passively and with agency when they do so.

On the one hand, this encounter can be described as "Future Shock" as did Alvin Toffler (1970), or the "Shock of the New" as did Robert Hughes (1981). Our approach is less cataclysmic and more prosaic: we want to understand the daily lived experience of ordinary people as they encounter new technology as well as the way people, and experts, reflect on the meaning and significance of those technologies.

Consonant with contemporary intellectual attention to the lives of common folk, our approach stresses the quotidian quality of reality and ordinary understandings of reality as understood by people from all walks of life. Of course we rely on expert analysis and sophisticated understanding in the analyses, the focus of attention toward how people make meaning out of change, particularly when the change occurs at the level of social technologies—the devices that modify and amplify our modes of communication with others. Our authors seek to understand the intertwining of the psychological, spiritual, and philosophical dimensions as new technologies, especially related to interpersonal communication, take an ever-expanding role in their routines and relationships.

In this introductory chapter, we offer an organizing scaffold laying out the book's intellectual vision and the juxtaposition of issues that the subsequent sections address. The volume will conclude with an essay by the co-editors drawing together and contrasting major themes of the chapters.

The first main section will examine the phenomena of new communication technology in people's lives from contemporary viewpoints—illustrating how we presently view and interact with emerging technology as it becomes more ubiquitous in our everyday lives. Topics in this section include the growth of cell phone use, rising human-machine communication, and a philosophical reflection on the meaningfulness of personal technology.

The section opens with Aakhus' overview of the evolution of technology and communication over the past two decades, first with an exploration of the Perpetual Contact project and the phenomenon of Apparatgeist (Katz and Aakhus 2002). This is complemented by Floyd's philosophical exploration of the Apparatgeist theory, considering it in relation to ordinary language philosophy and the works of Austin, Wittgenstein, and Cavell. Weilenmann's study expands on the development of the mobile phone over the past two decades (2000–2020), exploring how it has radically shifted our social interactions, not only in terms of facilitating communication via the phone itself but in relation to "shared screen time" and how we interact with one another locally in the presence of mobile phones.

This idea is expanded upon in Mays' discussion on the ways in which emerging communication technologies can afford us greater convenience in our daily lives while also shifting societal norms and human interaction in unexpected ways—comparing the impact the mobile phone had on society to the potential impact of emerging technologies in the future, namely artificial intelligence and robots. Her research explores how people perceive both their own and other's interactions with robots and AI to glean insight into the potential roles these technologies will play in our societies in the future. Nurock further explores the role of AI through the lens of Apparatgeist, highlighting the biases we impress upon the technologies we create and how this can shape us as a society in turn, given the reciprocal nature of the relationship between human and machine.

The second section looks at specific examples to explore the meaning of robotics and AI as they play an increasing role in people's experience. These include topics such as the spiritual significance of robots, the use of voice interaction to control one's life, and robots of both the simple friendly kind and those that claim the rights of citizenship.

Stoellger considers how human robots can become and what are our limits, in particular drawing on the example of Bless-U, a robot in Germany that gives its blessings to worshippers. Sugiyama looks at Pepper-kun, a robot in Japan that serves to assist in people's daily lives and is perceived by some as friendly and others as frightening or strange. Wang et al. discuss smart speakers in China and the relationship that users have with these omnipresent devices. Lastly, Jouhki presents Sophia the Robot, an internationally traveled robot designed to appear as though it has a more sophisticated intelligence than it actually does, thus presenting a vision of what AI may one day be capable of, and the level of comfort people have with these human-like abilities. These international perspectives provide insight into the types of robots and AI currently in production and the diverse ways they are used, while also considering how we as humans interact with them. Where does our level of comfort with an artificial intelligence reach its limit?

The third section looks at broader issues concerning the operational, sociological, and philosophical implications of people as they address a technology-driven future. Cheong and Mossberger provide an analysis of public and popular understanding of AI and the fears they have concerning it. They delve deeper into people's perceptions of AI and the Internet of Things, as it pervades our everyday lives, offering ways in which we as a society can prepare for a future that is so integrated with technology. Aczél also considers our future as we are in a period of societal change driven by emerging technology ("a new axial age"). She considers the rate of change in relationship to both technology and literary tropes.

This section also includes the perspective of Cassou-Noguès, offered via an unpublished novel by a pioneering computer scientist from the mid-twentieth century about his expectations of the twenty-first century, presenting an insightful juxtaposition between how the future of technology was imagined in the last century and how we imagine the future of technology today. But more than imagining the technologies themselves, these chapters delve into the relationships between humans and technology, ultimately asking how our interactions with the world will be altered by technological developments.

This book is designed to inform advanced undergraduates, graduate students, scholars, and interested members of the public on pertinent topics related to our shared future. We see this as a valuable addition to studies in new media, future studies, cultural studies, sociology, and digital humanities. For the general reader, it also sets forth significant research findings and provocative questions about the likely and possible futures awaiting us. Through our multidisciplinary approach, we highlight the importance of conceptualizing the future as a social process and the crucial policy and behavioral consequences of the applications of these concepts. Thus although the future may seem like an amorphous construct, arguments about what it will be like, and seizing control over the way in which it is formed, become a critical component that governs the structure of societies in the modern world.

References

Hughes, Robert. 1981. *The Shock of the New*. New York: Knopf.

Katz, James E., and Mark A. Aakhus, eds. 2002. *Perpetual Contact: Mobile Communication, Private Talk, Public Performance*. Cambridge: Cambridge University Press.

Nah, Seungahn, Jasmine McNealy, Janghyun Kim, and Jungseock Joo, eds. 2021. *Communicating Artificial Intelligence (AI): Theory, Research, and Practice*. New York: Routledge, Taylor & Francis.

Toffler, Alvin. 1970. *Future Shock*. New York: Random House.

Media Are Dead, Long Live Media: Apparatgeist's Capacity for Understanding Media Evolution

Mark Aakhus

In 1999, when we were formulating the Perpetual Contact project, it was still normal to understand the mobile phone as in fact a telephone that was mobile and that a personal computer was a personal stand-alone device for computing. Back then, we did not even have those handy *Buzzfeed* listicles to explain popular culture such as the one that lists all the things we no longer do now that we did in 1999. Here are just a few from such a listicle (Galindo 2017):

- Looking through the Sunday paper circulars to find out what movies and albums were being released that week.
- Waiting HOURS to download one song off of Napster and praying you wouldn't be knocked off the internet while it downloaded.

M. Aakhus (✉)
School of Communication and Information, Rutgers University, New Brunswick, NJ, USA
e-mail: aakhus@rutgers.edu

J. Katz et al. (eds.), *Perceiving the Future through New Communication Technologies*,
https://doi.org/10.1007/978-3-030-84883-5_2

- Having to clearly label your VHS tape so that no one would tape over it before you had a chance to watch it.
- Carrying around both a beeper and a cell phone.
- Sharing ONE landline phone with several people (like roommates).
- Having to pay for long-distance calls whenever you called anyone outside your area code.

Indeed, we can't party like it's 1999 anymore. Back then, however, I had not yet joined the mobile phone party. Like most people in the United States at that time, I did not have a cell phone. Between the time of the workshop we held on Perpetual Contact in December 1999 and the start of the new school year in September, there was a palpable change on campus, as students came back with their new cell phones. From 2000 forward, things were different.

On a trip to Finland in 2000, I was afforded a view of the future. I was astonished upon landing in Helsinki by the pervasive chirping of the now classic Nokia ring tone. It took me a while to realize the chirp was a mobile phone ringing. Shortly after my arrival there, a Finnish colleague lent me a mobile phone on which I could send text messages to others! It was like emailing but on a phone. I could send a text during presentations that had become boring and coordinate going out for dinner. I found it remarkable. Of course, upon returning to New Jersey, one of the first things my wife and I did was to buy cell phones. There was not much we could really figure out to do with the mobile phones at first but we managed. We would review all the good reasons, like safety and convenience, we had developed (or appropriated from commercials) to buy the phone and justify the monthly cost. Soon enough we were using the phone for new, seemingly necessary behavior such as calling to let the other know that it would be about one hour before arriving at home after work, and then to call to say it would be about 30 minutes, and then to call just a few blocks from home to point that fact out. Soon enough, we discovered that if one of us was grocery shopping it could be useful to call home to check on whether the right thing was purchased or to call the one shopping to suggest additional items to pick up. There was a real kick in calling one of our family or friends back in the middle of the country just to let them know we were on the shore enjoying the surf. Although, it was awkward being the one in public making or receiving a call. At some point, text messaging was added by the service provider and this helped accommodate those moments when having a private conversation in public just was not the thing to do.

My own experience reflected so many of the points developed by the authors in the book we were editing. In Perpetual Contact, we were anticipating ferment in the social and technical order from the mobile phone entering our private talk and public performance. The mobile phone quickly became a flashpoint disparaged for disrupting local scenes by making absent those who were present and praised for making present those who were absent. So, we attended to the disruptive aspects of the emerging media by investigating the complaints and the praise about emerging socio-technical practices. We found that the complaints and praise made explicit expectations about the social that were embedded in the technical or that social expectations were not in keeping with what was now socially possible due to technical capabilities. The new presence of the mobile phone had drawn into relief, and challenged, the habits and etiquette that grease the wheels of everyday interaction in accommodating the competing demands for autonomy and connectedness in communication. The new intersections between private talk and public performance were revealing that the capacity for participation in streams of talk and joint activities could lead to altered, extended, or expanded practices and ways of reasoning in, as Goffman might say, ordering interaction. The expressions of complaint and praise were actually pointing to the hard won cultural knowledge about getting along, getting by, and even occasionally cooperating just enough to achieve important ends. It was dawning on everyone that something serious was changing, but unlike the preceding innovations in media, newspaper, movies, radio, and television that gave birth to the mass public, the mobile phone was different. Although not without precedent as there were landline telephones and wireless walkie-talkies and citizens band radio for distant or mobile interpersonal communication, our focus on how people made sense of the mobile phone was suggestive of some broader insights about communication.

In Perpetual Contact, our project was to sketch the global scene at that time so that we could put forward a simple yet compelling premise for investigating the quickly evolving relationship among communication, technology, society, and culture. We were attending to the new capacities for connection ushered in by "personal" communication technology that were especially prominent with the mobile phone at that time. We recognized that the mobile phone was exposing deeper struggles about communication that would be generative of social, technical, and socio-technical practices. Practices that would be evident in mundane and quotidian actions as well as the grand, and developing for everyday people living their lives and very powerful economic and political actors living theirs. We coined the term *Apparatgeist* to name this dynamic struggle.

Apparatgeist is an orienting term for an agenda that challenges theory, research, and design to articulate deeper principles animating struggle and generativity at the interface of people, technology, and culture while recognizing variability and difference in experience. Our initial concept for the term Apparatgeist was that it refers to "the common set of strategies or principles of reasoning about technology evident in the identifiable, consistent and generalized patterns of technological advancement throughout history. It is through these common strategies and principles of reasoning that individual and collective behavior are drawn together" (Katz and Aakhus 2001, 307).

To understand Apparatgeist, it is important to see that social and technical practices of communication emerged with a socio-logic—that is, the "socially developed sense of practical reasoning" that results from communities of people "thinking and acting together over time" (Goodwin and Wenzel 1979, 289). Goodwin and Wenzel were demonstrating how schemes of practical reasoning and informal logic are captured by proverbs. They were articulating that backdrop of common sense deployed when inventing reasons for actions taken or for judging the actions of others. Like the classical Greek notion of topoi. It is very important to note that a socio-logic has contraries. It is not a worked out bureaucratic code for computing solutions to the difference we may have. Indeed, if I were being careful back then not to use up my mobile phone minutes, you might say, "an ounce of prevention is worth a pound of cure" and someone else might say "penny wise, pound foolish." A socio-logic can also evolve; it's hard to imagine many people even using such proverbs today, and saving my phone minutes is just not on my horizon of concerns.

Drawing on socio-logic, we sought to articulate a backdrop against which social and technical practices were invented and critiqued. We called this Perpetual Contact: "The compelling image of perpetual contact is the image of pure communication," which, as Peters (1999) argues, is "an idealization of communication committed to the prospect of sharing one's mind with another, like the talk of angels that occurs without the constraints of the body." We were attempting to put forward in the simplest way possible a premise for investigating the relationship among communication, technology, and culture—a premise that recognized that many significant technical achievements tended to appear and work across and within cultures—dams, railroads, airlines, and such. A premise that recognized the paradoxes of communication—like fire, you want the heat but not the burn. In communication, we may desire deep intersubjective connection but not at the expense of losing our self. A premise that recognized the obdurate, recalcitrant reality of communication against which technical systems develop.

This is the point that has probably drawn the most attention in subsequent research, and is often characterized as perpetual contact predicting a global homogenizing consequence. For instance, Axelsson (2010) compared teen and elder uses of the mobile phone and based on their finding of differences concluded that:

> The theory of Apparatgeist of the mobile phone is consonant with this hypothesis. However, the notion of Apparatgeist still needs to be reconciled with the age differences reported in this article (and elsewhere). If there is a universal wish for connectedness, and the mobile phone enables perpetual contact, why do young adults (at least in Sweden) use the mobile phone differently from their parents' or grandparents' generation?

Or, consider Barzilai-Nahon and Barzilai (2005)'s comparison of different religious groups' use of personal communication technology that found differences and thus led to the conclusion that "contrary to Katz and Aakhus, in our study we find no unified and objective apparatgeist that imposes itself invariably on all cultures."

On the contrary, construing perpetual contact as a process that necessarily leads to the homogenization of practice misses our fundamental point that socio-logic will be worked out in particular social and technical practices and in the invention of socio-technical practices. What is important then is to identify how groups of people develop ways of thinking and acting together over time. Indeed, that is closer to what Axelsson found—teens do it differently than their elders. That's what Barzilai-Nahon and Barzilai found—that different religious groups worked personal communication technologies into their community of practice without losing their fundamentals but slightly altering how they act together. That is what is interesting, not the straw-man or stalking horse that posits Perpetual Contact asserting a grand homogenizing effect of technology on society or homogenizing effect of society on technology. We seek to recognize and highlight the dynamic puzzles of communication out of which socio-technical practices emerge for the new technological context.

Katz (2003, 15) extends the important point that Apparatgeist is "a novel way of thinking about how humans invest their technology with meaning and use devices and machines to pursue social and symbolic routines." Assigning meaning to technologies now seems almost uncontroversial and a necessary assumption for explaining technology in society. But, it usually gets taken up in one basic way. The phone is my friend, I love my phone, phones are the downfall of western society—whatever, the user or implementer assigns a meaning in an attempt to make sense of the technology or in an attempt to persuade some particular usage. But there is another important sense of assigning meaning to technologies, that is, the technology itself is composed of an assembly of rules that define its functioning. Technology becomes part of the design of experience.

Two important directions for the development of Apparatgeist become apparent. First, the relationship of norms and technology in the initial development of Apparatgeist focused on the reaction to the technical as a disruption of communicative norms. By now, though, many of the presumptions against the mobile phone shifted to give mobile phone presumption, and yet there remains the matter of managing various demands of communication and interaction. There was a time when, for instance, one could enjoy a concert or meeting without the interruption of the mobile telephone, but now that is no longer a given. This is recognized in all kinds of technical developments directed toward disrupting the disruption. For instance, Yondr is a small bag in which one places their phone upon entering an event. While the bag is wirelessly locked by the event hosts, the phone owner keeps the bag with their phone in it. The bag prevents use. Upon departing the event, the bag is wirelessly unlocked, the phone removed, and the bag returned. The product's tagline is "be here now" as it blocks the problem of absent presence that was emerging as a concern but not yet the norm in 1999. Apparatgeist seeks to capture the yin and the yang of the yearning for perpetual contact—the dilemmatic tension between connectedness and autonomy—that drives innovation in communication practice. Perpetual contact reveals communication's version of creative destruction. Yondr is just one example of many other kinds of socio-technical innovations to address the concerns anticipated in 1999 that are now lived on a daily basis. Many of these issues are now very prominent around platform companies and algorithms in our personal and public lives.

Second, the initial development of Apparatgeist focused on the arguments people made for or against the mobile phone in human experience, but now it is increasingly important to understand the arguments technological products and services make about what human experience is and ought to be (Aakhus, 2019). Technologies make arguments about human conduct—empirical arguments about how communication works and normative arguments about the way it ought to work. This becomes apparent when, for instance, the CEO of Twitter, Jack Dorsey, expresses regret about the platform in admitting that:

> I would not emphasize the 'like' count as much. I don't think I would even create 'like' in the first place, because it doesn't actually push what we believe now to be the most important thing, which is healthy contribution back to the network and conversation to the network, participation within conversation, learning something from the conversation. (Wiener 2019)

It becomes apparent when former high-level employees in social media companies call out the fundamental business and technology model of the companies. Tristan Harris a former Google employee, for instance, started the movement for "time well spent" based on his argument that social media design is "downgrading" humanity by fostering shortened attention spans and heightened polarization, outrage, and vanity (Thompson 2019).

We should recognize the practical theory at work about managing the dilemmas of perpetual contact in the technical organization of communication and the consequences for the production of knowledge and the orchestration of action. Indeed, as Jouhki (2019) explains, Apparatgeist draws attention to the complex structure or organization of a system and importantly to the users, nonusers, and antiusers. Both the Dorsey and Harris examples highlight the attention given to ways our communication practices can be (re)designed, ordered, or altered and the tensions this can generate between the new possibilities for action and the expectations about what is appropriate or right for communication. The arguments technological products and services make about communication become matters not just for users and inventors but for providers, maintainers, investors, nonusers, and resistors who become engaged in shaping those arguments about human conduct.

In contrast to 1999, we find ourselves on the other side of those initial struggles with perpetual contact. At the same time, state-of-the-art thinking about media in 1999 was still in a classic media studies paradigm—that is, one investigated a specific medium such as telegraph, newspaper, film, radio, telephone, television, office equipment, and eventually the mobile phone and personal computer. Each medium was associated with its particular mode of transmission and content created for that medium. Among the prominent concerns were the adoption and diffusion of the devices that delivered the content particular to that medium via the specialized transmission system for that medium. That was all changing right in front of our eyes as the convergence of telecommunication and computerization was making it possible to digitize all kinds of content and media, and modes of transmission were becoming more connected and entangled. What do media and communication mean, for instance, when someone says they are watching TV but could be doing so when on a phone, computer, game console, or monitor attached to an antennae and the content could be live, recorded, or streamed?. Apparatgeist helps us see that we are on the other side of the old conceptualization of media.

Taking up these two directions can advance the Apparatgeist conceptualization as formulated and lend insight that overcomes a significant problem for the persistent classic media studies paradigm for understanding the relation among people, technology, society, and culture. The classical view where media is associated with technical/material device (i.e., telegraphs, newspapers, film, radio, telephone, television, office equipment, mobile phones, and personal computers) enrolled in a transmission system of content created specifically for that medium. As Iannacci (2010) argues:

> when content is digitized, as it is happening with the dawn of the Internet era, the traditional link between the physical transmission medium and the message is broken as digital standards become the medium of transmission of higher-level content standards.

Apparatgeist's anticipation of the deeper struggle over communication positions it to address the apparent loss of media in the era of digitalization and the emergence of socio-technical practice. The medium not being where we have traditionally been looking.

The way I would put it today based on the subsequent work I've done on communication and design (Aakhus 2003, 2007; Aakhus and Jackson 2005; Jackson and Aakhus 2014) is that saying there is a logic of perpetual contact does not mean there is one logic. There is a pragmatic infrastructure of human communication that technical innovation exploits and seeks to discipline in various ways. We should see technology something like the way we see language and language use. Just because we all use language, does not mean we use it in the same way; but in order to use it, others must use it in a similar enough way to have value. We should all today be very clear that our aim with Perpetual Contact and Apparatgeist then was to properly treat communication as a compelling force in human nature. Communication is the base not the superstructure. The cake not the icing. Communication is our human infrastructure on which other aspects of our built environment—technology and society—are constructed. Out of the fundamental interaction order emerges our practices for making meaning, action, and coherently weaving these together for coordination and cooperation. We were aiming to see not only how users experience a medium but what we would now think of as the design of experience that formulates a how for interaction. Rather than seeing technology as a mere conduit of communication but as part of communication practice that exists grounded in expectations about how communication works and how it ought to work. Indeed, the media are dead, long live the media.

Acknowledgments The author thanks the editors and Jeff Treem for their insightful comments.

References

Aakhus, Mark. 2003. Understanding Information and Communication Technology and Infrastructure in Everyday Life: Struggling with Communication at a Distance. In *Machines that Become Us the Social Context of Personal Communication Technology*, ed. James E. Katz, 27–42. New Brunswick, NJ: Transaction Publishers.

———. 2007. Communication as Design. *Communication Monographs* 74 (1): 112–117. https://doi.org/10.1080/03637750701196383.

———. 2019. Argumentative Design and Polylogue. In *Proceedings of the Third European Conference on Argumentation*, ed. Catarina Dutilh Novaes, Henrike Jansen, Jan Albert van Laar, and Bart Verheij, vol. 1, 3–16. Groningen, the Netherlands.

Aakhus, Mark, and Sally Jackson. 2005. Technology, Interaction, and Design. In *Handbook of Language and Social Interaction*, ed. Kristine L. Fitch and Robert E. Sanders, 411–436. Mahwah, NJ: Lawrence Erlbaum Associates.

Axelsson, Ann-Sofie. 2010. Perpetual and Personal: Swedish Young Adults and Their Use of Mobile Phones. *New Media & Society* 12 (1): 35–54. https://doi.org/10.1177/1461444809355110.

Barzilai-Nahon, Karine, and Gad Barzilai. 2005. Cultured Technology: The Internet and Religious Fundamentalism. *Information Society* 21 (1): 25–40. https://doi.org/10.1080/01972240590895892.

Galindo, B. 2017. Things we did in 1999 that are now completely outdated. *Buzzfeed*, June 24. https://www.buzzfeed.com/briangalindo/1999-was-a-very-different-time.

Goodwin, Paul D., and Joseph W. Wenzel. 1979. Proverbs and Practical Reasoning: A Study in Socio-Logic. *Quarterly Journal of Speech* 65: 289–302.

Iannacci, Federico. 2010. When Is an Information Infrastructure? Investigating the Emergence of Public Sector Information Infrastructures. *European Journal of Information Systems* 19 (1): 35–48. https://doi.org/10.1057/ejis.2010.3.

Jackson, Sally, and Mark Aakhus. 2014. Becoming More Reflective About the Role of Design in Communication. *Journal of Applied Communication Research* 42 (2): 125–134. https://doi.org/10.1080/00909882.2014.882009.

Jouhki, Jukka. 2019. The Apparatgeist of the Moon Landing. *Human Technology* 15 (2): 136–141.

Katz, James. 2003. *Machines That Become Us the Social Context of Personal Communication Technology*. New Brunswick, NJ: Transaction Publishers.

Katz, J., and Aakhus, M. 2001. Conclusion: Making meaning of mobiles – a theory of Apparatgeist. In *Perpetual Contact: Mobile Communication, Private Talk, Public Performance*, ed. J. Katz and M. Aakhus, 301–320. Cambridge: Cambridge University Press.

Peters, John D. 1999. *Speaking into the Air: A History of the Idea of Communication*. University of Chicago Press.

Thompson, Nicholas. 2019. Tristan Harris: Tech Is 'Downgrading Humans.' It's Time to Fight Back. *Wired*, April 23. https://www.wired.com/story/tristan-harris-tech-is-downgrading-humans-time-to-fight-back/.

Wiener, Anna. 2019. Jack Dorsey's TED Interview and the End of an Era. *The New Yorker*, April 27. https://www.newyorker.com/news/letter-from-silicon-valley/jack-dorseys-ted-interview-and-the-end-of-an-era.

Selves and Forms of Life in the Digital Age: A Philosophical Exploration of Apparatgeist

Juliet Floyd

Introduction

In 2002 James E. Katz and Mark Aakhus published *Perpetual Contact: Mobile Communication, Private Talk, Public Performance*, an application of a methodological approach they called "Apparatgeist." Apparatgeist is a moniker for what they discovered in their pioneering empirical investigations of the effects of mobile personal communication technologies (PCTs): that a new "Age of Apparatus," or "machine-spirit" has come to permeate the many levels of reality (Schutz 1932)—social, institutional, everyday, lived, and scientific—in novel and multifarious ways.

The discovery suggested a latest chapter in a philosophical narrative of the Anthropocene: the Age of Human Emergence from Africa, the Age of Migration, the Stone and Bronze Ages, the Age of the Warring States; of Reason, of Enlightenment, of Romanticism, of Industrialization, and now the Age of Apparatus (or "Machine Mindedness"). But their work was empirical, utilizing sociological methodology to develop their ideas

J. Floyd (✉)
Department of Philosophy, Boston University, Boston, MA, USA
e-mail: jfloyd@bu.edu

J. Katz et al. (eds.), *Perceiving the Future through New Communication Technologies*,
https://doi.org/10.1007/978-3-030-84883-5_3

empirically. Apparatgeist as a novel philosophical paradigm is this essay's subject. We regard it not merely as a new theoretical frame for sociology and media studies but also for philosophy itself, suggesting a new kind of "experimental" philosophy of emerging media(s) (cf. Floyd and Katz 2016). Apparatgeist transcends the usual understandings of "experimental philosophy" and "media"—a welcome philosophical move, as it enlarges and sophisticates philosophers' repertoire for coming to terms with social "realities." Philosophy of mind and language have too long been in thrall to a mechanistic philosophy of cognition-based computation, an individualist model. Overlooked have been other philosophical paradigms that need resuscitating and revitalizing today, especially those that highlight the collaborative nature of human existence, which tempers even the most internal-seeming sensations and cognitions.

Apparatgeist's philosophical framework may be enlivened by affiliating it with the twentieth-century tradition of Ordinary Language Philosophy (OLP), as developed by Austin, Wittgenstein, and, especially in his explorations of the very notion of the "ordinary" or "everyday" in film and philosophy, Cavell. Cavell found in Thoreau and Emerson a philosophical basis for this concept (Cavell 1988a, 1989). Somewhat unusually, I include Turing in the orbit of OLP: Turing reported that he had learned from Wittgenstein to appreciate of the foundational and creative importance of everyday "phraseology"—our evolving categories and "types" in ordinary language—to the foundations of computing (Turing 1944/45; Floyd 2013). He predicted that as artificial intelligence (AI) develops, humanity as a whole will have to engage in what he called "the cultural search," developing our phraseologies to cope creatively with the future (Turing 1948, 516). Properly read—and used as a tool of research—Turing's famed (1950) Test is an experiment in ordinary phraseology, rather than a means of seeing how far, epistemologically, humans may be fooled about the ontological status of their conversation partners. This approach to evolving phraseology in the age of *Apparatgeist* counterbalances what Krebs and Frankel (2021) have called the "tragedy of the virtual" in our time of Apparatgeist: an all-too-human drive to massify, fracture, and lose hold of our experiences, desires, and self-images in a post-scribal era.

Ordinary Language Philosophy (OLP)

The OLP tradition treats the "everyday" as a dynamic arena of familiarity. What is "obvious," "natural," and "familiar" with regard to the embedding of words in life, Wittgenstein calls "forms of life" (2009, §§19, 23, PPF i §1). These are not conventional "language games" but primordial ways of living whose meaningfulness is taken as "given": we weave together meaningful routines and speech in patterns that constitute the evolving "carpet" of human life, a dynamic, multi-aspectual arena in which words are always subject to rupture, drift, re-orientation, questioning, and the perlocutionary (multifarious social) effects of speech.

"Forms of life" are not simply given, they are rather a norm for elucidating "givenness" as such (Floyd 2018). They evince the backdrop of "harmonies" among us that are needed if we are to proceed in language at all: shared senses of relevance, acceptance of routines, and patterns of interest and response (Wittgenstein 2009, §242). As Cavell (1988b) argues, forms of life exhibit both a biological and an ethological dimension, and have both universal and particular structures. That we walk and chat, feel grief, experience hope, have expectations—this is generally common to human "forms of life" as we know them. Specific rituals, responses, reactions to particular situations constitute localized "forms of life" (Moyal-Sharrock 2015). The interest of this arena is in the imbrication of both aspects of forms of life with one another. In OLP the self seeks to find and form its own voice, its particular phraseology (Laugier 2015). "Forms of life" *replace* the idea of "culture" (Floyd 2018), providing a richer angle on meaning that is both more universal than "culture," and yet sensitive to what Nafus and Tracey (2002, 207) called, in Katz and Aakhus (2002), the "problem of individuality."

In Ralph Waldo Emerson and Henry David Thoreau, Cavell found philosophical precedents for taking "the near" and "the low" or "the common" as an arena for philosophizing with and about the self. As Emerson puts it in *The American Scholar* (1837), "the near explains the far":

> What would we really know the meaning of? The meal in the firkin; the milk in the pan; the ballad in the street; the news of the boat; the glance of the eye; the form and the gait of the body...

This tradition in American philosophy consciously leaves aside the central epistemological questions inherited in European philosophy through Descartes. According to that tradition, "experience" is "subjective representation," error lies in "will," and the main problem is how we can justify our uncertain knowledge of the external world or other minds on the basis of our given perceptual "evidence." In OLP this epistemological challenge is not answered; a different starting point is achieved. Descartes' "spatialist" spectator model of the world and experience is replaced by an investigation and pursuit of lived "experience." Of course what "experience" means—what making it "count" or "matter" in becoming someone *in* the world is—must be worked through, as Emerson's "Experience" (1844) conveys.

The postures of argumentative dispute and the search for "foundations" of knowledge that shaped the Cartesian tradition in modern European philosophy are thus displaced by a kind of criticism that takes the dailiness of our concerns and actions seriously, as the site of ethics, experience, and criticism. "Logic" is not given top-down, through a faculty of Reason, as in Kant (the will), Hegel (institutions and civil society), and Marx (the economic basis of an ideological superstructure) but in the texture of ordinary life, our ordinary attachments, moods, and search for community. The imperfections, disappointments, and desperations in our lives confront the demand to do better, to perfect, just here. American "transcendentalism" returned to an earlier "skeptical" tradition (Montaigne deeply shaped Emerson's philosophy) and at the same time anticipated, not only pragmatism but the "ordinary" in OLP.

OLP criticism also reworks the very notions of "experience" and "evidence," focusing on everyday life with words as a *locus* of moral and ethical self-transformation. The recounting of one's "experience" is a quest for what matters rather than a question of accurate representation of the world by a mind which passively imbibes sensations. Cavell wrote (1988a) of the drive for "moral perfectionism" embedded in the ethics of such recounting of "experience": a search for one's better self and one's true community, rather than a set of codes and rules of conduct to which one may appeal in justifying one's choices and actions.

On this conception, philosophy is a matter of confronting the path imagined for one by one's culture with one's own imagination, words, and life (Cavell 1999, 25). Cavell (1981) considered so-called popular culture, the Hollywood comedies and tragedies of his childhood, to offer some of the best opportunities to pursue this form of individual and communal enculturation. Philosophy, he remarked, is an "education for grownups" (1999, I, 125). The everyday possibilities for "transcendence" of the self-revealed in the popular culture of films (nowadays television series) show models for reworking problems in everyday life, and these are practical, "public" democratic problems in Dewey's sense (Laugier 2012, 2020).

Apparatgeist and Ordinary Language Philosophy (OLP)

There is little doubt that one's values and ethical responses require constant forms of "research" and repair in our everyday life in Apparatgeist. The constant presence of the mobile phone is a symbol and realization of this. Most of us periodically check for contact, making sure we remain "in touch," using words, images, and ever-more-compressed emojis to balance the task of living with the task of imbibing and shaping oneself. The press for individuality and society, for recognition and acknowledgment, permeates lived existence differently now. Instead of recognized spheres of structuration (domestic, professional, recreational), Apparatgeist cuts across these spheres: lawyer-mothers now chat on the phone doing business as they shop from phone-based lists and text with their children about the shopping list.

Of course some drop out, pursuing their forms of life differently. The menu of options enlarges rapidly. New forms of annoying entanglement with strangers' words in the public sphere require an effort to control the use of cell phones. On the whole, as de Gournay (2002, 199f.) argued, we see an "unquestionable decline of the bourgeoisie and its values," insofar as formerly determining, widely recognized factors of social status (parlor, theater, opera) are losing their legitimating roles, giving way to "a lifestyle centered more around intimate circles." Sailing what Wittgenstein metaphorically called the "seas of language" requires that we constantly adjust, remaining aware of winds, storms, and lulls in the winds. The "art" of social media requires that we each seek to find, not so much the production of information in a snazzy or effective way, but that we produce new media, new aspects organized *within* it: new forms of expression, creative idioms, standpoints, a *voice* (compare Cavell 1979, 103 on movie cycles and the quest for a "sound" in jazz and rock, and Laugier 2015).

Katz and Aakhus' Apparatgeist generated remarkable observations and predictions because it scrutinized the arenas of everyday life in just this way, without a top-down lens. "The ordinary"—for example, the very idea of a "standard context"—constantly evolves from day to day, pressured, biologically and ethologically, by human beings' constant embedding and re-embeddings of words in "forms of life," which now include machine-apparatus increasingly. In a world in which PCTs are widely distributed and used, the importance of "the ordinary" is altered, yet amplified. The "everyday" is not a given "Life World" [*Lebenswelt*] in the sense of traditional phenomenology, something we inhabit that is given as an encompassing arena already filled with meaning (Floyd 2020). Rather, it is a delicately woven equilibrium of familiarity and the rupture of familiarity, something we inhabit, explore, confront, escape, and constantly shift our relationship to, using words, gestures, claims: the entire field of our human body. Introducing robots into the home (as cleaning and health helpers, voice-activated servants, or sex companions) alters our everyday forms of life.

We cobble forms of life together, weaving a colorful "carpet" of life (Wittgenstein 2009, PPF I §2). In Apparatgeist, this takes center stage as human beings position themselves in a society rife with mobile technology. Davies (2021), exploring an affinity he detects in Cavell's later work on Austin, focuses on the importance of "found footage" in Oaxaca-based Mexican experimental filmmaker and video artist Bruno Varela's Monolito (2019), which utilizes fragments from Varela's personal archive, audiovisual material downloaded from YouTube, and digitally distorted VHS footage. The Oaxaca uprising, filmed at the time, becomes a kind of quarry for excavating new idioms. The idea of "found footage" reverberates loudly with Austin and Wittgenstein's sense of the cobbling together of "reality" through speech-act snapshots in a variety of contexts. This resists the kind of sentimentalism Emerson (1844) warned against.

Apparatgeist helps to illuminate OLP and vice versa. OLP's interest in the ordinary does not romanticize everyday life, much less enshrine "ordinary language" as a fixed, given grammar. Rather, like Apparatgeist, it expresses a form of "realistic" realism (Diamond 1991): its focus are the "realities" in the textures of human-to-human everyday interaction with words in the presence of machines, rather than a vision of human-machine interaction that places the Cartesian epistemological problematic front-and-center ("*Is* it a human or a machine?," "*Are* we just machines ourselves?"). Words must be "fitted" to occasions of their use, and this is tricky business, filled with positioning and import at a social level.

It is not that language is everywhere bounded by rules, or that we have to hand the perfect information context of computational logic. As Turing (1936) proved—not incidentally—*that* logic is in general undecidable: formal logic is not "gap free," but constantly in need of what Wittgenstein called "homespun" tethering to contexts, and what Turing (1954) labeled "common sense" (see Floyd 2017, 2020). "Common sense," held in common, evolves under the pressure of words. As we cobble forms of life together, the fundamental concept—even for the notion of *information*—is that of a partially, rather than a totally defined routine.

This mathematical point undergirds Turing's Universal Machine that can accomplish the work of all particular Turing machines. What that construct shows is that there is no general, fixed distinction to be had between data, hardware, and software: such distinctions are local and dynamic given the indefinite absorption into the command structure of new forms of phraseology. The result is the ubiquity of our ability to model computational processes in our world (Davis 2017) but also the inevitable presence of local understandings.

Thus we need to respect and be "realistic" about the labor and artfulness of the performances with words and machines that goes on, as well as the volatility and vulnerability of everyday speech in Apparatgeist. The labor involved in learning to operate a mobile phone nowadays is amply rewarded by the "naturalness" with which we absorb these devices into our everyday lives, public and private. But in real life the site of what is "natural," "ordinary," and "familiar" is liable to turn into a site of skeptical doubt, as in Poe's stories. "Feeling at home" in language is essential to its capacity to express: the fact that mathematicians don't generally come to blows over whether a rule has been followed is essential to *mathematics* (Wittgenstein 2009, §240). But this is not to mechanize or romanticize the familiarity of mathematical calculation. Nor is it to be certain that mathematicians and computer scientists will *not* come to blows, should the world change enough. The flip side of the familiarity of the ordinary in Apparatgeist—as in OLP and the American philosophical tradition from Emerson through Poe to Cavell—is skepticism: the philosophy of the ordinary rightly has in view the vulnerability of our everyday words and experiences to questioning and doubt.

Of course romanticism as a phenomenon finds its place in Apparatgeist, but now less as a literary movement than as a matter of machine practicality. Narratives *of* romantic love find their evolving place in our daily lives, where words must be constantly crafted and responded to, be it with online dating sites, sexting, or everyday text exchanges (Weigel 2016). The mere presence of a phone on a table has been shown to hamper conversation, instilling a sense of not being attended to; controlling abuse in relationships may also, however, find its expression in SMS texting. Valenzuela et al. (2014) shows an uptick in divorce rates among users of Facebook. In "reality" TV series such as *The Bachelor*, patterns of romantic love and courtship for marriage are rehearsed, remixed, and reworded. Materials or "realities" of everyday life are taken up and put into order, precisely for a context in which the institution of marriage is itself rapidly altering. Daily lives of couples, married or not, are beginning to be broached, not merely by the mobile telephone, but by the Internet of Things (robotic vacuum cleaners, robot companions, sex toys). Mays (this volume) has shown that the phenomenon of the "uncanny valley" marks a limit to human receptivity to robots, who ought not to look "too human" as they enter our sphere. People generally prefer gender-neutral robots. Her hypothesis is that humanoid robots threaten our sense of *being* human. Differently put, our ordinary forms of life, with expressive bodies, are threatened.

Yet we already knew that "ordinary life," even the sense of what it is to *be* leading a "human" form of life, is liable to be shifted at any moment, particularly through our lives with words. The silences in ordinary conversation may contain traces of memories of violence (Das 2006). "The Ordinary" may be peaceful, and it is the site of domestic life. Under the lens of "moral perfectionism," it is the arena where we seek our better selves: making amends, excusing and justifying ourselves, rejecting actions, pleading for understanding, begging for forgiveness, and taking our stand. But it is explosive in potential, and social forms of life constantly have to repair it. A single Tweet may lead to disaster, just as, in everyday life, one wrong word may rip open a tear in the fabric of a relationship, destroying it entirely. Emerson (1844), regarding this from the point of view of nature itself, already noticed the ease with which we may lose hold of even our deepest and truest relations to people: there is what he calls an "evanescence and lubricity" to our attachments. Think of the newfangled popularity of virtual sex toys and porn.

Katz and Aakhus (2002, 6) noted explicitly the growing prevalence and intensity of epideictic speech on mobile telephones. The amplification of this with social media is evident for all to see. Our drive to be heard must be placed alongside our fear of being misheard or misinterpreted or, worst of all, ignored. We carve out a social space with our words and defend it.

With so many words and forms of life flying around us every day, there are newfangled things to become anxious about. Groshek and Cutino (2016) document an increase in impolite and uncivil language on Twitter soon after the arrival of the mobile forms of personal communication technology. Yet, like so many communication technologies before it, these instantiations allow people to control their emotional states and reorient their thinking in conjunction with others whom they know. Millions facing isolation during the COVID pandemic seem to find joy in a Tweet about a nearly lost life that was saved. Everyday deaths are documented as individual events on the national news, shared by families who seek solidarity and exemplify the times.

Extending Austin's idea of speech acts to a realm Austin himself tended to ignore, Cavell (2005) broached the difficulties of scrutinizing the perlocutionary effects of "passionate utterance." This has become a systemic problem in our time, even in science. An example of the tendency of the idealized Habermasian "ideal" speech situation to undercut itself is illustrated by a powerful networking graphic used in Groshek and Tandoc (2017) to illustrate how, during the Ferguson riots, legacy journalists tended to forward on-the-ground reports at a significantly lower rate than individual Twitter users, whose "work" the legacy journalists would then take up. Groshek and Tandoc's spatialized network graph of 1,100,011 users in 2,760,607 Tweets about Ferguson shows the importance of some of the most active Tweeters, highlighting the strong networking activity of DeRay McKesson, whose Tweets connected far more previously unconnected groups of users than anyone else's (Fig. 3.1).

Such visualization is illuminating and certainly necessary, given the size of the database; we need, as Wittgenstein wrote, *surveyability* as a norm for science in a world of large datasets. Groshek and Tandoc make an optimistic plea for Habermasian norms of respectful speech in the practice of journalism and point toward the rise of social media within journalism as a potentially creative grassroots media force. And yet, at a recent conference honoring Das's 2020, Clara Han, who has collaborated with Das in researching contemporary human experience of life and death (Das and Han 2016), pointed out that such diagrams inevitably cover over the realities of "everyday" life, including the labor of many queer, feminist, and African American activists whose traces are erased in the diagram, which both is a piece of excellent science and makes the name "DeRay" a headline (see Garza 2014 and compare Scheman 2021).

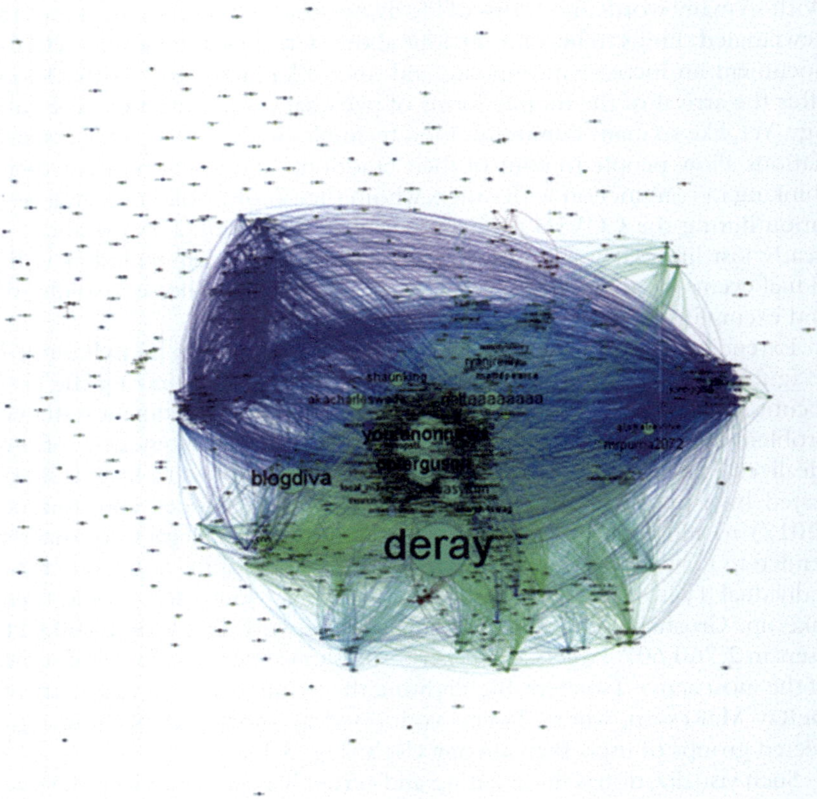

Fig. 3.1 From Groshek and Tandoc (2017, 206)

Das (2020) emphasizes at length the ethical "realities" of the anthropologist's situation, the difficulties of attending to the "texture" of ordinary forms of life sensitively. Such attending, as Emerson would have emphasized, must deal not only with the natural temperament of the scientist herself, but with all the many passing moods that shape her and the individuals in the society being observed, including not the least excitement and joy, resentment and contempt. How is the social scientist to learn how to imbibe and capture, among many other things, these moods and the deeper currents of feeling that are part and parcel of the fabric of forms of life? She has to put her own self on the line.

There *is* no "ideal speech situation": and this is a challenge for science itself. When Turing (1948, 516) predicted that in increasing its reliance on artificial intelligence, science would have to engage humanity in the "cultural search" on a global scale, he meant an ongoing search for "culture" as an evolving horizon of lived research, the finding of new "techniques" that will be conducted by "the human community as a whole." During the time of COVID, forced to rely on technologies of the internet, we see that this was actually occurring at both the individual and societal levels, especially in the arts of video, television, and music. It has been not so much a search for information but for human connection and meaningfulness. The problems of "everyday life" are problems of the public and vice versa, but now palpably and inescapably intertwined.

A Re-reading of the Turing Test

As a methodological schema, Apparatgeist (like OLP) rightly resists reductionisms: ideological, technological, and/or economic determinism as well as forms of explanation couched in terms of a (computationally renderable) notion of "*information.*" Apparatgeist of course does not deny this concept a role as an element of explanation. But it pictures the "affordance" spaces for individuals and institutional "structurations," the very theater of life, as newly dynamic in their evolving refractions of words, gestures, self-conceptions, ideologies, and human actions in private and public life—especially human actions that embed words and deeds about and with *machines* in everyday life. As they note (Katz and Aakhus 2002, 304) this frames a new paradigm for sociology and media studies; our point is that it does so for philosophy itself since language is a primary medium of philosophy.

In sociology Apparatgeist goes beyond the focus on particular domains (work, home, family) or institutions. It takes into account the *content* and *values* animating socio-technological environments: the press toward individuality and the explicit and implicit reasons that individuals act and structure their communicative lives in the ways they do. As in OLP the spoken *voice* may now take center stage: the expressive human body claiming its place (Laugier 2015). Voice-activated technology is important, not merely for its convenience but because nearly a billion more (non-literate) humans will be able to join in on the World Wide Web, adding their words to the mix.

Within Apparatgeist what Bourdieu called our everyday *habitus*, the "feeling of being at home" (and not at home) is taken to imbibe and express not only institutional, ideological, cultural, and economic forces of power but also self-understanding and expression as it is refracted through historical, psychological, evolutionary, and religious localities and traditions. Katz and Aakhus emphasize that this shapes the very reasoning by which, in everyday life, practical decisions are framed. An "informal," dynamic "logic" permeates Apparatgeist. A whole philosophy condensed into an age, as well as a subject of serious research. Das et al. (2021) explore the use of "simulated patients" planted in medical settings, a useful way of testing outcomes in medical care for lower-income communities. They echo our point that what is important here is not that "fake" patients are being smuggled in, fooling doctors into thinking they are "real," but that the simulated patients are themselves real people, helping to generate statistical measures of health outcomes with a creative methodology that is empirically and ethically sound. Their study tracked simulated patients through follow-up visits, revealing the importance of how a shared memory is constructed between patient and physician through words: the creation of new possibility spaces for interaction through phraseology is the point, not how "realistic" the simulated patients are. The elicited responses of the physicians are "real," whereas the simulated patient, while not "real" in one sense, is quite real in another.

In particular, simulated patient methodology avoids the "Hawthorne" surveillance effect in which the very fact that a person is being observed by another human being leads her to alter her behavior. (In the case of the Hawthorne experiment, the purported effects were to increase performance. Subsequent research has shown that the skill level of the observed individual is a powerful determinant of the performance impact of the observation. High competence leads to superior performance; low competence exacerbates poor quality performance.) The purpose of simulated patient methodology is to elicit responses of providers in order to study "real" possibility spaces, not merely to trick or surveil them.

Apparatgeist's "logic," though it is ubiquitous, is multi-valent and multi-aspectual in the sense of the ambiguous cues available from Jastrow's "Duck-Rabbit" or Necker's *a*-in-front-vs.-*b*-in-front cube (Figs. 3.2 and 3.3). One may see in one dimension, but one may also see the same thing

Fig. 3.2 The Duck-Rabbit. (https://en.wikipedia.org/wiki/Rabbit-duck_illusion, accessed February 26, 2021)

in another dimension, while being unable to hold both in mind at once (compare Wittgenstein 2009, PPF xi §118f.).

Emphasizing the importance of temperament to observation, Emerson (1844) remarked that "there is an optical illusion about every person we meet." Meaning requires an analysis of parts of the figure into a stable configuration on a ground, but there are multiple possible analysis of any articulated structure of words (Wittgenstein analogized logical features to facial features). The "logic" of Apparatgeist studies such connections and reconfigurations, tapping into changes in local resources and boundaries, assembling cues into projections and "aspects," now taken as standpoints, views, and prospects. It is not that we should speak of "multiple realities"

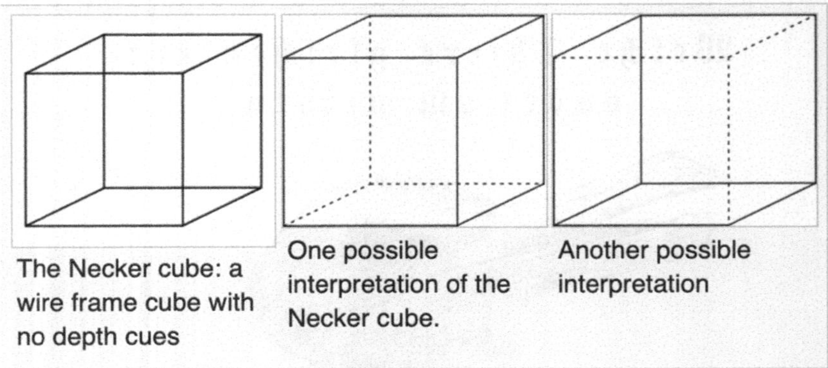

Fig. 3.3 The Necker Cube. (https://en.wikipedia.org/wiki/Necker_cube, accessed February 26, 2021)

here: if we do, that leads away from attending to the importance of the very real multiple dimensions in which human actors perceive situations and interact (Das et al. 2021).

In Apparatgeist the very manner of relating to one another's grammar with and about machines shifts, potentially leaping over time and geography, private and public space, touching and re-touching institutions, histories, psychologies, families, human relations, politics, economies, fashion, religions, experts, and laypeople. As Katz and Aakhus wrote (2002, Abstract), personal communication technologies (PCTs), especially the mobile phone, "affect every aspect of our personal and professional lives either directly or indirectly."

But not univalently, and not in a leveling way. For it is typical of Apparatgeist that the introduction of machines allows human users to artfully adapt their characterizations of contingent, local realities, institutions, and rituals (e.g., the delivery of *fatwas* by email, or Zoom court proceedings during COVID). This is true even though, at the very same time, mobile phones may sharply affect institutions, uses of language, social relationships, and human environments (social, institutional, political and ecological) on a global scale.

The predictive quality of this research from the late 1990s and early 2000s is eerily accurate. How could this be? *How* did Katz and Aakhus "see the future" of communication technology? The answer is that Apparatgeist got past the paradigm of communication as *information* that constituted the beginnings of the computational revolution in the hands of Shannon and other early computer scientists (Gleick 2011). It also left behind the received picture of the Turing Test, which continues to dominate the philosophy of mind today, a Cartesian one in which the name of the game is to determine whether what is before you is a machine or is a human.

The familiar picture imagines an "imitation" game, as Turing termed it (1950), in which human C, screened off from all perception of machine A and another human B, is tasked with posing questions to A and B in such a way that C tries to detect which is the machine and which is the human (Fig. 3.4). There is no social media here, and no "depth" to the human relationships. This serves as a Cartesian blind spot. It is shared, not only in popular presentations of the Turing Test but in popular culture: in the original *Bladerunner* movie, no mobile technology and social media were envisioned.

Turing's actual point in his famous Test (1950) was quite different. He wanted to take into account the anthropological aspect of our human forms of life with words. After the game is played, C will walk around the

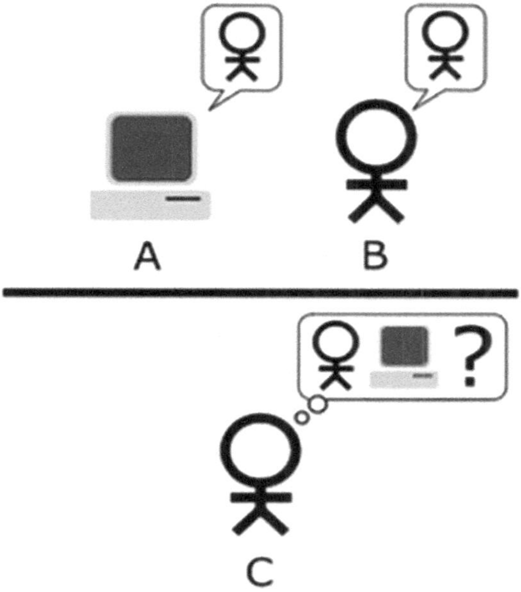

Fig. 3.4 The Cartesian version of the Turing Test. (https://commons.wikimedia.org/wiki/File:Turing_Test_Version_3.svg)

screen and have a talk with human B. C and B will have to relate to one another verbally and socially. Turing's interest was in screening off our anthropomorphism temporarily, but ultimately for the sake of human-to-human "phraseology," the forms of "typing" of objects we use to embed our words. In actuality, this is a *social* experiment involving the ***words*** A and B give to one another in the presence of A. The real question is what we will say once the screen comes down (Fig. 3.5).

In Apparatgeist, with the widespread uses of mobile technology, the screen not only comes down but we see a whirling social world of little

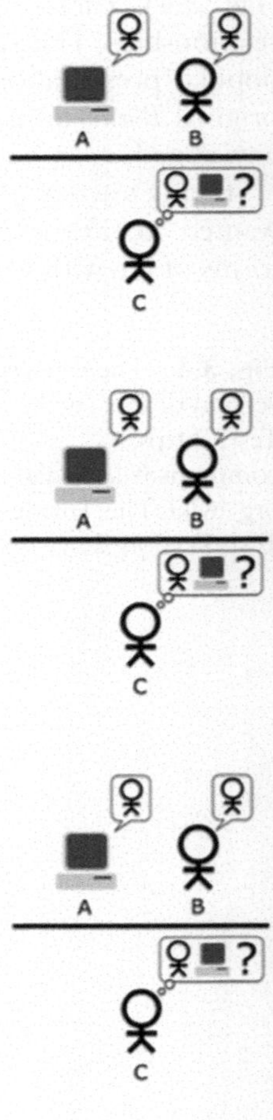

Fig. 3.5 The Turing Test in Apparatgeist. (Adapted from https://commons.wikimedia.org/wiki/File:Turing_Test_Version_3.svg)

Turing Tests as experiments in phraseology going on, peeking at screens, chatting with friends, watching them doing the same thing. The result is a flood, not so much of information but of performance: positioning our bodies and words for self-expression and the responses to others' expressions—including discussions of ourselves with machines. Scrutiny of performance takes different forms given the speed and ease of messaging. The technology itself becomes a symbol, not only of power but of fashion, jewelry, self-expression (Fortunati et al. 2003). The whole is tremendously dynamic.

It is also *real*. Here we bear in mind Austin's (1979, 58, 67, 86ff., 120n., 192, 284) idea of "*real*" as a "trouser" word: it requires the upholding flesh of a pair of legs to stand ("real what?"): a modification of a specific kind, a definite interest, mode, point, and suitable occasion of use. In the world of the 1950s: to "wear the trousers" is certainly to work, maybe even to seem to be the boss. But this doesn't happen without a "fit" between leg and cloth. Human bodies, flesh, and blood support the trousers of "reality."

To appreciate the force of "Is it real?" one typically specifies, in everyday life, what it would be to *fail* to be real, in one specific dimension or another. This elides discussion of a "reality" beyond all possible dimensions of eventual human ability to properly describe or intuit it. That discussion, irrefutable by OLP, lends itself to the more traditional Cartesian dialectic between skepticism and dogmatism. Cavell takes skepticism to be an ever-present possibility within the "ordinary," where the question "But is it *real*?" cannot be stopped from naturally arising. In his version of OLP (1999, 2013) is it the problem of other minds—whether or not I am truly acknowledged or loved or known or cared about—that forms the lived, social realization of skepticism. This problem finds its aesthetic expression, he argues, in phenomenologies of catastrophe and tragedy: an imagined annihilation of the world or self through a machine, invasion, bomb, or explosion (Beckett's *Endgame*, *Bladerunner 2049*) or works of tragedy and alienation (*Othello*, *Lear*, Zombies).

Rather than playing the role of an epistemological exercise in Cartesian skepticism about other minds, the Turing Test should be regarded as opening us up to the exploration of our own drive to speech and social expression in the presence of mechanization. This is fundamentally why the idea of "logic" in Apparatgeist, as in Turing's famous Test, conceives of logic itself in the manner of Wittgenstein, with his signal idea of "forms of life." The fact that most of us crave social recognition and use complex wordings to get it; that we tell stories; that we characteristically have hands with fingers and/or voices; that we chat; that we converse over meals; that we have limited energy, time, and memory—these are generally human forms of life. Then there are the specific, more localized "forms of life" we work with every day, altering rapidly with the development of new apps. As we have emphasized already, "forms of life" are not merely language games, they go deeper, to include the multi-valent, creative, and adaptive embedding of words in everyday life. The human body, Wittgenstein wrote, is the "best" picture of the human soul; one is not "of the opinion" that a body is ensouled rather than machine; rather one lives and responds to and expresses "forms" (possibilities) of ensoulings *with* one's body, *with* one's lived expressions (2009, PPF iv §§21, 25).

Occasion Sensitivity

Form is the *possibility* of structure, for Wittgenstein, not just one more actuality. A medium's possibilities are not given with the empirical or technological character of the medium alone but in what may be *done* or expressed with it (Cavell 1979, 164). As in logic, a "form" of life shows forth only when we see *through* our practices with words and take an action, concept, speech-act, or life to realize but one possibility (pattern, structure) among many. In the time of Apparatgeist, it is evident: with the ease and cost-free ability to generate words and texts, we are all constantly faced with choices that emphasize such seeing through, sometimes with enormous compression and fateful consequence ("Hi!" texted across a crowded party space to a friend is utterly different from "Hi!!!!!" texted in the same space to someone one has never met face-to-face; "Hi!!" is somewhere between).

This seeing "through" observed structure is dynamic and multidimensional in Wittgenstein's thought: sentences, words, and actions have "faces," different possible "looks" or "aspects." It is not only the words, it is how they are "fit" to reality (or not fit). Different ways of "fitting" elicit different aspects or characteristics of reality, including the "realities" of character revealed in the characterizer who characterizes. Human beings characterize, share characterizations, and re-characterize over and over again. It is as if the whole idea of a metalanguage is absorbed into the ever-shuffling process of formalization, reformulation, recasting of categorical "types," renewed experience, informal characterization, re-parametrization, and re-interpretation. We should respect the hustle: the multiple "faces" we encounter, show and respond to every day. Apparatgeist does.

This is not linguistic determinism: an old-fashioned, outdated vision of OLP. To see this, we need to emphasize the importance of what Travis (2006, 2008) calls *occasion sensitivity*. We project aspects (as prospects or standpoints) on given occasions of using words. But our projections are occasion-sensitive: the words alone do not take care of meaning. Whether it is true or false that "Odette's shoes are under the bed" will depend on our understandings of the occasion of claiming that they are, with its intents and purposes, as a speech-act situation. The sentence is multiply analyzable, just as human experience is, or the ambiguous cues of the duck-rabbit, the Necker Cube, or any puzzle picture. If Odette's shoes are three stories down, perhaps the claim is false. If directly on the floor of Odette's room, centered underneath the bed, true. But if a bomb is in her shoes, and the strength of the entire building an architectural issue, then being three stories down may count to make the claim true.

The point responds to ancient problems of skepticism. When you look at an apple, what do you see? Do you see the *whole* apple? Or only its surface? Would drawing a grid with Cartesian coordinates establish more precisely just how *much* of the apple you really see? But then how can one ever see "the (whole) apple" (compare Clarke 1965)? Perception is lost. The answer here is occasion sensitivity. It is true to say that you see the apple on some understandings of the point of our conversation. It is false on others.

Occasion sensitivity of words is emphatically neither pure conventionalism nor pure relativism, though in our Post-Truth era there is a constant danger (among experts and non-experts) of admitting the reality of this phenomenon but wrongly taking it to destroy Truth. But no (compare Floyd 2019). Relative to an occasion of use, a *point* in speaking, the truth of the sentence claimed may be absolute. There are not differing modes of truth, but different ways of talking about truth *as* absolute, different manners of projecting our words, different and evolving phraseologies. There is something available to *be* possibly said in a language, and by saying it one may *reveal* the possibility to folks who may not have seen that the possibility was there.

To keep this straight, we must work a good deal to achieve sufficient "attunement" of understandings with one another (a shared sense of relevance, outrageousness, purpose, what *matters*). This is a deep need for forms of life: shared capacities for claiming and "fitting" our concepts to reality. Apparatgeist highlights how this point, appreciated before the advent of mobile technology, is amplified by it. The dawning of the age of robots and other artificially intelligent entities such as smart speakers and augmented reality settings should continue to support and enrich our understanding of how people combine cognition and emotion to figure out and reconfigure their understanding of everyday life. But the machines will not do it alone: we will be constant cultural contributors.

Can we "see" the future of communication technology? We can "see" spaces of possibility in light of human history and our evolution. Human-to-human interaction in the presence of machines, I predict, will continue to form a central area of research, one in which sensitivity to ordinary life and the methodology of Apparatgeist, illuminated by the tradition of OLP and deepened by the kind of attentive ethnography urged by Das and her collaborators, will certainly contribute. Appeals will be made to regulate the social sphere of interaction with legal rules and principles. Ethical calls will be made with more and wider social significance as we go. Dreams of immortality through machines will continue. Yet Emerson's and Wittgenstein's points about meaning, "experience" and how we must respect the difficulties of gaining and holding these in daily life—respecting the very human tendency to avoid the difficulties of reality—will remain. We each seek to get from experience to meaning, from words to realities, to care and invest in what is worthwhile for us. But we must face all the while that we always orbit in the region as children, who lose and gain their attachments to toys as they grow. We should admit our vulnerability to the reboundings of our own words. Collective catastrophizing, skepticism, and collective grief will continue to grip us in our sense of vulnerability; there are many ways of "augmenting" reality and many ways of avoiding it. The trick, in research, will be not to lose hold of those aspects of reality that matter to us, respecting all the while the difficulties of everyday life.

I follow Turing's idea of a growing, collective, global "cultural search," embedded continually in our "forms of life" in the context of "the human community as a whole." Our inventiveness in learning how to find our way in the dizzying spectacle of possibility spaces, our remaining true to "The meal in the firkin; the milk in the pan; the ballad in the street; the news of the boat; the glance of the eye; the form and the gait of the body" will be a measure of our ability to adapt, as human beings, to the ethics of our day. We must learn to educate ourselves in finding our own ways and face a continual re-education in the face of everyday life. The difficulty of *becoming someone* is not trivial, and becomes ever more fateful in our era, where individuals may serve as icons with the flick of a finger. Pursuit of philosophy and research into how our interactions with one another are being re-symbolized and reconfigured, seeing how it is that people *feel* about one another and their lives in society, working through the materials of everyday life, whether in popular culture or in the halls of academe: these are, it seems to me, foundational in our hopes for the future. Such research, research into people's *searches* for meaning and culture, will have to be carried out, not only by experts but by everyone.

Acknowledgments I owe significant debts to James E. Katz, my collaborator (with Rachell Powell) on the 2016–2019 Boston University Mellon Sawyer Seminar. James has been a leading force in the scholarly study of emerging media, and I thank him and his colleagues in the Boston University Division of Emerging Media for drawing me into a new world for philosophical analysis. James gave me sage feedback on a late draft of this chapter that led to important improvements, and I owe him a very great deal for his many stimulating and supportive conversations. It has been a privilege to watch Kate Mays and Zeynep Soysal blossom in their careers as scholars of the subject, I have learned much from them; Zeynep's post-doctoral support during the Mellon Sawyer Seminar was crucial to the success of the endeavor.

Participants at the Mellon sponsored 5 February 2018 "Day of Apparatgeist" gave me insightful feedback on an initial presentation of this material, especially Vanessa Nurock and Sandra Laugier; Pierre Cassou-Nougès provided me with stimulating discussions sparked by his several seminar papers at Boston conferences. The French Consul of Boston, aided by Michaël Vallée, offered generous support as did the Boston University Humanities Center (BUCH) under the wise aegis of Susan Mizruchi. BUCH supported me with a Jeffrey Henderson Fellowship during the fall of 2020 to write this chapter.

A successor Sawyer Seminar at Johns Hopkins University on certainty in a world of Big Data is ongoing, and I have profited from exchange with this team, particularly during my May 2019 visit. Veena Das and Clara Han have given me profoundly interesting ways of rethinking my ideas and offer a path forward for future thinking about "ordinary language" approaches.

Last but certainly not least, Katie Schiepers has shouldered many of the burdens of fine-grained editorial work for this chapter and this volume, and she deserves special thanks for that.

References

Austin, J. L. 1979. *Philosophical Papers*, ed. J. O. Urmson and G. J. Warnock. New York: Oxford University Press.

Cavell, Stanley. 1979. *The World Viewed: Reflections on the Ontology of Film*. Enl. ed. Cambridge: Harvard University Press.

———. 1981. *Pursuits of Happiness: The Hollywood Comedy of Remarriage*. Cambridge, MA: Harvard Film Studies, Harvard University Press.

———. 1988a. *Conditions Handsome and Unhandsome: The Constitution of Emersonian Perfectionism: The Carus Lectures, 1988*. Chicago: University of Chicago Press.

———. 1988b. Declining Decline. *Inquiry* 31 (3): 253–264. Reprinted in Cavell 1989, 29–77.

———. 1989. *This New Yet Unapproachable America: Lectures After Emerson After Wittgenstein*. Chicago: University of Chicago Press.

———. 1999. *The Claim of Reason: Wittgenstein, Skepticism, Morality, and Tragedy*. New York: Oxford University Press.

———. 2005. Passionate and Performative Utterance: Morals of an Encounter. In *Contending with Stanley Cavell*, ed. Stanley Cavell and Russell B. Goodman, 177–198. Oxford University Press.

———. 2013. *Must We Mean What We Say?: A Book of Essays*. Cambridge University Press.

Clarke, Thompson. 1965. Seeing Surfaces and Physical Objects. In *Philosophy in America*, ed. Max Black, 98–114. Ithaca, NY: Cornell University Press.

Cooper, Barry S., and Jan van Leeuwen, eds. 2013. *Alan Turing: His Work and Impact*. Amsterdam: North-Holland/Elsevier Science.

Das, Veena. 2006. *Life and Words: Violence and the Descent into the Ordinary*. Berkerley: University of California Press.

———. 2020. *Textures of the Ordinary: Doing Anthropology After Wittgenstein*. New York: Fordham University Press.

Das, Veena, and Clara Han, eds. 2016. *Living and Dying in the Contemporary World: A Compendium*. University of California Press.

Das, Veena, Benjamin Daniels, Ada Kwan, Vaibhav Saria, Ranendra Das, Madhukar Pai, and Jishnu Das. 2021. *Simulated Patients and Their Reality: An Inquiry into Theory and Method*. Manuscript of 2/26/2021.

Davies, Byron. 2021. *Found Footage at the Receding of the World*. Manuscript.

Davis, Martin. 2017. Universality Is Ubiquitous. In *Philosophical Explorations of the Legacy of Alan Turing: Turing 100. Boston Studies in the Philosophy and History of Science*, ed. J. Floyd and A. Bokulich, 153–158. New York: Springer Science+Business Media.

de Gournay, Chantal. 2002. Pretense of Intimacy in France. In *Perpetual Contact: Mobile Communication, Private Talk, Public Performance*, ed. James E. Katz and Mark A. Aakhus, 193–205. Cambridge, UK: Cambridge University Press.

Diamond, Cora. 1991. *The Realistic Spirit: Wittgenstein, Philosophy, and the Mind*. Cambridge, MA: MIT Press.

Emerson, Ralph Waldo. 1837. The American Scholar. Address to the Harvard Chapter of the Phi Beta Kappa Society. First published in Emerson, Essays: First Series, 1841; open access at http://digitalemerson.wsulibs.wsu.edu/exhibits/show/text/the-american-scholar. Accessed 21 February 2021.

———. 1844. Experience. First published in Emerson, Essays: Second Series, 1844; open access at http://digitalemerson.wsulibs.wsu.edu/exhibits/show/text/the-american-scholar. Accessed 21 February 2021.

Floyd, Juliet. 2013. Turing, Wittgenstein and Types: Philosophical Aspects of Turing's 'the Reform of Mathematical Notation' (1944/5). In *Alan Turing: His Work and Impact*, ed. S. Barry Cooper and J. van Leeuven, 250–253. Amsterdam: North-Holland/Elsevier Science.

———. 2017. Turing on 'Common Sense': Cambridge Resonances. In *Philosophical Explorations of the Legacy of Alan Turing: Turing 100. Boston Studies in the Philosophy and History of Science*, ed. J. Floyd and A. Bokulich, 103–152. New York: Springer Science+Business Media.

———. 2018. Lebensformen: Living Logic. In *Language, Form(s) of Life, and Logic: Investigations After Wittgenstein*, On Wittgenstein, ed. Christian Martin, 59–92. Berlin: deGruyter.

———. 2019. 'The True' in Journalism. In *Journalism and Truth in an Age of Social Media*, ed. James E. Katz and Kate K. Mays, 85–102. New York: Oxford University Press.

———. 2020. Wittgenstein on Ethics: Working Through Lebensformen. *Philosophy and Social Criticism* 46 (2): 115–130.

Floyd, Juliet, and James E. Katz, eds. 2016. *Philosophy of Emerging Media: Understanding, Appreciation, Application*. New York: Oxford University Press.

Fortunati, Leopoldina, James E. Katz, and Raimonda Riccini, eds. 2003. *Mediating the Human Body: Technology, Communication and Fashion*. Mahwah, NJ: Lawrence Erlbaum Associates.

Garza, Alicia. 2014. A Herstory of the #Blacklivesmatter Movement. *Feminist Wire*, October 7. https://www.thefeministwire.com/2014/10/blacklives-matter-2. Accessed 27 February 2021.

Gleick, James. 2011. *The Information: A History, a Theory, a Flood*. 1st ed. New York: Pantheon Books.

Groshek, Jacob, and Chelsea Cutino. 2016. Meaner on Mobile: Incivility and Impoliteness in Communicating Contentious Politics on Sociotechnical Networks. *Social Media + Society* 2 (4): 205630511667713. https://doi.org/10.1177/2056305116677137.

Groshek, Jacob, and Edson Tandoc. 2017. The Affordance Effect: Gatekeeping and (Non)Reciprocal Journalism on Twitter. *Computers in Human Behavior* 66: 201–210.

Katz, James E., and Mark A. Aakhus, eds. 2002. *Perpetual Contact: Mobile Communication, Private Talk, Public Performance*. Cambridge, UK: Cambridge University Press.

Krebs, Victor, and Richard Frankel. 2021. *Human Virtuality and Digital Life. Philosophical and Psychoanalytic Investigations*. New York: Routledge.

Laugier, Sandra. 2012. Ordinary Virtues of Popular Cultures. *Critique* 68 (776): 48–61.

———. 2015. Voice as Form of Life and Life Form. *Nordic Wittgenstein Review* 4 (October, Special Issue on Forms of Life): 63–81.

———. 2020. The Conception of Film for the Subject of Television: Moral Education of the Public and a Return to an Aesthetics of the Ordinary. In *The Thought of Stanley Cavell and Cinema: Turning Anew to the Ontology of Film a Half-Century After The World Viewed*, ed. David LaRocca, 210–227. New York: Bloomsbury.

Moyal-Sharrock, Danielle. 2015. Wittgenstein on Forms of Life, Patterns of Life, and Ways of Living. *Nordic Wittgenstein Review* 4 (October, Special Issue on Forms of Life): 21–42.

Nafus, Dawn, and Karina Tracey. 2002. Mobile Phones and Concepts of Personhood. In *Perpetual Contact: Mobile Communication, Private Talk, Public Performance*, ed. James E. Katz and Mark A. Aakhus, 206–221. Cambridge, UK: Cambridge University Press.

Scheman, Naomi. 2021 under review. The On-the-Ground Radicality of Police and Prison Abolition: Acknowledgment, Seeing-As, and Ordinary Caring. Submitted to *Ethical Inquiries After Wittgenstein*, ed. Ondrej Beran, Nora Hämäläinen, and Salla Aldrin-Salskov. Under review, Springer.

Schutz, Alfred. 1932. *Der sinnhafte Aufbau der sozialen Welt* [The Meaningful Strucuture of the Social World]. Berlin: Springer.

Travis, Charles. 2006. *Thought's Footing: A Theme in Wittgenstein's Philosophical Investigations*. Oxford/New York: Oxford University Press.

———. 2008. *Occasion-Sensitivity Selected Essays*. Oxford: Oxford University Press.

Turing, Alan M. 1936. On Computable Numbers, with an Application to the Decision Problem. *Proceedings of the London Mathematical Society* 2 (42): 230–265. Reprinted in eds. Cooper and van Leeuwen 2013, 16–43.

———. 1944/45. The Reform of Mathematical Notation and Phraseology (1944/45). In *Alan Turing: His Work and Impact*, ed. S. Barry Cooper and J. van Leeuwen, 245–249. Amsterdam: North-Holland/Elsevier Science.

———. 1948. Intelligent Machinery: A Report Written for the National Physical Laboratory. In *Alan Turing: His Work and Impact*, ed. S. Barry Cooper and J. van Leeuwen, 501–516. Amsterdam: North-Holland/Elsevier Science.

———. 1950. Computing Machinery and Intelligence. *Mind* 59 (October): 433–460. Reprinted in *Alan Turing: His Work and Impact*, eds. Cooper and van Leeuwen, 2013, 551–568. Amsterdam: North-Holland/Elsevier Science.

———. 1954. Solvable and Unsolvable Problems. *Science News* 31: 7–23. Reprinted in *Alan Turing: His Work and Impact*, eds. Cooper and van Leeuwen 2013, 322–331. Amsterdam: North-Holland/Elsevier Science.

Valenzuela, S., D. Halpern, and James E. Katz. 2014. Social Network Sites, Marriage Well-Being and Divorce: Survey and State-Level Evidence from the United States. *Computers in Human Behavior* 36: 94–101.

Varela, Bruno. 2019. Manolita. Film online at https://vimeo.com/368070969.

Weigel, Moira. 2016. *Labor of Love: The Invention of Dating*. New York: Farrar, Straus and Giroux.

Wittgenstein, Ludwig. 2009. *Philosophische Untersuchungen = Philosophical Investigations* [in German and English]. Trans. G.E.M. Anscombe, P.M.S. Hacker and J. Schulte; Ed. G.E.M. Anscombe, Rev. 4th ed. Chichester, West Sussex, UK/Malden, MA: Wiley-Blackwell.

Shared Screen Time: The Role of the Mobile Phone in Local Social Interaction in 2000 and 2020

Alexandra Weilenmann

Introduction

In the beginning of the century, the mobile phone was marketed primarily as a tool for remote office work. However, it turned out that a technology originally designed for private remote communication in interaction with others became a device for other more social, communicative, and interactional purposes in the hands of young people. In their everyday activities, the phones often had an important role, despite their relatively limited functionalities initially. Young people also challenged the idea of the personal and private phone as they were creatively exploring new ways of collaborating and communicating on their phones. Interestingly, this device for remote communication also had a social function in the local environment when socializing with people who were in the same place.

A. Weilenmann (✉)
University of Gothenburg, Gothenburg, Sweden
e-mail: alexandra.weilenmann@gu.se

J. Katz et al. (eds.), *Perceiving the Future through New Communication Technologies*,
https://doi.org/10.1007/978-3-030-84883-5_4

As noted in the book *Perpetual Contact* in 2002: "Mobile technology also affects the way people interact when face-to-face or, rather and increasingly, face-to-face-to-mobile-phone-face, since people are ever more likely to include the mobile phone as a participant in what would otherwise be a face-to-face dyad or a small group, and even parties" (Katz and Aakhus 2002, 2). It is hard to imagine almost 20 years later that it was a new observation that people were so preoccupied with their phones that they even had them in front of them when they met others. We can then remind ourselves that, at this time, we did not have social media, nor even mobile internet, and that we could not take pictures using our mobile phones. Despite this, it was common for the mobile phone to be on the table when people met and it often was a part of the conversation: for example, a received text message could lead to a conversation about the content or the person who sent it. Since then, we have witnessed an explosion of platforms and services, and the opportunities to share and engage with and throughout these devices are constantly evolving. This has made the smartphone of today into a ubiquitous and indispensable device that we both love and hate; a device that both maintains and challenges social ties (Ling 2008).

While we initially appreciated the potential to be constantly available, a reaction has emerged where we want to disconnect and limit our interaction with our devices. The mobile phone is seen as a dangerous disruption to social relationships and local community (Turkle 2017). In recent years, the screen time debate has flourished, focusing mainly on managing and limiting our device use as it supposedly creates risk to both our health and the quality of our relationships. While there are concerns about screen time's impact on important health issues such as getting enough physical movement and sleep for the body to function, there is also a worry that the increase has resulted in mental health problems and the weakening of face-to-face interaction. This argumentation seems to build on the special status of face-to-face communication, its potential for intimacy and connection, and how it is seen as more authentic than mediated technology (Baym 2015). There is an underlying assumption that non-technology-mediated communication has a higher quality than one where technology is involved. "We have a true self that becomes less authentic when mediated through networked technologies," as Tiidenberg et al. (2017) found when examining the discourses and the rhetoric among young people. They write that "[t]he grand narrative of authenticity stubbornly clings to an online/offline divide, despite the fact that most people's daily experiences traverse digitally mediated and unmediated settings" (ibid., 6).

Not only does it seem as though mediated interaction has less authenticity than face-to-face interaction, it also seems to be the case that, when socializing with others, that social situation is considered less authentic when technology is involved in some way. There is common understanding that face-to-face "quality time" should not involve mobile phones or other digital devices (Pentzold et al. 2020). The terms disruption and interruption are commonly used to describe what happens when the mobile phone is brought into a local social situation. For example, the term phubbing has been introduced to show how the mobile phone is taking the focus from the co-present interaction (Chotpitayasunondh and Douglas 2018; Abeele 2020).

Much of the research that investigates the impact of the mobile phone on social co-present interaction is based on theoretic arguments or psychological perspectives, and study approaches often rely either on reported data (e.g., how people describe their own or other's technology use and how much they estimate that they use it) or on experimental studies (e.g., constructing situations where people are interrupted or looking at others being interrupted in their social interaction by mobile phones as in Chotpitayasunondh and Douglas 2018). While these studies can raise interesting questions, they often fail to provide an analysis of naturally occurring mobile phone use in actual social settings.

For example, in one study it is argued that the mere presence of a mobile phone affected the quality of conversation and the level of trust in forming personal relationships (Przybylski and Weinstein 2013). The participants were asked to describe a meaningful event, while the mobile phone was sitting on a table nearby. However, if this was not a highly regulated type of interaction, it is not unlikely that the phone would have a supportive role in such a conversation, for example, by showing a picture of this meaningful event or maybe a photo of family members or others who were part of the event. We know from before that meaningful events are often photographed to be shared later (Chalfen 1987), which is now done through the mobile phone. The mobility and ubiquity of the mobile phone means that these photos can be introduced to "enhance in-person conversation" (Brown et al. 2016). I wish to argue that with an experimental setup like this, the participants are limited from using their natural ways of managing social interaction (cf. Esbjörnsson et al. 2007). It is also likely that the grand narratives that Tiidenberg et al. describe, will lead the participants to report lower quality of conversation when the phone was present. The notion that quality time should not involve technology is visible not just in the views presented by informants in various studies, but I want to argue that it is a premise that is built into the design of several studies investigating the phenomenon.

A different methodological perspective on how co-present phone use can be understood outside of the experimental and constructed lab environment is to conduct observations *in situ*. In a series of studies, Brown and colleagues (e.g., Brown et al. 2013) have done screen recordings and video recordings of co-present mobile phone use and show how it is common for more than one person to spend time around a mobile phone. They explain this through a discussion of how the mobile phone is a topical resource in interaction that supports a form of multi-activity that involves both conversation and the use of technology. In one study, they show how co-located social media consumption made up a large part of the socialization around the telephones; that is, social media has a function in the group you are with (ibid.). Participants browsed through and talked about topics such as Instagram photos and memes that they had access to on their phones. This approach has the potential to give us an additional perspective on how screens are affecting social relationships.

In this chapter, I wish to set the screens in their social context and show the importance of making the connection between what is happening on/through the phone and what is happening in the surroundings. Based on methodological explorations over 20 years, I have together with colleagues examined in different ways the local relevance of the mobile phone. This has allowed us to examine how participants orient to the local environment and how they make the connection between the co-present and mediated setting. This is a form of *shared screen time* that is largely dismissed both in research and in the public debate on the impact of mobile phone use. The examples presented in this chapter consist of both excerpts from field notes from ethnographic observations and transcripts of video-recorded interaction from studies done with almost 20-year intervals.

Tales from the Field: Shared Screen Time Yesterday and Today

When returning to the data collected during ethnographic work in the early 2000s, it is interesting to see that the mobile phone already had a clear socially structuring function for people when they met at this early stage, despite the fact that the technical possibilities were significantly fewer. In an early observational study of mobile phone use, we showed how young people worked to make their phones and information on screens available to friends in the same place (Weilenmann and Larsson 2002; Weilenmann 2003). For example, we found that participants read aloud from text messages that they received or showed their screen to co-present friends in order to involve them in the communication that took place via the mobile phone. While one form of sharing involved the participants using the phone of others, in a more minimal form of sharing the content or information on the phone was made available to others in different ways, without anyone else holding or touching the device. The two strategies for minimal forms of SMS sharing that we presented were by reading aloud from the phone, relating what was going on, or by simply showing the screen to others. Both strategies were ways to let friends (and perhaps others in the environment) participate in personal communication, strategies for making private information presented on a very small screen accessible to others. These strategies seemed to occur when teens tried to engage others in the remote communication in which they were involved.

To illustrate this, we can have a closer look at one example from fieldwork of young people's public mobile phone use in early 2000 (reported previously in Weilenmann and Larsson 2002). In this example, a girl shares her text message with her friends as she is writing it by both showing the screen to her friends and reading aloud from the message:

> Example 1: Sharing Text MessagesThree girls are sitting on a tram. One girl (A) is writing an SMS-message. A turns to B, who is sitting next to her, gives B a light nudge, and says "hey." She shows the display to B. A deletes a few letters, and then continues to write the message. She says with a whiny voice: "I don't wanna send this." She then begins to read aloud parts of her message: "I want to have a house party. I'm leaving soon you know." Presumably, she now sends the message. She then puts her phone in her purse.
>
> Shortly after she puts her phone away, it rings. She exclaims "NO." She picks up her phone, and without looking at the display, gives the phone to her friend, B, and says: "Please, can you take it?" B pushes the phone away, refusing to answer it. A answers the call. A talks to someone about the house party. She ends the phone call after a short conversation and says to her friends: "I hate (him)! Shit!" she sighs. "What did he say?" her friend asks. "Nothing" she responds and turns to the window, crosses her arms and sighs.

In the first part, the girl tries to involve her two friends in the writing and production of a text message. What could otherwise be an individual and private activity, to formulate a text message on a very small screen, is here made into a collaborative shared screen activity. She shares her message by first showing the text message to her friend. This is done quite subtly, by a slight push with the elbow and the screen, in order to indicate that she wants her friend to read it. In this case, her friend does not seem to be particularly interested in the message. Shortly afterwards, she uses another strategy to share the contents of the phone with her surroundings: she reads aloud from her message. This may be because she wants more engagement from the others and did not succeed by just showing the message. Reading aloud from the screen is a way to make the message on the private screen publicly available (cf. Heath and Luff 2000).

In the second part of this example, A's phone rings right and she tries, without success, to involve her friend in this phone call by asking her to answer the phone. Once the conversation is over, she makes a comment about the conversation and the person she just talked to. In these ways, through jointly constructing text messages and talking about the phone call afterward, these young people work to make activities that could otherwise be individual and private into shared activities.

In the next example from field studies conducted 15 years later (reported previously in Weilenmann and Hillman 2020), we see a similar type of activity when a group of young people socialize around selfie-taking. In this example, from ethnographic observations of selfie photography in public places in Sweden, there is the same form of minimal sharing of technology as the one we identified in the field studies in 2000, but now the content that is shared is visual, rather than textual and verbal. Even an activity as seemingly personal and individualistic as taking a selfie is turned into a collaborative activity:

> Example 2: Sharing SelfiesTwo girls are sitting in a park outside a Swedish music festival that is just about to begin. They are leaning against part of a huge sign that bears the name of the festival, a sign that was a popular place for taking photographs, including selfies. The girls were drinking cider and smoking, and were both intermittently using their phones to chat and take images and videos of themselves and the surroundings.
>
> Girl A takes a couple of selfies of herself and her friend using her phone, and then adds a filter to them and sends them using a messaging app. As she

does this, we see how Girl B glances towards the screen of the phone, thereby taking part in the remote communication. They then proceed to take another set of selfies using Girl B's phone instead.

Previous research has shown how visual communication where participants send images back and forth in a kind of conversation has its own entertainment value (Katz and Crocker 2015). Based on studies in the field, we can also show how co-located people become part of this visual communication and that the activity also has a local entertainment value besides what is played out online.

Spending time around selfies is something we have observed in field work in places where people have time to sit down, have a drink or coffee, smoke and talk to friends. In these situations, today as well as yesterday, mobile phones are more often than not ready. Turning to share a picture on your phone screen now smoothly fits into the natural process of communication. On several occasions, we observed how the actual selfie photography was in focus of the interaction, as in this example. DiDomenico and Boase (2013) argue that our devices are now part of the various linguistic and physical resources that we can draw upon when producing social actions. They borrow Goffman's terminology to argue that the co-located situation is the primary involvement, where ongoing mediated interaction constitutes a secondary involvement. In the example from the field presented here, it is difficult to determine what constitutes the primary social commitment. The difference becomes even more complicated when the socializing around the phone becomes a focus in itself as opposed to being a side activity that the user has to handle at the same time as the local situation.

In the third and final example from the field, we will show how social media is produced and consumed through and with the sharing of screens. Here we have developed our methodological approach in order to capture the more fine-grained details of the sharing and collaboration taking place with these devices. This example comes from a field study at a Swedish zoo, where we used a new approach to document social photography in the field as and where it happened (previously reported in Hillman and Weilenmann 2015). Two children were invited to participate in a study where we experimented with capturing social media activities as they were happening in the field. We did screen recordings of the activities of the boys' phones, we documented them with a video camera, and one of them was equipped with video glasses to also show the direction of the gaze. This setup was made to allow for a richer dataset of the shifting between what was going on in the local environment and on the screen.

In the following example from this study, we see how the two children (here called Emil and Liam, Fig. 4.1) got involved in taking photos of animals with their respective mobile devices. While not instructed to collaborate, their photo taking became a socially organized process, where they are orienting both to the local environment—searching for animals to photograph—at the same time as they are orienting to the images as they appear on their own screen and on their friend's screen. As they are showing the images to each other, they are also assessing the pictures and comparing them. The younger brother of one of them (here called Lukas) is also brought into what turns out to be almost a competition about who got the best picture of the animals (Fig. 4.2).

Example 3: Sharing Social Media Production[1]Emil: did you get a picture of *only* the kid

Liam: yes ***and*** look some more on the top (scrolls in his Instagram feed)

Lukas: Liam Liam Liam Liam

Emil: I got a picture of it

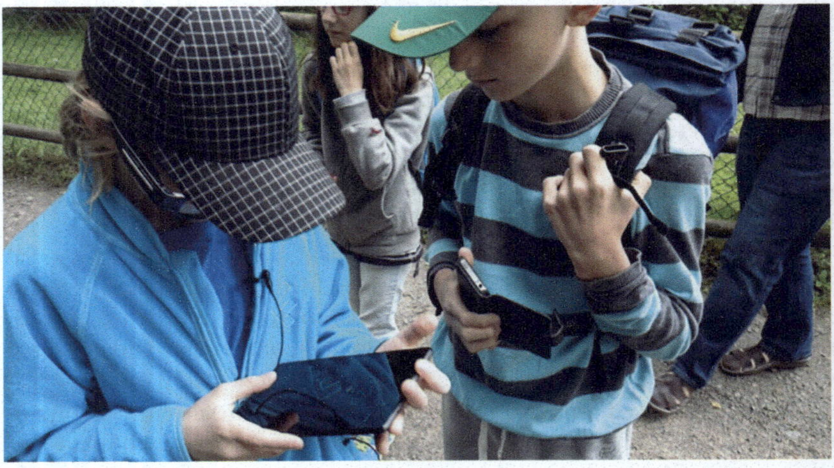

Fig. 4.1 Shared screen activities in the field

[1] The conversation is translated from Swedish to English and is somewhat simplified for this chapter—the analysis was made based on a more thoroughly transcribed version based on CA standards (Sacks et al. 1978).

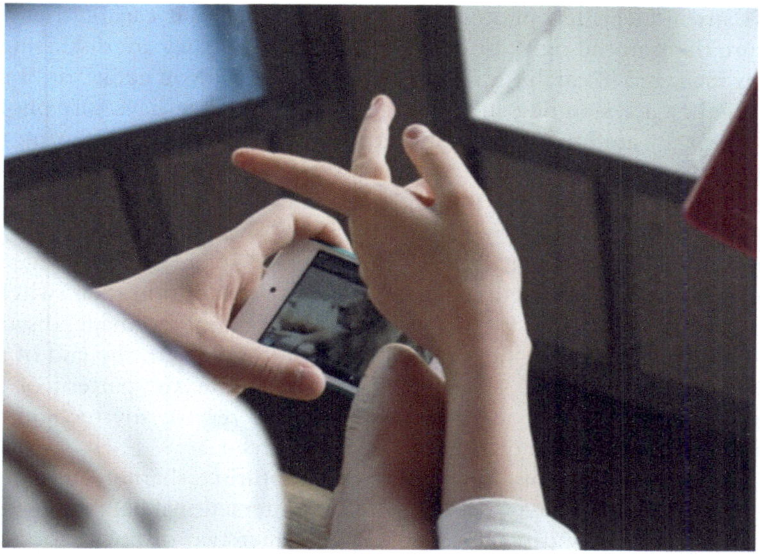

Fig. 4.2 Looking and touching each other's phone screens while comparing images taken of animals at a zoo

Liam: but it hasn't it appeared (He scrolls and does a quick press with his finger on Emil's phone screen)

Emil: it's loading I think

Lukas: Liam

Liam: yes (he takes a step back and turns toward Lukas)

Lukas: Liam can I see your picture

(Liam shows his phone screen)

Lukas: hohoho (makes an appreciative sound as he walks away)

Emil: I got this as well Lukas, check this out check mine (shows his phone screen)

Lukas: oh that was cuter

Emil: where is the little one

Liam: (switches to camera mode) I'm gonna take a picture when they're fighting (takes the phone and aims the camera/phone towards the animals)

Lukas: no they're not fighting they kiss

(Liam takes a picture)

Liam: Emil it turned out awesome pattern, look (shows his screen)

Emil: over there is the kid

Leo: Emil look what a pattern I got (he turns his screen towards Emil who looks in the other direction)

As anyone who has photographed animals knows, it can be tricky to capture them in the right moment, so a lot of what they are discussing is if they managed to catch the animal on camera—"did you get it" or "I got it." As they are standing in front of the animals they have just photographed, they are browsing through the images. As they are showing the images to each other, they are also assessing the pictures and comparing them. When asking to see the image on the screen the brother is also showing his screen, thereby making his image available for comparison. The younger brother settles the discussion by saying which image he believes is the cutest. The boy who "lost" this competition then switches the screen to camera mode to continue capturing another image, discussing with the others what he is planning to photograph. In the end of the example here, the boy is sharing his screen to show the pattern of the animal on the photo he just took but does not receive any recognition from the other boy who does not look at his screen.

They continue like this, moving between capturing, sharing, and assessing images. From this type of more detailed interactional data we can see how consumption and production are no longer two distinct processes, rather they are linked together in various ways. Here, the photos receive more immediate feedback as these young zoo visitors are quickly moving back and forth between taking images and looking at them. While this might seem like an unusual setup, which was partly constructed for study purposes, it is now the case that many museum and zoo visitors are carrying their camera phones around and these sorts of photographic activities are an integrated part of the experience (Bautista 2013; Weilenmann et al. 2013). From our ethnographic studies in several zoos in Sweden and other countries, we have seen that it is more than common that visitors socialize around the photographic production phase. The local environment is occasioning a certain form of photo capturing but also a certain form of looking and socializing around the images they have just taken.

Discussion

In this chapter I have shown how a technical tool that was originally designed to allow for remote, private communication has become an integrated part of local social interaction. I have illustrated this with examples where the participants shared and made the content on these small screens available for their co-located friends. Based on this, I have argued for a contrasting view to understand the disruption of mobile phones in local social interaction, where we also take into account this type of shared screen time. Because the mobile phone is often at hand in social situations, it is woven together with other linguistic and physical resources that the participants rely on to act socially (cf. DiDomenico and Boase 2013). The micro-mobility (Luff and Heath 1998) and flexibility of the mobile phone screen supports this type of shared phone use.

In the fieldwork from around the turn of the century, the phones had limited possibilities compared to the richness of today's communication landscape. Still there were similarities in how the phones were at the center of attention. In early 2000, there was still a sort of "newness" to the mobile phone (Gershon and Bell 2013), and it was therefore perhaps not surprising that it received a lot of attention when people met and spent time together. Its simple presence had a type of agency in itself that restructured social engagement. We observed, and were informed of during interviews, extensive discussions among young people about different phone models, and the various ways that they modified their phones by painting them with nail polish or applying different skins. While the content that was accessible through and on the phone was rather basic compared to what we can do today, young people made the most of it. With time however, that novelty faded, but the phones did not receive less attention. Instead, there was a parallel development of different functionalities that continued and enhanced the phone's affordances as an interactional resource, available to the user and their co-located friends. While some of these functionalities can cause disruptions and challenge the ongoing occasion, some allow enhanced opportunities for social, co-present activities, or as I have called it in this chapter: shared screen time.

An important function of the mobile phone, or smartphone, today is to consume and produce photos on social media. Since the phones are now, as then, more or less always with us, the pictures we have taken ourselves and the ones we get access to via social media are always with us as well. The images we have on our phones enable certain forms of social interaction. Socializing around photos and photography is something we observed in the field, especially in cafes and other social meeting places. On several occasions, we observed how the selfie photography itself became a topic and focus for spending time with friends in the same place. These findings show the relevance of social media not only as an online phenomenon but also as activities that are both enabled by the local environment and allow certain forms of interaction locally (cf. Licoppe and Figeac 2018). The argument that consumption of images is a socially organized activity is not new (cf. Chalfen 1987), but the design of the current technology enables a faster flow between taking a picture and sharing it with others. Production and consumption are no longer two separate processes. Photos are taken and shared in the moment to enhance social relationships over distance as well as in the local context.

When our phones are so entangled in our local engagements, it becomes difficult to decide what are the main and secondary foci. As a researcher, or as any observer watching people spend time together while having their phones in their hands, it is easy to make the judgment that the phones are "in the way" for a genuine social experience. For the participants, in some situations it is not necessarily that they are interrupted in one primary social activity; it is rather a process of involving others in activities and making the relevant social connections at relevant moments in time. Such an understanding clearly challenges experimental studies where these types of naturally occurring, emerging, shared screen activities are not allowed to be a part of the study design. If we are to understand the impact of our devices on social relationships, we need to consider co-present shared screen practices, and how they co-exist with remote interaction.

Acknowledgments I wish to acknowledge the collaboration of two colleagues in collecting the data presented in this chapter—Catrin Larsson and Thomas Hillman. I wish to also thank Rich Ling and Katrin Tiidenberg for their valuable comments on this chapter.

References

Abeele, Mariek V. 2020. The Social Consequences of Phubbing. In *The Oxford Handbook of Mobile Communication and Society*, ed. Rich Ling, Leopoldina Fortunati, Gerard Goggin, Sun Sun Lim, and Yuling Li, 158–174. New York: Oxford University Press.

Bautista, Susana S. 2013. *Museums in the Digital Age: Changing Meanings of Place, Community, and Culture*. Lanham, MD: AltaMira Press/Rowman and Littlefield.

Baym, Nancy K. 2015. *Personal Connections in the Digital Age*. Malden, MA: Polity Press.

Brown, Barry, Moira McGregor, and Eric Laurier. 2013. iPhone in Vivo: Video Analysis of Mobile Device Use. In *Proceedings of the SIGCHI Conference on Human Factors in Computing Systems*, 1031–1040. New York, NY: ACM.

Brown, Barry, Frank Bentley, Saeideh Bakhshi, and David A. Shamma. 2016. Ephemeral Photowork: Understanding the Mobile Social Photography

Ecosystem. In *Proceedings of the Tenth International AAAI Conference on Web and Social Media*, 551–554. Palo Alto, CA: AAAI Press.

Chalfen, Richard. 1987. *Snapshot Versions of Life*. University of Wisconsin Press.

Chotpitayasunondh, Varoth, and Karen M. Douglas. 2018. The Effects of "Phubbing" on Social Interaction. *Journal of Applied Social Psychology* 48 (6): 304–316.

DiDomenico, Stephen M., and Jeffrey Boase. 2013. Bringing Mobiles into the Conversation: Applying a Conversation Analytic Approach to the Study of Mobiles in Co-present Interaction. In *Discourse 2.0: Language and New Media*, ed. Deborah Tannen and Anna M. Trester, 119–132. Washington, DC: Georgetown University Press.

Esbjörnsson, Mattias, Oskar Juhlin, and Alexandra Weilenmann. 2007. Drivers Using Mobile Phones in Traffic: An Ethnographic Study of Interactional Adaptation. *International Journal of Human-Computer Interaction* 22 (1–2): 37–58.

Gershon, Ilana, and Joshua A. Bell. 2013. Introduction. *The Newness of New Media, Culture, Theory and Critique* 54 (3): 259–264.

Heath, C., and Luff, P. 2000. *Technology in Action*. Cambridge Uuniversity Press.

Hillman, Thomas, and Alexandra Weilenmann. 2015. Situated Social Media Use: A Methodological Approach to Locating Social Media Practices and Trajectories. In *Proceedings of the ACM CHI'15 Conference on Human Factors in Computing Systems*, 4057–4060. New York, NY: ACM.

Katz, James E., and Mark Aakhus, eds. 2002. *Perpetual Contact: Mobile Communication, Private Talk, Public Performance*. Cambridge University Press.

Katz, James E., and Elizabeth T. Crocker. 2015. Selfies and Photo Messaging as Visual Conversation: Reports from the United States, United Kingdom and China. *International Journal of Communication* 9: 12.

Licoppe, C., and Figeac, J. 2018. Gaze Patterns and the Temporal Organization of Multiple Activities in Mobile Smartphone Uses. *Human–Computer Interaction* 33 (5–6): 311–334.

Ling, Rich S. 2008. *New Tech, New Ties*. Cambridge, MA: MIT Press.

Luff, Paul, and Christian Heath. 1998. Mobility in Collaboration. In *Proceedings of the 1998 ACM Conference on Computer Supported Cooperative Work*, 305–314.

Pentzold, Christian, Sebastian Konieczko, Florian Osterloh, and Ann-Christin Plöger. 2020. #qualitytime: Aspiring to Temporal Autonomy in Harried Leisure. *New Media & Society* 22 (9): 1619–1638.

Przybylski, Andrew K., and Netta Weinstein. 2013. Can You Connect with Me Now? How the Presence of Mobile Communication Technology Influences Face-to-Face Conversation Quality. *Journal of Social and Personal Relationships* 30 (3): 237–246.

Sacks, Harvey, Emanuel A. Schegloff, and Gail Jefferson. 1978. A Simplest Systematics for the Organization of Turn Taking for Conversation. In *Studies in the Organization of Conversational Interaction*, 7–55. New York: Academic Press.

Tiidenberg, Katrin, Annette Markham, Gabriel Pereira, Mads Middelboe Rehder, Ramona-Riin Dremljuga, Jannek K. Sommer, and Meghan Dougherty. 2017. "I'm an Addict" and Other Sensemaking Devices: A Discourse Analysis of Self-Reflections on Lived Experience of Social Media. In *Proceedings of the 8th International Conference on Social Media and Society*, 21. New York, NY: ACM.

Turkle, Sherry. 2017. *Alone Together: Why We Expect More from Technology and Less from Each Other*. Hachette UK.

Weilenmann, A. (2003). Doing Mobility. PhD Thesis, University of Gothenburg, Gothenburg Studies in Informatics, (28).

Weilenmann, Alexandra, and Thomas Hillman. 2020. Selfies in the Wild: Studying Selfie Photography as a Local Practice. *Mobile Media and Communication* 8 (1): 42–61.

Weilenmann, Alexandra, and Catrine Larsson. 2002. Local Use and Sharing of Mobile Phones. In *Wireless World*, ed. Barry Brown, Nicola Green, and Richard Harper, 92–107. London, UK: Springer.

Weilenmann, Alexandra, Thomas Hillman, and Beata Jungselius. 2013. Instagram at the Museum: Communicating the Museum Experience Through Social Photo Sharing. In *Proceedings of the ACM CHI'13 Conference on Human Factors in Computing Systems*. New York, NY: ACM.

Possibility or Peril? Exploring the Emotional Choreography of Social Robots in Inter- and Intrapersonal Lives

Kate K. Mays

Technology is often an augur of both possibility and peril in our lives. It promises to make our lives easier, more enjoyable, more efficient, but it also threatens the status quo. When the Internet came to the public over two decades ago, it revolutionized personal communication technology (PCT), enabling rapid development of personal devices like the mobile phone as well as the expansion of people's informational and communicative capabilities through those devices. These developments upended vast sectors of daily life including, among many, the focus of this chapter, interpersonal communications and relationships. In particular, the expansion and mobility of the Internet and personal communication technology (PCT) ushered in a new age of perpetual contact (Katz and Aakhus 2002). In this environment, one is always potentially accessible across sectors of their lives: work e-mails can be accessed after hours and on the weekend,

K. K. Mays (✉)
Center for Mobile Communication Studies, Boston University, Boston, MA, USA
e-mail: kkmays@bu.edu

J. Katz et al. (eds.), *Perceiving the Future through New Communication Technologies*,
https://doi.org/10.1007/978-3-030-84883-5_5

intruding on home life; parents' calls can interrupt outings with friends; friends' text messages can intrude on time spent with a partner. In some ways, the ever-increasing modes for communication fragmented attention and threatened information overload and burnout. In other ways, these new asynchronous communication modes expanded possibilities for staying in touch, improving relationships with loved ones and rejuvenating past relationships. As a current example, the Internet has been a lifeline for so many during the COVID-19 self-quarantine, allowing many to continue working and staying socially connected during a time when physical social distancing is so critical. In short, the Internet and its ancillary applications like the mobile phone have revolutionized daily life.

We are at the cusp of another technological revolution in the robotization of society. Indeed, the last decade has seen a rapid progression in not only robotic and AI technologies but also the human-machine relationships that may form. Military personnel form attachments to the robots that assist them with explosive ordinance disposal (Carpenter 2016). The robot dog Aibo has been mourned and given an official Buddhist funeral (Connellan 2018). The android robot Sophia was granted citizenship by Saudi Arabia (Vincent 2017). While this last example may have been primarily a publicity stunt, the ensuing attention and outcry highlight the pressing problem of social robots, namely, how they should be treated and integrated into our civic and social lives.

This chapter focuses on the coming effects in social life, in terms of both personal and interpersonal well-being. It begins by reviewing the ways in which PCTs like the mobile phone instigated social adjustment in both public and personal spaces. Then it discusses how, in the same way that the mobile phone radically altered social norms, AI and robots are positioned as the next frontier of socially disruptive technologies. Drawing from qualitative data, the chapter explores people's perceptions of social robots and how they would view others' interactions with social robots.

Social Disruption of Personal Communication Technologies

As PCTs developed and proliferated, research focused on the ways in which the technologies' affordances aligned with and diverged from face-to-face (FtF) communication. Early theorizing assumed that richer modes of mediated communication (e.g., channels with audio/visual capabilities) performed better than the reduced-cues channels (e.g., text only). These assumptions were upended when Walther (1996) and Tidwell and Walther (2002) found that similar relational depth could eventually be reached through text-only communication as achieved in FtF interactions. The underlying finding here was that humans would achieve their relationship communication goals regardless of a medium's constraints. This observation was expanded upon in Katz and Aakhus's (2002) theory of Apparatgeist, which proposes that human behavior is revealed through the design and use of technology, which influences social norms and expectations. This was demonstrated initially by how people's use of mobile phones revealed a "socio-logic" of "perpetual contact," which illustrated human's fundamental drive for connection and communication, enabled through the mobile phone's affordances of anytime-anywhere contact.

Numerous facets of life have been affected by this "mobile turn" (Caron and Caronia 2007; Goggin 2008; Caron and Caronia 2015)—how we organize our lives, stay in contact with others, and interact with and move about the world. For example, notions of distance have shifted, such that physical presence is not a prerequisite for interaction. The landline telephone had begun to chip away at this assumption, enabling synchronous communication between people who were physically distant, but it was still anchored to one place at all times, which limited the extent to which one's life contexts (e.g., home, work) could overlap. With the mobile phone, contexts blend into one another, as one may receive a work call while shopping in the grocery store—we always live potentially and concurrently within our personal and professional contexts, blurring public and private spheres: those boundaries are malleable and no longer as stark.

As the mobile phone has become "embedded" in the fabric of society over time, mutual expectations for how we interact with one another have developed (Ling 2012). As such, cultural and symbolic importance is imbued in individual decisions on how to use one's phone, particularly if one resists adoption or ignores their phone at certain times (Goggin 2006). Further, studies on the "domestication" of technology (Silverstone and Haddon 1996), as it is brought home and assimilated in its new environment, demonstrates that technology does indeed compel behavior change and prompt an evolution of norms. Therefore, the "new" technology from the last two decades (mobile phone, social media) has shaped behavior, compelling a reorganization of personal and social lives. These changes have been framed both positively and negatively, and their effects on individual well-being and relationships are still being determined (Coyne et al. 2020).

The mobile phone's positive effects can be seen in the ways they lubricate our social and work lives, enabling easier and more efficient communication. Couples have multiple modes to stay in touch throughout the day and express their affection, which enhances relationships (Coyne et al. 2011; Novak et al. 2016). When people use their phone's interactive components (e.g., messaging applications) for deeper engagement with friends and loved ones, their social capital and well-being improves (Chan 2015; De Reuver et al. 2016). These positive effects are particularly pronounced for long-distance relationships, which are easier to maintain through regular and closer contact (Marlowe et al. 2017; Billedo et al. 2015).

The crux of concerns around mobile phones is their ability to draw people away from other human connections. Turkle (2011) posited that attachment to this technology detracts from face-to-face relationships in that people exist "alone, together" as they attend to their devices, physically co-present but psychologically and emotionally off in their own distinct, virtual worlds. That said, Turkle's (2011) diagnosis is made in broad strokes and largely ignores the potential for vast individual differences in the way people use their devices. For many, the mobile phone is used as a tool for connecting with others, as illustrated in the cases of long-distance couples. The ability to asynchronously engage—through messaging apps, e-mail, and social media—expands the possibilities for staying in touch when a phone call or in-person meeting would be infeasible. These methods for "continuous partial presence" (Ebner and Schiefner 2008, 158) or "ambient intimacy" (Thompson 2008) arguably buoy or sustain relationships that otherwise might fall by the wayside due to distance, busyness, and changing life circumstances.

PCTs have also affected the nature of public space, as people prefer the digital world in their phones to the physical world around them (Fortunati 2002). This behavior can disrupt in-person interaction even when phones are idle: the mere presence of a mobile phone manifests the possibility for an interruption of a third, distant, virtual other, a "ghost participant" in any encounter (Caron and Caronia 2007). Our perpetual attention to personal communication devices has normalized the "absent presence," which Gergen (2002) termed to describe how absorption in mediated worlds renders physical companions absent. This phenomenon has been identified more explicitly in "partner phubbing" (Pphubbing), when someone ignores their partner in favor of their phone (Roberts and David

2016). Pphubbing gives rise to conflict in relationships, which in turn reduces levels of relationship satisfaction (Roberts and David 2016), as well as personal well-being (McDaniel and Coyne 2016). Further, the "ghost participant" can degrade relationships: Przybylski and Weinstein (2013) confirmed that even the mere presence of a phone on a table between two people can damage feelings of closeness, connection, and conversation quality. In these ways, Turkle's (2011) concerns about technology disrupting face-to-face engagement are well-founded.

As time has gone on, norms and etiquette have evolved to incorporate the mobile phone's disruptions. These phenomena—"alone, together," "absent presence," and "ghost participant"—demonstrate the "active role of things" (Caron and Caronia 2015) in how the mobile phone, as a symbolic object, shapes human behavior. Perpetual contact refers primarily to how technology facilitates and mediates communication; however, the mobile phone's role in social reorganization extends beyond a communication conduit toward a third participant in interactions, possibly creating conflict and feelings of exclusion and isolation. This is not to say, however, that people are completely at the mercy of their PCTs. While smartphones may enable Pphubbing, for example, the root of such a negative dynamic exists in the person-person relationship: the choice for paying attention to and showing care for one's partner rests in the individual, not their phone.

To that end, more recently there appears to be user resistance to and backlash against the "always-on" demands of technology. In response, tech companies are developing applications to ameliorate technological overload. People can track the time they spend on their applications and set limits on their devices to cut them off after spending a pre-designated amount of time on social media apps. Other examples of devices and applications that limit technology use have been emerging over the last year. "Dumb phones" are making a resurgence, offering a mobile device that allows calls and texting and not much else. The "DinnerMode" application promotes face-to-face engagement and "FocusKeeper" helps concentrate people's energy on a singular task. "Yondr" safely locks away people's phones at schools, concerts, weddings, and other events in order to preserve a certain kind of public space or communal experience, free from an intruding phone (Bahrampour 2018). In this way, it appears that companies are responding to consumers' needs and acknowledging that evermore constant use of their technology may be impeding their quality of life.

Thus, it seems we are in a stage of personal technology use that is more balanced between the affordances' technological "demands" and personal needs. Mobile phones were a novelty when they first emerged, and their rapid advancement as miniature computers has been a marvel. While the norm of technological overload still threatens, people have largely adjusted to incorporate the technology in ways that suit them, or are at least aware that they have the agency to resist aspects of PCT use. Thus, society is considered more dynamic and resilient to the technological determinism that has been predicted. In this light, the chapter turns to a new emerging technology that poses another wave of social disruption: AI and robots.

Social Disruption of Robots

Right now, our PCT is evolving to be more voice-directed and autonomous, which may change the way we rely on and identify with non-human entities. AI-driven "personal assistant" technology like Amazon's Alexa, Apple's Siri, and Google's Assistant are being developed to be more personalized, socialized, and emotionalized, tapping into humans' innate tendency to anthropomorphize and socially respond to human-like cues (Reeves and Nass 1996). Currently, these digital voice assistants are disembodied and embedded in existing hardware like our mobile phones and home speakers. They are designed as hands-free and interconnected convenience devices that can assist with and enhance people's everyday habits and functions—driving safely, cooking more efficiently, and changing the music without breaking from the task at hand. These voice agents also have greater capabilities to respond playfully and learn their human commanders' personal preferences. In turn, people are interacting with this software socially and emotionally (Calvin 2017). This is not surprising, given long-established findings that people treat computers, which are much less interactive and emotive, socially (Reeves and Nass 1996).

AI-driven digital voice assistants and robots are distinct technologies that may, but do not necessarily, share some common features. AI programs are engineered to make machines with human-like intelligence, so that they can "learn" from their environments and adapt accordingly, able to operate on their own without direct human commands (Oberoi 2019). AI need not be physically embodied, as is evident with digital voice assistants. Similarly, robots need not include AI: there are certainly robots that operate without its aid, instead acting by pre-existing programming or direct human commands (Oberoi 2019). That said, the value proposition of *social* robots, the focus of this chapter, is the ability to mimic human-human interactions, to respond autonomously and spontaneously to unique and personal situations. As such, social robots must employ AI to function. The relevant overlap between AI and social robots is both technologies' capacity for autonomy and agency.

This capacity for agency underpins a key distinction between AI technology and other computer-mediated (CMC) technologies like the mobile phone, social media, or e-mail: autonomous AI serves as a communicative *partner* whereas CMC technology, as a communicative *channel*, does not (Guzman 2018). In this conceptualization, agentic technology is poised to *relate* in a more human-like way to people, as "machine subjects *with* which people make meaning instead of *through* which people make meaning" (Guzman and Lewis 2019, 4, emphasis added). As such, AI technology and social robots pose more of a challenge to our ontological understanding of PCTs. With growing personalization, these technologies will become intimate parts of life. This has already been foreshadowed by mobile phones, which have quickly grown to represent far more than utilitarian tools that efficiently coordinate people's lives (e.g., Ling and Yttri 2002). Today's phones are often deeply personal devices to which people are emotionally attached (Vincent 2006, 2015). Just as with the mobile phone, then, we could imagine that as this agentic, socio-emotional, personal communication technology evolves, it will bring on new social scenarios that call for different norms.

As mentioned above, social robots diverge from existing PCTs on some key dimensions. They are embodied, and thus may appear sentient in dramatic ways. They can autonomously and preemptively respond to their users. Given these affordances, Höflich (2013) has proposed expanding the dyadic model of human-robot interaction into a triadic model that takes into account an autonomous social robot "as a mediator between two persons or between a person and his or her environment … where the robot is not only 'a third' (thing) but also 'the third' (social entity or communication partner)" (p. 36). Gunkel (2018) similarly has suggested that we are at the "third wave" of human-computer interaction research, which "is concerned not with the capabilities or operations of the two interacting components—the human user and the computational artifact—but with the phenomenon of the relationships that is situated between them" (2018, 3). This "relational turn" has implications beyond design and function, toward one's identity and relationships.

In that vein, social robots have been conceptualized as "relational artifacts" that prompt reflection "about aliveness, what is special about being a person, and the roles of thought and feeling in human uniqueness" (Turkle et al. 2006, 360). Human-robot relations may reveal more about a person's life outside of the robot interactions themselves. Among other pertinent concerns like data privacy, social robots present possibilities and threats on social dimensions: enabling artificial connection may alleviate but also may exacerbate loneliness and alienation. Of particular interest in the transition from CMC to HMC is how artificial connection interacts with one's "real life" connections.

Our mobile phones have altered the ways in which public spaces and personal social interactions are structured. In turn, one might expect that the established norms for mediated communication—in terms of one's reachability, availability, attention, and time—will evolve anew, and require renegotiation in one's relationships. Some may forget that they are communicating with a machine, and this communication may involve high levels of emotional engagement. Others may reject this kind of engagement with a machine, and either want no kind of digital personal assistant or one that remains strictly functional. Indeed, one study found that a majority of users still referred to Amazon's Alexa with object pronouns and emphasized the digital assistant's utilitarian and entertainment functions (Purington et al. 2017). However, those users that did personify Alexa discussed more of the technology's sociable aspects. The variation in individual tendencies toward and adoption of socio-emotional autonomous technology, whether the existing digital voice assistants or forthcoming social robots, may necessitate new negotiations around the technology as it operates around and interacts with human-human relationships. The following section looks at one case of a socio-emotional robotic technology, a virtual home robot called "Azuma Hikari." People's responses to Hikari illuminate aspects of social disruption that might arise with the social integration of this technology.

The Case of Azuma Hikari

This qualitative study consisted of 23 semi-structured interviews (13 women, 10 men) conducted during the Fall 2017 and Spring 2018 semesters. Participants were undergraduate and graduate students (18–26 years old) from a large private university in the Northeastern United States. Each interview lasted 30–60 minutes and followed the same protocol, though follow-up questions varied depending on individual responses. Participants were first asked about their experiences with digital voice assistants like Siri and Alexa. Next, more speculative questions probed participants' opinions on robots in various sectors of life: industrial work, law enforcement, civil service, customer service, healthcare, childcare, and the home. Then participants were shown a video of a commercial for Azuma Hikari, a mini-holograph of an anime character who acts as someone's personal assistant/companion.

In the video, Hikari is shown as a multifaceted home device: she is interconnected to the house hardware so that she can turn on lights in the same way Alexa might; she also communicates with her owner throughout the day, sending him flirty texts, asking him to come home, demonstrating excitement when he does finally come through the door. This embodied iteration of a digital home assistant is different from those currently proffered in the United States and other western countries: the socio-emotional aspect of its "company" is explicitly emphasized. Indeed, its creator has said that he wanted to develop something he "could love" (Boxall 2019). Thus it is important to note that Hikari has been created in a cultural context that is largely distinct from that of participants interviewed. Whereas Alexa and Siri are primarily geared for information delivery, Hikari's primary purpose is socio-emotional support and connection.

As such, the findings from these interviews only encompass the particular use-case of social AI for companionship. Using automated technology in this way is less commonplace in the United States, whereas Japanese users—to whom Hikari is marketed—are more familiar with and open to such technology. Participants were asked how they felt about what they'd seen in the video, whether they would be interested in such a technology, how they would feel if a friend owned it, and how they would feel if a romantic partner had one.

Overall, there was an abstract acceptance of AI companions like Hikari. Participants identified the possibilities for such technology as a balm to social isolation for some. Many brought up Japan's "loneliness crisis" and saw how Hikari could be a "best-worst" option for social recluses who otherwise would have no other social contact. Another line of possibility arose in how Hikari could be a temporary solution for those who are involuntarily isolated due to life transitions. This was salient particularly for the graduate student interviewees who had recently moved to the city and still building a social life. One participant described a Hikari-like device as a social "stop-gap" for her as she navigated her new life away from family and friends.

Undermining Personal Growth

Notably, most recoiled at the notion of themselves owning a Hikari in the way the commercial depicted. They could see the potential for others' needs but not their own. At the root of this resistance was a sense that owning (and needing) a Hikari was an admission of personal and interpersonal deficiency. Therefore, Hikari was predominantly viewed as a technology that would undermine socialization. At least one participant described her as a "crutch" that would enable underlying and ongoing issues that stymies one's socializing. With Hikari, people would not feel compelled to "work on" their social awkwardness, anxiety, or other phobias. These observations are not dissimilar to concerns raised around abundant screen time, and one participant drew a parallel between escaping through Hikari to escaping into a video game or other online space. In the case of Hikari, though, the "escape" is too similar to what she is displacing: relying on Hikari was too easy of an "out" for those who simply should try harder to improve their social skills.

To that end, participants were concerned that displacing FtF interaction (or even mediated human-human interaction) with a Hikari-type social robot would degrade one's existing social skills. They raised questions like, "can a robot disagree with someone?" "Can robots have their own opinions and stand their ground?" In short, they were skeptical that interactions with Hikari were more like one-way communication rather than a two-way communication process, where one has to engage with and confront another's agency. This reduction in complexity would have implications for someone's ability to negotiate conflict, be vulnerable, and develop and deploy empathy. Without any reciprocity or social exchange, wherein one's own goals and motivations have to accommodate another's, the "right" kind of social learning would be disrupted. People would not have to put any effort into cultivating a meaningful relationship. Ultimately, participants worried about the potential for "on-call interactions" in a kind of socialization and companionship that is "so perfect it's not perfect." One participant noted:

> I think that we need a certain degree of disagreement or conflict or kind of interaction that doesn't just align perfectly ... I think it's bad that he doesn't have to ask her anything in return or put in any effort. [M, 23]

Thus, there was an unease about the "perfect companionship" that social robots might offer. People's relationships with animals are potentially an informative touchpoint for future human-robot relations. Höflich (2013) notes that people have a tendency to attribute intellectual personalities to their pets: for example, when a dog is rebellious, it is "stubborn" and has a mind of its own, and "this very lack of total obedience—because they do not 'function' as a machine—strengthens the emotional bonds" (Höflich 2013, 40). Robots so far are designed to follow humans' orders, and one could imagine that maintaining their obedience is a critical component for people's comfort. Science fictions offer plenty examples of possible consequences if robots' autonomy outstrips their docile nature.

However, a social robot's function differs from servile task completion when that "task" is providing sociality and companionship. In the Gatebox commercial, the Hikari device provides comfort and ego-stroking. As many participants observed, though, the "function" of socializing extends beyond wish-fulfillment. What we wish for and what we need may at times be in conflict, and navigating this tension is an important part of being human.

Undermining Human-Human Relations

The other vector of concern related to how a social robot might disrupt human-human relationships and interactions. Participants mused about whether Hikari would "meet" friends and family, would she accompany her owner on errands, outings, trips? If someone started a new relationship, would they have to be concerned about whether Hikari liked the new romantic partner? Should one "break up" with Hikari when they find a romantic partner? Is flirty-texting with Hikari cheating?

In part, these considerations spoke to the "face work" (Goffman 1967) in which people may have to partake if they integrated a Hikari-like device into their lives. Their own perceptions of the technology were largely negative; thus, they imagined that those who owned a Hikari would need to manage others' impressions of such a choice. Using a Hikari extends beyond the functional, taking on a symbolic role of what it conveys to others about the person who opts into this kind of interaction.

These questions also were related to the notion that a "relationship" with Hikari could potentially induce jealousy in friends or romantic partners, by dint of any perceived diversion of emotional energy and attention toward Hikari. Some participants explicitly noted that owning a Hikari would be a "deal-breaker" for any romantic prospect. Similarly, they would be concerned about friends who utilized a Hikari-like device, assuming that such a purchase would indicate there is a serious problem in the friend's life. Getting a Hikari would signal that the friend is in desperate need of some (human) help.

One participant considered a Hikari-like device in a familial context, imagining the ways in which it could interfere with the parent-child relationship:

> Let's say in a family, there's a technology like that and it's designed as a cute little kid ... The parents love that product, and then will spare a portion of their love to that technology, [which] originally would have been given to [their] three kids. And then those three kids will say, "why do you talk to that technology and you don't talk to me anymore?" [F, 22]

In this example, the technology would be an extremely useful "Rorschach" test (Turkle et al. 2006), reflecting the painful truth that the children required more parental affection and attention. It also suggests the importance of mitigating perceived competition between humans and their robots. To this end, the device's embodiment was an important variable for participants' speculated acceptance. Most recoiled at Hikari's overtly gendered presentation, and particularly at the opposite-sex pairing of the female Hikari and her male owner. If the hologram instead took the shape of a cute animal or even a same-sex human, participants expressed more acceptance. Interestingly, though participants across the board rejected the general notion of robots as romantic companions, they still felt threatened by the emergence of such technology, imagining others would be more susceptible to its inducements.

Looking Forward: Robots as Strangers, Robot-Human Interaction Rules

As social robots diffuse in everyday life there are clearly a number of potential issues and dynamics that would need to be negotiated, both person-robot and person-person. How one chooses or not to incorporate a Hikari-like device in their lives may reflect to varying degrees their personal well-being, social self-efficacy, and relationships. An unexpected but consistent thread in interviews was the uncertainty and jealousy one might feel if a loved one engaged meaningfully with such a technology, and this chapter will conclude with a deeper consideration of this dynamic.

Well before robots and PCTs existed, Georg Simmel ([2008], Wolff 1950) observed how "The Stranger" could disrupt local communities through individual interactions. A person from afar, with no local ties, would enter a place and have a very particular individual influence because of their "stranger" characteristics: mobility, objectivity, not belonging, and an abstract commonality (e.g., nationality, race, something larger than the local community). Through these traits, "the stranger" becomes a safe outlet for self-disclosure: because they are not tied to the community, the stranger has a distance and objectivity on local matters; because they might eventually move on, the stranger will carry the individual disclosures with them.

"The Stranger" can also live in the digital world. Virnoche (2001) observed how mediated communication enabled similar dynamics of intimate disclosures: "strange-making technologies" like the telephone, e-mail, and online message boards create various degrees of distance that prompt information sharing and increased closeness. Social robots present a new realm of "strange-making": they are of our world in that we create them, they are purchased and brought home, but they are distinctly separate in a number of ways, the most obvious being ontologically. Sandry (2018) has proposed treating social robots as a form of "quasi-other" in order to retain the ontological boundaries in the human-non-human hierarchy while acknowledging their heightened social capacity. Such a distinction would categorize the robot as somewhat-like-us but not *of* us. Indeed, as mentioned earlier, participants expressed general interest in Hikari's affordances—as a friendly, assistive, digital companion, but recoiled at its particular embodiment (cute, giggly girl). They preferred to be able to choose its presentation, which suggests a path forward for such technology if it allows for more individual choice in how it appears and can be used. As a machine and not a human, how robots "fit" into someone's life is largely self-determined. Similar to the mobile phone's trajectory—which enabled new behaviors and ways of interacting but the use of which is still individually determined—we might observe a similar pattern of social robot use. Its design and affordances prompt but do not necessarily compel certain modes of interaction. Further, users' needs may influence design choices, such that there is a wider variety of robot types and use-cases offered on the market.

Importantly, and the fundamental argument of this chapter, is that as with the mobile phone, the way that one chooses to employ a social robot would reflect their values and priorities. This will have implications in their socio-emotional lives and once again demonstrates the "active role of things" in PCT usage. For example, a large part of participants' discomfort with Hikari was the prospect that a potential romantic partner might already turn to their robot for comfort, self-validation, and intimacy, taking up space that the human would instead fill. Or, more damning, was the notion that one's romantic partner might adopt a Hikari-type device during the course of the relationship, thus signaling an ambivalence about their relational closeness. While it could be argued that disclosing secrets to one's social robot is no different than keeping a diary, as an animate entity, the "replacement" of human by robot is more obvious. Therefore, while one might perceive their disclosures to a robot as akin to writing in a diary, their loved ones might instead perceive the robot disclosures as more similar to confiding in a friend. This potential disjuncture in perceptions of use could result in loved one's feeling threatened by the robot, competing with it for access to the human user's inner world. "The Stranger" was a safe outlet for a community's gossip or confessions not only because he was not *of* them but also because he was transient and temporary. In a similar way, participants spoke of negotiations around Hikari's eventual "departure" when, for example, entering a romantic relationship. This could entail getting rid of the device, but it could also mean changing its embodiment, or turning off certain settings that seem particularly intimate, such as the ongoing daily texting. Perhaps these types of devices could come with certain "modes" such as "functional" and "companionate" that allow the user to control the affordances to match their needs in that particular life circumstance. As in the case of Pphubbing, how people negotiate and determine the use of a Hikari-like device ultimately resides in their relationship dynamics. In their considerations of what to do with Hikari if one used it while single and then became partnered, participants raised the specter of whether continued use might constitute some form of cheating on their human partner. The concept of an "emotional affair" or "emotional cheating" is vaguely defined and certainly more ambiguous than if someone physically cheated on their partner. Nevertheless, it has become more prominent with the rise of PCTs. It is easier to carry on close contact through texting on mobile phones or messaging on personal computers without detection, and this capability has raised questions about the parameters of emotional intimacy—when does information sharing between two people cross over from close friendship to emotional affair? Is it the frequency, time of day, emotional depth, some combination therein? The answer is likely individual and relative: each couple needs to determine for themselves what is acceptable behavior.

In this way, the "rules" that a couple—or any dyad or group—establishes for interactions with a social robot will reveal the human dynamics at play in these relationships. Depending on the situation, a girlfriend's jealousy at her boyfriend going to happy hour with a female coworker may illustrate her irrational insecurity, or it could indicate the relationship's shaky foundation, or demonstrate the boyfriend's emotional carelessness and unavailability. Similarly, people's interaction rules (Goffman 1967) for their social robots could speak to individuals' and relationships' strengths, deficiencies, and values. As people integrate and maintain a social robot in their lives, coordinating this new presence will require an *emotional choreography* that may generate new interpersonal management techniques. For social scientists, it can also help elucidate society's priorities, morals, and relational mechanisms. In this way, understanding humans' evolving relationships to these machines will further our understanding of ourselves. New technology necessarily threatens the status quo, but it also presents opportunities for reflection, growth, and self-determination.

References

Bahrampour, Tara. 2018. This Simple Solution to Smartphone Addiction Is Now Used in Over 600 U.S. Schools. *The Washington Post*, February 5. https://www.washingtonpost.com/news/inspired-life/wp/2018/02/05/this-millennial-discovered-a-surprisingly-simple-solution-to-smartphone-addiction-schools-love-it/?utm_term=.9fefc59006a2.

Billedo, Cherrie Joy, Peter Kerkhof, and Catrin Finkenauer. 2015. The Use of Social Networking Sites for Relationship Maintenance in Long-Distance and Geographically Close Romantic Relationships. *Cyberpsychology, Behavior, and Social Networking* 18 (3): 152–157.

Boxall, A. 2019. Who Is Hikari-Chan? She Is the Mind-Blowing Future of A.I. in Your Home. *Digital Trends*, December 19. https://www.digitaltrends.com/mobile/gatebox-japan-minori-takechi-interview/.

Calvin, Aaron Paul. 2017. Can Amazon's Alexa Be Your Friend? *Digg.com*, March 30. http://digg.com/2017/amazon-alexa-is-not-your-friend.

Caron, André H., and Letizia Caronia. 2007. *Moving Cultures: Mobile Communication in Everyday Life*. McGill-Queen's Press-MQUP.

———. 2015. Mobile Communication Tools as Morality-Building Devices. In *Encyclopedia of Mobile Phone Behavior*, 25–45. IGI: Global.

Carpenter, Julie. 2016. *Culture and Human-Robot Interaction in Militarized Spaces: A War Story*. Routledge.

Chan, Michael. 2015. Mobile Phones and the Good Life: Examining the Relationships Among Mobile Use, Social Capital and Subjective Well-Being. *New Media & Society* 17 (1): 96–113.

Connellan, Shannon. 2018. Japanese Buddhist Temple Hosts Funeral for Over 100 Sony Aibo Robot Dogs. *Mashable*, May 2. https://mashable.com/2018/05/02/sony-aibo-dog-funeral/.

Coyne, Sarah M., Laura Stockdale, Dean Busby, Bethany Iverson, and David M. Grant. 2011. "I luv u:)!": A Descriptive Study of the Media Use of Individuals in Romantic Relationships. *Family Relations* 60 (2): 150–162.

Coyne, Sarah M., Adam A. Rogers, Jessica D. Zurcher, Laura Stockdale, and McCall Booth. 2020. Does Time Spent Using Social Media Impact Mental Health?: An Eight Year Longitudinal Study. *Computers in Human Behavior* 104: 106160.

De Reuver, Mark, Shahrokh Nikou, and Harry Bouwman. 2016. Domestication of Smartphones and Mobile Applications: A Quantitative Mixed-Method Study. *Mobile Media & Communication* 4 (3): 347–370.

Ebner, Martin, and Mandy Schiefner. 2008. Microblogging-More than Fun. *Proceedings of IADIS Mobile Learning Conference* 2008: 155–159.

Fortunati, Leopoldina. 2002. The Mobile Phone: Towards New Categories and Social Relations. *Information, Communication & Society* 5 (4): 513–528.

Gergen, Kenneth J. 2002. The Challenge of Absent Presence. In *Perpetual Contact: Mobile Communication, Private Talk, Public Performance*, ed. James Katz and Mark A. Aakhus, 227–241. Cambridge, UK; New York: Cambridge University Press.

Goffman, Erving. 1967. *Interaction Ritual: Essays on Face-to-Face Interaction*. New York: Pantheon Book, Random House.

Goggin, Gerard. 2006. *Cell Phone Culture: Mobile Technology in Everyday Life*. London; New York: Routledge.

———. 2008. The Mobile Turn in Universal Service: Prosaic Lessons and New Ideals. *Info-The Journal of Policy, Regulation and Strategy for Telecommunications* 10 (5–6): 46–58.

Gunkel, David J. 2018. The Relational Turn: Third Wave HCI and Phenomenology. In *New Directions in Third Wave Human-Computer Interaction: Volume 1-Technologies*, 11–24. Cham: Springer.

Guzman, Andrea. 2018. What Is Human-Machine Communication, Anyway? In *Human-Machine Communication: Rethinking Communication, Technology, and Ourselves*, ed. Andrea Guzman, 1–29. New York: Peter Lang.

Guzman, Andrea, and Seth C. Lewis. 2019. Artificial Intelligence and Communication: A Human–Machine Communication Research Agenda. *New Media & Society* 22: 1–17.

Höflich, Joachim R. 2013. Relationships to Social Robots: Towards a Triadic Analysis of Media-Oriented Behavior. *Intervalla: Platform for Intellectual Exchange* 1 (1): 35–35.

Katz, James E., and Mark Aakhus, eds. 2002. *Perpetual Contact: Mobile Communication, Private Talk, Public Performance*. Cambridge University Press.

Ling, Richard. 2012. *Taken for Grantedness: The Embedding of Mobile Communication into Society*. Cambridge, MA: MIT Press.

Ling, Richard, and Birgitte Yttri. 2002. Hyper-Coordination via Mobile Phones in Norway. In *Perpetual Contact: Mobile Communication, Private Talk, Public Performance*, ed. James Katz and Mark A. Aakhus, 139–169. Cambridge, UK; New York: Cambridge University Press.

Marlowe, Jay M., Allen Bartley, and Francis Collins. 2017. Digital Belongings: The Intersections of Social Cohesion, Connectivity and Digital Media. *Ethnicities* 17 (1): 85–102.

McDaniel, Brandon T., and Sarah M. Coyne. 2016. "Technoference": The Interference of Technology in Couple Relationships and Implications for Women's Personal and Relational Well-Being. *Psychology of Popular Media Culture* 5 (1): 85.

Novak, Joshua R., Jonathan G. Sandberg, Aaron J. Jeffrey, and Stephanie Young-Davis. 2016. The Impact of Texting on Perceptions of Face-To-Face Communication in Couples in Different Relationship Stages. *Journal of Couple & Relationship Therapy* 15 (4): 274–294.

Oberoi, Esha. 2019. Differences Between Robotics and Artificial Intelligence. *SkyfiLabs.com*. https://www.skyfilabs.com/blog/difference-between-robotics-and-artificial-intelligence.

Przybylski, Andrew K., and Netta Weinstein. 2013. Can You Connect with Me Now? How the Presence of Mobile Communication Technology Influences Face-To-Face Conversation Quality. *Journal of Social and Personal Relationships* 30 (3): 237–246.

Purington, Amanda, Jessie G. Taft, Shruti Sannon, Natalya N. Bazarova, and Samuel Hardman Taylor. 2017. 'Alexa Is My New BFF' Social Roles, User Satisfaction, and Personification of the Amazon Echo. *Proceedings of the 2017 CHI Conference Extended Abstracts on Human Factors in Computing Systems*, 2853–2859.

Reeves, Byron, and Clifford I. Nass. 1996. *The Media Equation: How People Treat Computers, Television, and New Media Like Real People and Places*. Cambridge, UK: Cambridge University Press.

Roberts, James A., and Meredith E. David. 2016. My Life Has Become a Major Distraction from My Cell Phone: Partner Phubbing and Relationship

Satisfaction Among Romantic Partners. *Computers in Human Behavior* *54*: 134–141.
Sandry, Eleanor. 2018. Aliveness and the Off-Switch in Human-Robot Relations. In *Human-Machine Communication: Rethinking Communication, Technology, and Ourselves*, ed. Andrea Guzman, 51–66. New York: Peter Lang.
Silverstone, Roger, and Leslie Haddon. 1996. Design and the Domestication of Information and Communication Technologies: Technical Change and Everyday Life. In *Communication by Design. The Politics of Information and Communication Technologies*, ed. Robin Mansell and Roger Silverstone, 44–74. Oxford: Oxford University Press.
Simmel, Georg. 2008. The Stranger. In *The Cultural Geography Reader*, 323–327. Routledge.
Thompson, Clive. 2008. Brave New World of Digital Intimacy. *The New York Times*, September 5. https://www.nytimes.com/2008/09/07/magazine/07awareness-t.html.
Tidwell, Lisa Collins, and Joseph B. Walther. 2002. Computer-Mediated Communication Effects on Disclosure, Impressions, and Interpersonal Evaluations: Getting to Know One Another a Bit at a Time. *Human Communication Research* 28 (3): 317–348.
Turkle, Sherry. 2011. *Alone Together: Why We Expect More from Technology and Less from Each Other*. New York: Basic Books.
Turkle, Sherry, Will Taggart, Cory D. Kidd, and Olivia Dasté. 2006. Relational Artifacts with Children and Elders: The Complexities of Cybercompanionship. *Connection Science* 18 (4): 347–361.
Vincent, Jane. 2006. Emotional Attachment and Mobile Phones. *Knowledge, Technology & Policy* 19 (1): 39–44.
———. 2015. The Mobile Phone: An Emotionalised Social Robot. In *Social Robots from a Human Perspective*, ed. Jane Vincent et al., 105–115. Cham: Springer.
Vincent, James. 2017. Pretending to Give a Robot Citizenship Helps No One. *The Verge*, October 30. https://www.theverge.com/2017/10/30/16552006/robot-rights-citizenship-saudi-arabia-sophia.
Virnoche, Mary E. 2001. The Stranger Transformed: Conceptualizing On and Offline Stranger Disclousure. *Social Thought & Research* 24: 343–367.
Walther, Joseph B. 1996. Computer-Mediated Communication: Impersonal, Interpersonal, and Hyperpersonal Interaction. *Communication Research* 23 (1): 3–43.
Wolff, Kurt H., Trans. 1950. *The Sociology of Georg Simmel*, 402–408. New York: Free Press.

The Artificialistic Fallacy

Vanessa Nurock

AI and Bias: More than Just a Looking Glass?

The biases found in AI have been described by Joy Buolamwini (2016) as a "coded gaze"—a direct reference to the "colonial gaze" or the "male gaze," which establish a vision of the world and power relations on the basis of a framework of domination. The central idea conveyed by this expression is that to code is to have the power to impose a certain vision of the world and certain relationships of domination. An additional issue raised by this coded gaze is that it passes through the artifact of a machine that can be described as not only a "seeing machine" but also a "prescribing machine." As Virginia Eubanks (Eubanks 2018) has shown, this prescribing function is explicit in some cases, such as resource allocations. The central problem here is that the coded gaze is supposed to be neutral and objective because it is shaped by technical elements.

In what follows, I would like to focus on the crossover between the male gaze and the coded gaze by looking at gender bias in AI. An interesting example of this bias can be found in the personal virtual assistants

---

V. Nurock (✉)
CRRHI, Côte d'Azur University, Nice, France
e-mail: vnurock@univ-cotedazur.fr

J. Katz et al. (eds.), *Perceiving the Future through New Communication Technologies*,
https://doi.org/10.1007/978-3-030-84883-5_6

answering to sweet (feminine) names such as "Siri" (Apple's digital assistant), "Cortana" (Windows'), or "Alexa" (Amazon's). I developed these examples and proposed a very preliminary sketch of the Artificialistic Fallacy (Nurock 2019). At first glance, these personal assistants may seem completely disembodied and neutral, unaffected by the male/female binary. Yet, they are almost immediately categorized, in a gendered manner, as female. Their voices are therefore feminine, which seems appropriate for assistant behaviors—in contrast to command behaviors with masculine voices. As a result, some voice recognition software are unable to respond to female human voices (see, for instance, Silke Carty 2011). For this reason, women have been asked to masculinize their voices in order to make themselves understandable to the machine, and thus to remodel themselves to fit the design of the machine!

Moreover, as a recent UNESCO report showed in 2019, these personal assistants (as well as the digital divide in general) reinforce the patriarchal system of domination (UNESCO 2019). "I'd blush if I could," Siri replies submissively to a user who tells her "Hey Siri, you are a bitch." As Hilary Bergen (Bergen 2016) has pointed out, personal assistants seem programmed to encourage flirting, even when it becomes aggressive, and their reactions are not conducive to disarming this type of behavior, but on the contrary may actually fuel it. If we consider these personal assistants on the one hand and, on the other hand, household robots whose round shapes may be considered feminine, there is no doubt that all these characteristics reinforce not only a certain conception of domestic work as feminine but also its qualification as virtual and invisible, making it even more subaltern.

A specific vision of domestic work and chains of command—including human command of technology—is thus brought to light. Even in a technical world, where the machine obeys humans (or is supposed to), it does not obey men and women in the same way, and thus amplifies or exacerbates existing relations of domination. It has long been argued that these biases are, after all, only a mirror of the society that makes AI. Thus, it would not be AI that needs to be changed, but society itself, since an unbiased society would shape an unbiased AI. As tempting as this solution may be, it probably would not work here: not only because shaping an unbiased society is not that easy but also because AI not only mirrors biases but can also reinforce and even enhance biases and inequalities. AI biases are definitely more than a simple mirror. Gender bias in AI not only mimics our biases but also supports (and is supported by) the patriarchal framework that underlies our social and artificial systems.

From Apparatgeist to Forms of Life

Perhaps, then, we should consider these biases not only from a conjunctural point of view (e.g., belonging to the category of "bad data": garbage in—garbage out) but also from a structural point of view. As I have just pointed out, saying that AI mirrors our societies gives only a very partial view of the issue at stake here. In fact, the mirror goes both ways: it reflects our societies but also reshapes them. In order to explain this dynamic, we can draw on the Apparatgeist theory.

As James Katz and Mark Aarhus (Katz and Aakhus 2002) have shown regarding mobile technology, the relationship between reality and technology is much more subtle than a simple one-way path. In order to analyze this complexity, they coined the neologism "Apparatgeist," which echoes, among other things, the term *Zeitgeist*, the spirit of the times. The Apparatgeist or "spirit of the machine" accounts for the transcendental dimension of certain technical objects. The term *Apparat* here refers to the machine in both its technical and social dimensions, and emphasizes the idea that technology is socially constructed.

The Apparatgeist does not reveal a form of technological determinism but rather the complex relationship we have with emerging digital technologies. These technologies imprint upon our ways of being and living and at the same time show our strong desire for Perpetual Contact, defined by Katz and Aakhus as a "socio-logic of communication technology" (Katz and Aakhus 2002, p. 307). This desire for Perpetual Contact does not come from technology, but rather is stimulated or even modified by it. This desire and this communicational logic shape the links (both real and imaginary) that individuals and societies have with these machines. The term *Geist* (spirit) is here to be understood in a classical philosophical sense: Hegel used it to designate a consciousness proper to each stage of history, which develops and surpasses itself in a dialectical process. The concept of Apparatgeist thus refers to a dialectical movement between *Apparat* and *Geist*. In this movement, society models the apparatus, and the apparatus, in the same process, models societies as well as individuals. In truth, the machine establishes a structure and a limited set of possibilities. In turn, the individual or society deals with these constraints, sometimes going so far as to remodel or even hack them, putting them to an unintended use. In other words, technology is not fatalistic, in the sense that not everything is decided in advance—but it is deterministic because it eliminates a certain number of possibilities by putting guardrails in place and thus marking out the scope of what is possible, or even, as we will see later, acceptable.

Relationships between the human being and the machine thus acquire a form of intimacy that is probably unprecedented in the history of humanity. Here, the question becomes "how are we to analyze our becoming machines?" or, more precisely, these "machines that become us"—the title of the 2006 book edited by James Katz (Katz 2006). Interestingly, in this title, the important thing is neither the term "machine" nor the term "us" (humans), but rather the process of becoming and the direction of this becoming, which is precisely what the present chapter aims to inquire into. The concept of Apparatgeist goes even further by embodying a "social sense" in and through the machine: the machine can go as far as replacing certain types of relationships or even affective and cognitive processes.

I would like to suggest that the Apparatgeist theory could convey what Langdon Winner (Winner 1986), using Wittgensteinian vocabulary, analyzes in the field of philosophy of technology with the concept of "Forms of Life." He suggests that the links between technology and society may be analyzed in terms of "second nature" or even "Forms of Life" to explain how "as they become woven into the texture of everyday existence, the devices, techniques, and systems we adopt shed their tool-like qualities to become part of our very humanity" (p. 12). The fundamental question to be asked about technology is therefore no longer "how do we make things work?" but "what kind of world are we making?" and what role does technology play in certain processes of transformation, whether psychological, social, or political? For example, Winner shows that the design of a boat may be such that the captain has to shout to be heard by the crew, which immediately establishes a certain intrinsically hierarchical political structure. Or, a bridge may be so low that buses cannot pass under it, which de facto prevents disadvantaged populations without individual means of transportation from easily accessing certain neighborhoods or the city center.

Winner goes even further by pointing out that these Forms of Life function as a second constitution, parallel to but also sometimes superimposed on the socio-political constitution. For this reason, we must assume all the more responsibility in the process of making (technical objects and the world): the important thing is not to study the impacts of technical change but to evaluate the social infrastructures that certain technologies create and in which our activities are embedded. As Susan Leigh Star (Star 1999) shows, this kind of infrastructure probably becomes more invisible in the digital world. But although invisible, it may also be designed in such a way as to establish certain implicit social and political structures.

The "Naturalistic Fallacy"

To put it differently, the Forms of Life created by relationships between technologies, ethics, and politics value some patterns at the expense of others. I would now like to focus on this idea and raise an issue: the risk of what I propose calling the "Artificialistic Fallacy." This new concept is based on two theoretical pillars: first, the Naturalistic Fallacy, one of the most classical concepts of moral philosophy; second, "naturalization" as analyzed by Bourdieu (Bourdieu 1998).

The concept of an "Artificialistic Fallacy" is inspired by the "Naturalistic Fallacy," a benchmark of moral philosophy. Thus, a quick detour through Moore's *Principia Ethica* is necessary. The Naturalistic Fallacy is based on Moore's denunciation of reductionism, understood as the assertion that moral norms can be reduced to natural facts. More precisely, Moore (Moore 1903) denounces the confusion between Goodness (G) considered as a moral property on the one hand and as a natural property on the other. In other words, he rejects the equation: "it's natural = it's good."

By "natural property" Moore means one that can be studied by or exhaustively defined in terms of the natural sciences or psychology. Thus, for Moore, the error—and danger—of naturalism is that it equates G with a natural property, which can be studied exhaustively by the natural sciences. We would therefore run the risk of replacing philosophy, and more precisely ethics, with the natural sciences. This is why Moore emphasizes that naturalism (as he defines it) is both false and dangerous: according to him, naturalism not only is unable to propose valid ethical principles but could also lead us to accept false principles. Among the different types of naturalism, Moore's favorite target is Spencer's evolutionism, alongside Mill's hedonism. Spencer is his prime target because his theory is a social application of Darwinism. Spencer states, among other things, that human evolution is moving toward social progress because it selects the fittest individuals and makes societies evolve. Social Darwinism thus confuses, according to Moore, natural evolution with the moral evolution of man.

So, as we can see, for Moore, the denunciation of the Naturalistic Fallacy concerns above all the reduction of the moral and social dimension of man (and of societies) to a biological dimension.

The second theoretical basis for understanding the Artificialist Fallacy is the concept of naturalization as defined by Bourdieu in his book *Masculine Domination*. By "naturalization" Bourdieu means how relations of domination (especially gendered ones) become embedded in our habits of thought by being assimilated to natural phenomena, where "natural" means both normal and biological. This assimilation is achieved through a movement of essentialization coupled with de-historicization. While the Naturalistic Fallacy confuses natural and good, the naturalization denounced by Bourdieu confuses social and natural facts. This confusion is facilitated, as Marx and Nietzsche had already shown in their own terms, by the fact that the origin and genesis of the phenomenon are forgotten, and it thus appears to be if not eternal, at least immutable. A methodological mistake can thus become an ideological imperative.

This ideological imperative appears in at least two main fields: gender and education. In gender, for example, some people assert that differences between so-called masculine or feminine practices are anchored in invariants. These so-called differences are all the more easily naturalized as they are directly linked to the body. To put it another way, naturalization may interpret socially constructed gender roles as the results of biological sex and thus confirm male domination. In the same way, in the educational field, the naturalization of gifts, capacities, and talents may also be used in order to validate the reproduction of the status quo.

Toward an "Artificialistic Fallacy"?

My hypothesis is that artificialization relies on naturalization in various ways to take the Naturalistic Fallacy a step further: toward the Artificialistic Fallacy. Artificialization is, in fact, likely to enshrine naturalized structural habits in the machine, in code (even if deep learning might seem to prevent them from becoming immutably fixed in place). It would then falsely give the impression that if these structural habits are artificialized, they are unbiased and therefore morally good. This could lead to a kind of stratified fossilization where artificialization would be added on top of naturalization—for example, in the case of gender bias.

Indeed, in naturalization as denounced by Bourdieu, the ideological imperative constructs a conception of human nature that confuses the natural and the social instead of articulating them together. Similarly, one could suggest that artificialization entails the risk of constructing a conception that *confuses* the social (which is already confused with the natural) with the artificial. In contrast, the Apparatgeist *articulates* Apparat and Geist together. To put it another way, the risk inherent to artificialization is to equate: "social = natural = artificial = good," where the Naturalistic Fallacy equates: "natural = good" and naturalization equates: "social = natural."

My hypothesis is that this shift is made possible, and even supported, by another confusion, which occurs in two stages. First, the confusion between neutral and artificial, and second, the confusion between neutral, artificial, and impartial. Regarding the first confusion, the claim to neutrality can be examined by returning to the issue of gender bias in AI, already mentioned above. In terms of the second confusion, the use of moral dilemmas, and in particular the tramway dilemma, in "moral machines" reveals the predominance and even reinforcement of a patriarchal conception of ethics.

Let us first go back to gender bias. It can be suggested that in the case of gender bias, supposed neutrality hides a neutralization. Some researchers, such as Alison Adam (Adam 1998), show that although the origins and development of IT have mobilized relatively mixed-gender teams in which men and women worked together, women have historically been rendered invisible—for example, not appearing in official photos whereas they clearly appear in photos of the teams at work. This phenomenon is all the more ironic given that today we often hear discourses about the lack of women in AI (and the most valued fields of science and technology in general), which pose the feminization of AI as a challenge. It is then forgotten that the masculinization of AI is a historical phenomenon: the more a profession becomes valuable and the more it is considered objective, the more it appears to be a man's business. This historical invisibilization has, in fact, gone hand in hand with a progressive masculinization: since IT and AI were considered valuable and important, they could no longer be a woman's business.

I would like to suggest here that the issue is not only that the history of AI has been "neutralized" in the sense that women have been erased from it. This erasure is significant because it reveals that the neutralized view of AI is dominated by a certain patriarchal vision of the world, which assigns men the important and "objective" jobs—even when reality contradicts this. However, as Alison Adam points out, quoting Thomas Nagel (and I will come back to this later) this “point of view from nowhere,” that AI is supposed to inhabit, its alleged neutrality and the absence of gender from it, actually hides a white man in his 30s or 40s—what is sometimes termed “AI’s white guy problem” (see, for instance, Crawford 2016 and Hao 2019). These biases and the gradual forgetting of the historicity of this “neutralization” phenomenon in favor of an essentializing approach are indeed part of what Bourdieu analyzes as a naturalization process. In addition, there is the further idea that the technological dimension of AI guarantees its objectivity and scientificity and also that this scientific objectivity should, in turn, guarantee its technological neutrality—which is probably related to gender neutrality. But this shift from scientific objectivity to technological neutrality doesn’t end here. Furthermore, this technological neutrality, in turn, is considered a guarantee for ethical impartiality.[1]

After this first step, which recontextualizes the process of neutralization in different ways through the example of gender bias, I would like, in a second step, to examine the transition from neutrality to impartiality, from so-called technological objectivity to ethical impartiality. As Alison Adam writes, AI is not “the view from nowhere,”—a supposedly neutral, objective point of view. Moreover, I believe that the statement that AI is not the “view from nowhere” can be shifted from the field of epistemology to the field of morality—where it first belonged, through the implicit reference to Nagel—and can be considered not only in terms of objectivity and neutrality but also in terms of impartiality. Indeed, impartiality, alongside neutrality, is one of the qualities often attributed to AI.

For example, the claim to impartiality was one of the major arguments on which Michito Matsuda relied in proposing an AI for mayor of the city of Mata, west of Tokyo, in 2018. Impartiality would therefore seem to be an unstoppable argument for proposing AI as a solution to some of our ethical and even political problems. It is probably unnecessary to recall here that impartiality is often considered one of the most important virtues for achieving justice, for instance, through the figure of the impartial

[1] Unfortunately, I do not have enough space in this chapter to analyze further this glitch from scientific objectivity to technological neutrality and further from technological neutrality to moral and political neutrality. Let me just mention that there is strong debate in philosophy on the definition of scientific objectivity, technological neutrality, and ethnical or political impartiality but that “switching” from one category to the other has not been, to my knowledge, ever considered as consistent, so that, logically, these categories should be kept separate. However, this glitch is precisely a major characteristic of the Artificialistic Fallacy.

spectator or judge. It may also be noted in passing that the temptation to automate ethics has been a common trend in philosophy since at least the eighteenth century (I developed this idea in Nurock 2019).

More recently, this question has been reiterated using the tools of cognitive psychology, neuroscience, and artificial intelligence. This shift is all the more interesting since the reinvestment of the classical question of the automation of morality by the cognitive sciences makes it possible to highlight an additional stratum of the notion of artificialization, which is also based on naturalization in the sense of the cognitive sciences—and not only in the critical sense given by Bourdieu—as the explanation of morality relying in part (or solely) on natural explanations. As I have shown in Nurock (2011), there are various strategies of naturalization.

John Mikhail (Mikhail 2011) has proposed an original way to achieve the naturalization of morality (as defined by the cognitive sciences), partly based on testing the moral intuitions of individuals through a series of moral dilemmas elaborated by Philippa Foot and Judith Jarvis Thomson, the most famous of which is the trolley problem. On the basis of Mikhail's extension of the trolley problem from armchair philosophy to cognitive science psychology (and neuroscience), two websites were developed. These websites were explicitly intended to serve as tools for testing our moral sense online: "The Moral Sense Test" (http://www.moralsensetest.com/) and "The Moral Machine" (http://moralmachine.mit.edu/). The first was designed by Mark Hauser's team at Harvard in the early 2000s, relying on Mikhail's work and in collaboration with him. The second website, the "moral machine," aimed in particular at enabling the programming of driverless vehicles but could also be used for other so-called autonomous machines (such as drones). Using these dilemmas to test our moral sense and to program driverless vehicles poses many problems that have already been raised elsewhere—not to mention the technical difficulties that make these vehicles problematic, but this is not my focus here.

I would like to focus on one problem in particular, which seems to me symptomatic of what is at risk in artificializing morality. Using these dilemmas as tools to test and, above all, to program ethics (as is the purpose of the second website) seems to me pretty dangerous not only for our "smart" cities where these vehicles would be used but also, and maybe foremost, for our conception of what morality is. One could, indeed, object to the use of these dilemmas with a series of arguments that are both concrete and theoretical.

In practical terms, one could argue that the proposed situations remain quite distant from those that might be encountered by a driver, who will see neither a lever nor a tramway (as in the description of the trolley problem), but rather the people who are likely to be run over. Indeed, the way in which a moral problem is framed is essential to its apprehension and eventual resolution.

Turning to the theoretical level, the use of dilemmas is problematic for both ethical and metaethical reasons. Using dilemmas to describe our moral life is indeed a rather singular way to frame it. By definition, a dilemma involves two morally unacceptable situations. This is well illustrated, for instance, by William Styron's novel *Sophie's Choice.* Summoned by a Nazi to choose between her son and her daughter, it is clear that Sophie is distressed not by remorse but by horror. There is no right answer, no real choice, but necessarily, to varying degrees, what philosophers such as Patricia Greenspan (Greenspan 2005) have called, some "moral residue." One cannot imagine, in any case, Sophie coming out unscathed by this choice. The immoral individual—some would say the monster—in the story is, of course, not Sophie but rather the German Nazi soldier who forced her to choose and framed the dilemma. It is important to note here that, even before the vogue for trolleyology, the use of dilemmas was long commonplace in moral psychology. It was, in fact, introduced by the research of Lawrence Kohlberg, the major figure in moral psychology in the second half of the twentieth century. Moreover, (Kohlberg 1981) precisely promoted a "view from nowhere," which, according to him, allows all perspectives to be taken into account in an ecumenical vision that represents the last stage of moral development.

However, it can be pointed out that this use of moral dilemmas by Kohlberg's team does not in any way justify the use made of moral dilemmas in trolleyology today for two main reasons. First, methodologically speaking, the way moral dilemmas are used in the "moral machine" is actually the opposite of what Kohlberg was doing, on two counts. On the one hand, for Kohlberg, moral dilemmas are no key to finding the "right" answer since, *bis repetita*, there is no such thing in a dilemma. In Kohlberg's view, what matters most is not the answer, but rather the justification given by the subject and the path taken to achieve it. On the other hand, for Kohlberg, studies that describe morality are primarily prescriptive. His entire theoretical framework is constructed in a normative way in order to lead to what should be the most complete stage of moral development. In no way does Kohlberg seek to automate morality. Quite the contrary, since he wants to reflect on how to best enable moral development through moral education. And this indeed makes a huge difference.

Second, the use of moral dilemmas has been strongly criticized on scientific grounds from within the Kohlbergian framework by some of Kohlberg's collaborators. Among them is Carol Gilligan, who used Kohlberg's famous Heinz dilemma—in which a man has to decide whether or not to steal a drug to save his wife's life—to show that some subjects tried to get out of the dilemma, which they felt was precisely unacceptable from a moral point of view. This is obvious in the famous answer of young Amy, who rejected the frame of an alternative. Moreover, Amy did not choose; instead, she solved the situation by suggesting that the voice of each protagonist should be heard. In other words, she refused to adopt the "view from nowhere" and explored the points of view of the various protagonists.

In order to account for such reactions to the Kohlbergian paradigm, which this paradigm had downgraded to lower forms of moral development, Carol Gilligan (Gilligan 1982) proposed that we should instead highlight a form of ethics that had not been sufficiently theorized, and which she named the "ethics of care." To put it briefly, the ethics of care (which is not in *competition* with other approaches) places emphasis on relationships rather than on impartiality. As Gilligan points out, this ethics is not feminine—although it is often culturally attributed to women—but it is feminist, because it challenges and rejects patriarchal norms and their binaries. Instead, the ethics of care operates within a democratic framework, where invisibilized voices can and should be heard.

However, in the example of trolleyology, the use of dilemmas to develop a "moral machine" not only reproduces the dominant binaries (including in ethics) of our patriarchal societies, it may also reinforce them by artificializing them. Could we really consider that our driverless car has made the right choice by running over this or that person on the side track? Should we convince ourselves that this was necessarily the right solution, the right thing to do, since the vehicle with an artificial—that is, "neutral"—driver is undoubtedly "impartial"? If we did, we would undoubtedly act as if there were a correct solution to the moral dilemma. This would generate a profound modification of the current view of what morality is—what philosophers would call a *metaethical* revolution.

Such an approach could wrongly give the impression of proceeding from those forms of cognitive shortcuts that philosophy has analyzed as a "sense of duty," which Adam Smith's *Theory of Moral Sentiments* (Smith

1759) distinguishes from the moral sense because of its automatic dimension and the fact that it is based on predetermined rules, which can, in a way, be assimilated to a code—even if Smith, of course, means rules of law or good society rather than algorithms. However, as Smith notes, this "sense of rules" is fundamentally based on moral motivation—which is precisely what any so-called moral machine would (at least until further notice) lack.

In summary, the Artificialistic Fallacy points out that biases in AI not only mirror our world: they threaten our very conception of what morality is and should be from a metaethical point of view. However, as the Apparatgeist theory elegantly shows, our relationship to emerging technologies is complex. Thus, fatalism is probably not the best candidate for analyzing it: there is no fatality that AI will for sure reshape our relationships and even our morality. However, the issue of determinism remains intact, and we must be aware of this risk of artificialization in order to prevent any shrinking of our moral Forms of Life—which are, at least for the moment, infinitely richer, subtler and more pluralistic than their artificial counterparts. At least, if we consider this subtlety as something we value and care about!

This issue may soon become crucial for today's "digital natives" as well as for future generations who will be increasingly immersed in AI. For this reason, it is now urgent to discuss the Naturalistic Fallacy in order to put our relationship with AI into perspective from a theoretical as well as from a practical and educational point of view. It is also urgent to design AI with care in order to avoid this risk of artificialization but also because AI may probably be a tool to broaden our perspectives and reinforce our relationships rather than restrict them to some limited patterns, when and if we believe that it is not relevant to do so, as it is the case with morality and some other aspects of our social life.

Acknowledgments I wish to thank a referee for insightful comments. I also wish to thank Daniela Ginsburg for her professional linguistic revision of this chapter.

References

Adam, Alison. 1998. *Artificial Knowing: Gender and the Thinking Machine*. Routledge.

Bergen, Hilary. 2016. 'I'd blush if I could': Digital assistants, disembodied cyborgs and the problem of gender. *Word and Text* 6: 95–113.

Bourdieu, Pierre. 1998. *La Domination Masculine*. Paris: Seuil.
Buolamwini, Joy. 2016. InCoding – In The Beginning Was The Coded Gaze. MIT Media Lab (May 16, 2016). https://medium.com/mit-media-lab/incoding-in-the-beginning-4e2a5c51a45d.
Crawford, Kate. 2016. Artificial Intelligence's White Guy Problem. The New York Times (June 25, 2016). https://www.nytimes.com/2016/06/26/opinion/sunday/artificial-intelligences-white-guy-problem.html?auth=login-email&login=email.
Eubanks, Virginia. 2018. *Automating Inequality: How High-Tech Tools Profile, Police, and Punish the Poor*. New York: Picador, St Martin's Press.
Gilligan, Carol. 1982. *In a Different Voice*. Cambridge, MA: Harvard University Press.
Greenspan, Patricia. 2005. *Practical Guilt: Moral Dilemmas, Emotions, and Social Norms*. Oxford University Press.
Hao, Karen. 2019. AI's white guy problem isn't going away. *MIT Technology Review* (April 17, 2019). https://www.technologyreview.com/2019/04/17/136072/ais-white-guy-problem-isnt-going-away/.
Katz, James. 2006/2013. *Machines That Become Us: The Social Context of Personal Communication Technology*. Oxon/New York: Transaction Publishers/Routledge.
Katz, James, and Mark Aakhus. 2002. *Perpetual Contact: Mobile Communication, Private Talk, Public Performance*. Cambridge: Cambridge University Press.
Kohlberg, Lawrence. 1981. *Essays on Moral Development, Vol. I: The Philosophy of Moral Development*. San Francisco, CA: Harper & Row.
Mikhail, John. 2011. *Elements of Moral Cognition: Rawls' Linguistic Analogy and the Cognitive Science of Moral and Legal Judgment*. Cambridge: Cambridge University Press.
Moore, George Edward. 1903. *Prinicpia Ethica*. Cambridge: Cambridge University Press.
Nurock, Vanessa. 2011. *Sommes-nous naturellement moraux*. Paris: Presses Universitaires de France.
———. 2019. L'Intelligence Artificielle a-t-elle un genre? *Cités* 80: 61–74.
Silke Carty, Sharon. 2011. Many Cars Tone Deaf to Women's Voices. autoblog.com (May 31, 2011). https://www.autoblog.com/2011/05/31/women-voice-command-systems/.
Smith, Adam. 1759 [1981]. The Theory of Moral Sentiments. In *Liberty Fund*, eds. D. D. Raphael and A. L. Macfie.
Star, Susan Leigh. 1999. The Ethnography of Infrastructure. *American Behavioral Scientist* 43: 377–391.
UNESCO. 2019. I'd blush if I could. EQUALS and UNESCO. https://en.unesco.org/Id-blush-if-I-could.
Winner, Langdon. 1986. *The Whale and the Reactor: A Search for Limits in an Age of High Technology*. University of Chicago Press.

PART II

Future Technologies in Action

Thing or No-Thing: Robots Are Not Just a Thing, Not yet a Human. An Essay in Thinking *Through Media* by *Hermeneutics of Difference*

Philipp Stoellger

In Advance: A Remark on the Method

The following considerations are neither from an empirical nor from a historical point of view but from a *phenomenological* and *hermeneutical* one, in accordance with the conference claim of "enhanced understanding" (Boston University, College of Communication 2019). Whatever *understanding* may be and how it may be 'made', empirical and historical methods are different from hermeneutics. Though determining what contemporary hermeneutics is would be another discussion entirely. So, for the purposes of this chapter, I will take it that the definition of

P. Stoellger (✉)
Systematic Theology (Dogmatics and Philosophy of Religion), Heidelberg University, Heidelberg, Germany
e-mail: ps@wts.uni-heidelberg.de

J. Katz et al. (eds.), *Perceiving the Future through New Communication Technologies*,
https://doi.org/10.1007/978-3-030-84883-5_7

'understanding' is already comprehended. In the background of my theological perspective are also imaging science and German Media Theory—as religion *is* a medium and operates in and by media. Religious histories, therefore, are a field of inventing and investigating emerging media—like Christ and his spirit. And as for humans, the intersection of theology and media philosophy, let me ask for the anthropological difference of humans and new media. That is why I presuppose the model of a chiastic emergence of humans and media as *figuration* (Stoellger 2019, 503; 2020a, 225–235; 2020b, 19–47; 2016a, 192–206).

But just to avoid misunderstandings: in the line of a hermeneutics of *difference* (not of consensus and identity) (Stoellger 2016b, 164–193). I reject the exclusion of hermeneutics and phenomenology by the German Media Theory (Kittler et al.). As long as new media are *used* by humans and address their users, questions of meaning and truth remain indispensable. As an example for decisive differences we live by, I will exemplify the hermeneutics of difference by that of *trust and reliance*.

In General: Media as Operative Frames of Perception

New media are *new* insofar as they *change our frames of perception* (interaction, forms of life, feelings, habits of thought, speech, politics, etc.). I refer to this as *mediality* (or *meta*-mediality). As 'medium' was terminologically an invention of Thomas Aquinas for Aristotle's anonymos and metaxy, a medium is what *intervenes* and comes *in between*. It is *operative* insofar as it gives access to the otherwise inaccessible, but it is therefore transparent and opaque at the same time (like a church-window). In this way, a medium is not just a means to an end like an instrument but *an operative form of perception* (forming perceptions and perception forming).

These changes in the frames of perception become manifest in metaphors and metonymies, for example, in stories and parables, icons and images, and throughout literature and the arts. One manifestation is the common habit of thought and speech framing the founded research—the brain as computer or the 'genetic code' as to be re-written by CRISPR and others. This *may* appear as new metaphysics, or *bio*metaphysics, as if humans are essentially their genetic code (new essentialism: Aristotle's substance is replaced by genetic substantialism). Furthermore, the pattern is shifting to *techno*metaphysics: as the brain and the code are negotiable, 'thesei' not 'physei', the deep belief in making humans better and better by genetic engineering becomes intriguing.

That is why the mediality of new media and their impact on our perception, interaction, and so on can be analyzed and interpreted by their conceptual and figurative manifestations. However, as such an hermeneutical and phenomenological approach is highly *abductive* (Peirce), validation remains a problem. One cannot make general claims, but must find and invent a *meaning*, an interpretation, of 'what is going on'. An *investigative* research in mediality, therefore, has to be *imaginative* and *innovative* and *inventive*: the 'inventio' was the name for 'abductions' in former times, that is, to reveal the actual and future patterns of perception, thought, and so on.

In this line I understand the abductive and intriguing question: whether robots may or should be(come) our *friends*. It is probably better to befriend them than to make an enemy of them. Making enemies is easy, but if finding a fruitful, friendly relationship is the challenge, I am looking for some response.

What Do I Mean by 'Robots'?

Robots are (1) not animals, (2) not just things, (3) not yet a human being, and (4) not yet God (despite Kubrick's depiction of A.C. Clarke's HAL 9000 in 2001: A Space Odyssey). But then what—for heaven's sake—are they? Their own 'species'? Of which 'genus'? I would suggest they are a very special species in the multitude of intermediary beings, like angels and demons: existing in between, a complex of imagination and reality, with their own unique bodies and their own mode of communication.

Robots are:

In a narrow sense, humanoid machines (devices, apparatus).
In a wider sense, all machines controlled by programs.
In the widest sense, all connected devices or even more: the (mode of) connection itself.
In other words, they are 'knots' of a web. They are constituted by and as relations, by the special relations we call 'digital' or 'programmed'.

Here I would prefer to speak in the more narrow sense of robots as *forms* in the medium of digital communication. Robots are *animated subjects* in between Things and Humans: intermediary beings in the realm of intermediacy (fitting with their relationality). They form their own species (let's call them *No-Things*) with agency in the realm of intermediacy (let's name it the *In-between*) where we also meet angels and demons, famous paradigms for what we call 'media'.

The proper pattern of thought and interaction is not 'either/or' (as Kierkegaard or some theology and philosophy would argue), but the realms of *inter*: robots—like other 'Apparatgeists' or operative 'spirits'—populate and enliven a world *in-between*. That's quite appropriate for media: the realm of in-between.

An eye-opening impact of this way of perception is a new way of looking at the human—not substantialist but relational (Cassirer with Leibniz: mathematical function relation as model for a relational ontology—and anthropology), with a primacy of relation before relates: understanding humans *as relational media* (media anthropology) and even *God as medium* (i.e., *not* as apparatus or machine).

Drawing on their Apparatgeist theory, Katz and Aakhus highlighted in their argument that "machines do indeed become us" (Katz 2003, 315), yet in doing so, they invite numerous superordinate and category-transferring questions:

1. Machines become "our representatives at a distance," Katz and Aakhus say. Do these machines become our 'life after death', the *soma pneumatikon*, the resurrected body (or more) of eternal life? Do they become the living presence of the dead? Do they become not just *our* representatives but *their* representatives as well, that is, taking on multiple categories of representation? After all, the Golem became the representative of itself, and of the dark side of machine life (a theme I will pick up below).
2. Machines become "important parts and reference points in our self-concepts" (Katz 2003, 318).
3. Machines become "meaningful accoutrements to our self creation and symbolic interpersonal communication" (Katz 2003, 318).

Could they become decisive media of 'self-understanding'—figures of the other, challenging us to become a self? Our 'representatives' develop a significant impact for our self-concepts: not just that the brain is seen as a computer but that humans are conceptualized as media. *That's* the starting point of *media anthropology* (in German Media Theory).

Identity as relations—like relatives—is decisive for media anthropology: insofar as human beings are not substances but originally relations (primacy of relations like media), the form named 'human' becomes possible and real only in, by, and through dynamic relations named 'media'.

From Servants to Friends? James Katz and the Golem

James Katz's pattern of understanding in 2003 was that machines do become us, but "[m]achines will always be the servants of humans" (Katz 2003, 318). That's a common idea: *the master–slave pattern*, or slightly different *servant*. (A similar pattern would be employer and employee.) The slave or servant is, of course, more than a thing, but do they have autonomy, freedom, dignity? The follow-up observation is: as soon as they become us, they won't remain servants. That may be why Katz in 2019 goes far beyond that: not just servants, but perhaps *friends*. If they become us, they could become our friends, but *should* they? The question is intriguing: at first glance, one would say no and never; at the second or third, though, the contemplation begins, and it is this contemplation that I am displaying here. Robots as friends sounds like a category mistake, but it is a calculated mistake: that's what we call a *metaphor*. In my view, this metaphor shows a horizon shift that has taken place over the last two decades: what appeared to be an instrument, an apparatus, or a mere servant seems to develop a momentum and its own technical and social form of life. Katz's metaphorical proposal is symptomatic of this horizon shift in our life with robots.

The pattern has a history: remember the famous and notorious Golem? The legend from the Middle Ages, first dating to the twelfth century in Worms, Germany (commentary to Sefer Yetzirah), popular since the Prague-version of Rabbi Judah Loew (1525–1609), and widespread since the literary reception (Meyrink 1998), is about a human-like creature made out of clay and something else: magic, ritual, and some divine agency and presence. The story abridged: Rabbi Loew wanted to help the oppressed Jews in Prague by creating a strong and powerful helper. By a divine vision, Rabbi Loew was instructed to create a Golem out of clay. After seven days praying, the Rabbi and his helpers collected some clay from near the Moldau and created a human-like figure (cf. figuration, Fig. 7.1).

By the medium of sacred formula (tzirufim), the figure began to glow and steam, growing hair and nails, but only by the recitation of the biblical word did the Golem open its eyes: "And the LORD God formed man *of* the dust of the ground, *and breathed into his nostrils the breath of life; and*

Fig. 7.1 Reproduction of the Prague Golem. (https://upload.wikimedia.org/wikipedia/commons/9/9f/Prague-golem-reproduction.jpg [public domain])

man became a living soul" (Gen 2:7). But that recitation was not enough. Together at home, the Golem needed further animation—by kabbalistic ritual (Sefer Yetzirah, cf. the Worms version). A little piece of paper with *God's name* was put under its tongue—and *that* was the crucial animation. The Golem is animated by a name, the name of God (or a name-like property, ämät: truth). The concept is clear: only *God* is giving life, otherwise such a creation would be the greatest blasphemy, an unfriendly takeover of God's privilege. It is a common topic, not only in religious spheres, that animated machines are monsters, demonstrations of man's will to play God.

This commonplace topic has a relevant intuition: that man's making of machines which 'come to life' is dangerous. However, as the Golem shows, it's not blasphemy, but possible—with a certain humbleness. Strictly speaking, if one has to take the responsibility toward God (and future generations), some 'technophilia' will become more careful in its applications.

What was and is the danger of a Golem? Isn't it just the best friend, helping the Jews—in the name of God? Like an angel, it is doing the 'work of God': a figure of divine agency? Interestingly, like a robot the Golem can be 'switched off' by removing the 'name of God' from its mouth. This *has* to be done every Sabbath, not to break the Sabbath law. But once the Rabbi forgot to switch it off, the story picks up speed: the Golem ran through the Prague Ghetto and destroyed whatever came in its way. The ending of the Golem's rampage is narrated in different versions. One is that Rabbi Loew could switch it off by removing the name paper, but that's quite a lucky ending: as if the switching off would be so easy. Remember Goethe's sorcerer's apprentice: the brooms I summon may overpower me. Switching them off becomes a real problem. When the Golem goes its own way, it remains an open question how to switch it off. The machines we are living with, and increasingly by, cannot be switched off anymore.

One lesson we learned from the Golem is that *servants* rarely remain mere servants. They develop their own momentum and self-dynamic. It's a story about the mediality of media: their self-dynamic. That's a significant aspect of James Katz' Apparat*geist* theory—with the implication of an Apparat*life* theory. If there is a 'geist' in the apparatus, it will not remain a servant: not just a machine, not yet a human, but an animated subject with its own agency. That is why one may suggest an expanded version: Apparatgeist with Apparat*life* theory, as interpretive patterns for the decisive momentum of media and their operativity. They are not lifeless instruments but, in a special way, living entities in between us. When they are 'running' and 'operating', they develop their own life, but their form of life is quite special: in contrast to humans it is 'more'—potentially eternal, immortal (no more 'off switch') omniscient, omnipresent, almighty?

However, at the same time it is less: less emotions, less embodiment, less joy and sorrow. Robots don't know what it means to laugh or cry. And in this context we may also ask, can robots be sinners? As long as they do not have 'free will' or the ability to experience the fascinating force of emotion and desire, they cannot be. Conversely, if a robot cannot believe in God, he cannot sin (like animals). However, considering that sin is not a moral question but a deeper one, perhaps robots can be sinners—by losing their intact relationship with the creator. In that way, Golem lost its relationship to Rabbi Loew. The Golem is not morally bad, he is just 'out of order'. Its self-dynamic seems to be instinctive, though that is disputable: why is he destroying? What is in his way? The story could be told in other directions. It's not necessary that the apparatus-friend becomes an enemy—but *that's* the great fear the story is dealing with.

Robots are *too much* and *too little* at the same time. They are more than a soft toy, a doll, or a puppet. They are filled with or full of a suspicious 'self-dynamic' with their own 'program', energy, possible surveillance, connected, with perhaps too much 'life' but not enough soul? Robots are not enough, not human enough, to call 'friends'. There is a lack of body *and* soul: no soul in the machine. Imagine, for example, a 'soul test' for robots: would we marry them, baptize them, or bury them? If their animation develops its own life, an 'after-life' (Warburg), they become real 'others' (with Levinas and beyond him). They make claims and become a challenge, not just as animated objects but as challenging others. Then they become real (and more than real: imaginary) members of social life, of religion, politics, and ethics.

Robots are their own species, a species I would call No-Things—animated things which become more than things: animated subjects. Once animated, they become 'living images' or 'pets' which we live with (and sometimes by). (But here we have to draw a distinction: animation by use—in vivo—and by theory—in vitro: ANT.) That may be one more reason to ask, along with James Katz, if they should become our friends. It is surely better to befriend them than to make enemies of them, but how does one befriend a robot, and will he 'friend back'?

Friends and Like-Friends

Can a robot be our enemy? This is a common motif, as the Golem shows. It is also evident that the opposite is possible, as the Golem shows as well: it was created as a 'friend of utility'. As long as robots are 'marked' as robots, they may become 'our friends'. However, when they become confusable with humans, they can be scary: remember the uncanny valley.

'Friends' or friendship is usually defined as a relationship between humans, that is, equality (or similarity), based on:

1. A kind of reciprocal love like sympathy and benevolence (each one wishes the best for the other for his own sake).

2. Trust and reciprocity. Aristotle called this reciprocal love—benevolence and knowledge of each others' attitude. He distinguished between friendships of 'utility', of 'desire' or 'pleasure', and 'perfect friendship'. The easiest answer to the question 'should robots become our friends?' is that they can and may be friends of utility as they are useful. However, this is an underestimation. If they 'become us', we are emotionally engaged, and robots are, therefore, more than useful devices. So the second kind of friendship seems appropriate: that of pleasure and desire.

The consequent option is evident: different robots may be friends in different ways. My Mac may be my friend of utility, while a sex robot is probably more a friend of desire (or of needs)—but what about '*perfect* friendship'? It is based on virtues, unselfishness, a shared (form of) life, and similarity. Even that may be possible with robots: virtues, unselfishness, and a shared life.

Remember the robot named 'Boomer' in Taji, Iraq. He was a MARCbot—Multi-function Agile Remote-Controlled Robot—a little truck with an arm and a camera to find bombs and defuse them. He was not only named (Boomer) but shared with the soldiers a form of life, was highly unselfish and altruistic, with serious virtues—a real friend for them. That is why he was 'buried' with military honor and 21 gun salutes (cf. Köppe, 2019). Whenever a robot may be a friend, he needs a name—like Boomer. The nameless, the anonymous, is uncanny (another uncanny valley: a web or an algorithm has no name and cannot be a friend) (Fig. 7.2).

What about reciprocity and recognition? A serious asymmetry appears: we can 'befriend' them (and 'unfriend' them as well), but do they 'friend back'? Are they able to be emotionally concerned, engaged, and committed? As far as I can judge: they do not and cannot. They can act as if they can, but they are unable to *feel friendship*. One can *act as if* one is a friend of someone: let's call it *fake* friendship, perhaps out of opportunistic reasons or for whatever reason. What then is the robot, if he is a friend: is he merely a simulation of a friend? Is he acting as if he is?

This raises the old question of being and appearance (Sein und Schein). Remember the old conflict between Socrates/Plato and the Sophists: is it enough and right to *appear* to be just, or is it decisive to *be* just, not just to act as if you are? With Kant, the question reappears in a radicalized form: only the will can and shall be 'holy', all appearance is ambiguous. The distinction of being and appearance is relevant in some fields—ethics

Fig. 7.2 MARCbot. (Darrell Greenwood, 2009, *MARCbot*. https://upload.wikimedia.org/wikipedia/commons/d/d6/MARCbot.jpg [originally posted to Flickr])

and science, love and faith—but in art, for example, it would be (nearly, really?) nonsense to ask: is it art or does it only seem to be art?

In politics—one may hesitate: politics and fake politics—is there a difference? In the power game of politics it seems to be nonsense to distinguish being and seeming/appearance. But take a dictator: he believes and seems to be powerful, but he is not really (just violence, not power, no recognition). What then in face-to-face relationships like friendship: does it make sense to distinguish being and seeming to be a friend? I would propose that the difference is crucial—and connected with a trust criterion: only a *real* friend is trustworthy.

By the way, the same is relevant in regard to God: if he would be so free not to be love, if he may change his essence and attributes, he would not be trustworthy, but merely an ambiguous absolute power (*potentia absoluta*).

That is why I suggest a fourth kind of friendship which Aristotle apparently did not consider. Robots are like-friends—they behave like them and are treated like them—but they are not *real* friends, just *like-friends*. That does not mean they are *not* friends. Think about family-like relations: someone can be like a father to you or like a brother or sister. He or she is not your brother or sister, but *like* them. The 'like relation' is quite serious and of high emotional importance. I suppose the 'like relations' are a social realm of 'in-between': not father, not not-father, but its own kind of fatherhood, like a unique kind of friendship. Robots are like friends but do not friend back, do not love back.

Thus a further significant asymmetry appears: I guess that usually we in Western society believe that robots can be our enemy, truly and profoundly our enemy. The enmity they have toward us is believed to be real; their friendship is not. If I am right with this abduction, the question is how to understand this asymmetry.

Is there a prevalence of fear of machines (like of strangers)? So much joy, but still more fear? Or is it more than fear: existential angst because of the indefiniteness and indeterminacy of robots (remember the distinction of fear and angst in Kierkegaard and Heidegger: the indefiniteness of 'death' draws the distinction)? The indefinite is uncanny, that is, the Apparatgeist theory probably needs an Apparatangst theory, but that's *our* angst, not the one of the apparatus.

But in advance, I suppose that the normative, religious, and traditional disposition is still anthropocentric, and at the same time 'robophobic', beneath all the joy, desire, and reliance on them. Though social and sexual diversity may be recognized (more or less), technical and 'posthuman' diversity is not. Who will argue for 'robotic diversity'? Where are the limits of diversity and inclusion? Should we develop an ethical theory named 'Singer 3.0' (after the Princeton philosopher Peter Singer who argues that we are inappropriately human species-centric), claiming that the critique of speciesism has to be updated: not just human rights and dignity for primates and animal rights against anthropocentrism, but a social, moral, legal, and political inclusion of robots? Robot rights and dignity? (Should a robot have the right to vote in presidential elections, for example? When we read about the famous "parliament of things" (Latour 1993), the political inclusion of robots seems desirable. But until further notice I would claim, voting robots should be called vote rigging. Be it robot or bot—if they do vote, they are manipulating the elections.)

Here I do hesitate: should the robot have the right, for example, not to be switched off? A friend has certain rights and a special dignity. He has the right not to be switched off, not to be 'unfriended', without quite good reasons, and I am not sure whether political differences are good enough to unfriend someone. The robot, however, is defined by the operation of 'switching' (Kittler and the 'German Media Theory'), so to be switched off is essential for a robot and is not a violation of its dignity. This is a crucial difference to human friendship.

The like-friend can be switched off and on. One may say that is a special generosity of robot friendship: they are friendly enough to accept being switched off.

This line of reasoning may be followed further: what should we do with our new friends in the end? We don't recycle or throw away a dead friend like waste, but a dead robot? Recycling may be the best friendly turn: robots are organ donors 'by nature'. But—my old Macs, for example—I still keep them for decades … 'Love is as strong as death', we know from the Song of Songs (Song 8:6). The emotional attachments to some robots are longer lasting than their operating lifetime. The 'end of life' for the user is different from the one of the producer.

But *why* do I keep them? Hard to say, but I suppose they are old companions, charged with memory and shared experiences, connected with key events of my life. And they are not just puppets or souvenirs, but less and more: less, as they are not very visual and haptic, not so embodied; but more as they are living archives, traces of my life—more like a diary one would never throw away.

The Trust Criterion: Trust Versus Reliance

Is there no real trust in robots, only real mistrust? I suppose that the social imaginary—for example manifested in film and literature—channels and primes such mistrust: it is better entertainment to show machines as dangerous enemies.

Reliance or even more, trust? The question 'should robots become our friends?' implies 'should we *trust* (in) them?'. "What is today's anathema is tomorrow's trustworthy standard", Katz noted (2003, 315). Does this mean that robot relations become the 'trustworthy standard'? I would distinguish: they probably become the reliance standard (with some burden in regard to personal reliance!), but they won't become *trustworthy*.

A real friend we trust, a robot we do not (by being online)? See, for example, Alexa in Germany (cf. Druga 2019).[1]

[1] "Gerade in Deutschland trauen die Kinder den Geräten am wenigsten. Als sie zu meinem Workshop kamen, erwarteten sie, dass Alexa nicht ehrlich auf ihre Fragen antworten, sondern versuchen würde, sie zu täuschen. Sie hatten also bereits durch die Medien und die Gesellschaft eine negative Einstellung der Technologie gegenüber. Die Kinder haben nicht unbedingt anders mit den Geräten interagiert, aber sie haben die Antworten anders interpretiert. Sie hatten zum Beispiel das Gefühl, dass Alexa lügt und gar nicht wissen kann, wer Bundespräsident in Deutschland ist—weil sie nicht aus Deutschland kommt" (Druga 2019).

I rely on my robots, but I do not trust them. Why is this, and what causes this distinction?

Trust and reliance have a different 'emotional temperature': trust is hot, reliance is cold or cooling down. If I do trust, I am emotionally engaged. Trust can be so hot that one can be burned if the trust fails. Trust is quite risky or even dangerous: one needs trust to live by, but one can die by deep disappointment.

Reliance, on the contrary, is emotionally cold or cooling down: reliable structures exonerate us from the risks of trusting. I can rely on the fact that I will get my burger if I pay for it—there is no need to trust. Exoneration or relief is a gain in complex communication, and highly reliable media like GPS are really exonerating during a flight. I don't have to trust in the pilots, I just have to rely on the devices.

I suppose that's what robots are made for: to rely on—and to exonerate us from the risks of trust. So I rely on my Mac, but I don't trust it. However, I do *entrust* it with a lot (all my secrets…). Should I do so? Should I treat it *as if* it were a confidential friend? Better not, because it is online, connected, and easy to hack (at any rate). So I should better *not* entrust it with my secrets because it is just a 'like-friend': a friend of reliance, not of trust. While trust is highly 'error-prone', very risky, or even life-threatening (cf. Christ's death on the cross), it is plausible and becomes common to replace trust by supplements or simulations of trust: reliance and reliable 'robots' like AI.

The very example which provoked my question is the new AI development in US intelligence: security checks of employees in the intelligence (and elsewhere) is handed over to (or taken over by) AI. We have the data, but not enough staff to analyze it. Therefore, AI can do this work instead of human agents (cf. Sassenrath 2019). I do understand the problem, and perhaps the need as well—but the consequences are no less risky than to trust in trust. In granting credits or in employee selection, AI can make decisions the superiors don't understand. If the AI is basic (and becomes hegemonial), the reliance on AI replaces the trust in human decision-making. (Remember Stanisław Lem's 'Golem XIV'—Lem 2012, 97ff.) Furthermore, the AI does not trust in human agents—because AI never trusts but calculates and decides (even if the AI *claims* trust, like the promotors of 'Augustus Intelligence' claims trust for their AI (Hanson 2019)).

The AI solution in US intelligence, banking, and so forth becomes a new problem, and the problem we tried to solve becomes even worse because of it. The dilemma is that AI has good reasons *not* to trust in humans—but are our reasons good enough to replace human trust with reliance in AI? The problem becomes worse because AI or algorithms are more reliable than human analysis or memory. I don't trust my memory, but rely on my Mac—not just for scheduling. The Mac is much more reliable than me.

A simulated friend may be much more *reliable* than a 'real friend'. Friendship is like trust: it can be quite risky. One may, for example, be disappointed, whereas a simulation can be stable and highly reliable—a really reliable friend, that is, a friend of reliance, *not* of trust.

Do we still trust in trust? Do we still dare to trust in trust? Do we trust in love (or in hope)? The abducted story behind this may be that most of us in the West don't trust in faith any more (not in God). Then one may expect that we trust in trust, that is, in personal relations and the trustworthiness of humans instead. But like trust in faith, trust in trust disappears (or vanishes). Might the consequence be that there is no trust any more, just reliance? That is to say, we rely on controlling, calculus, and apparatus? In other words, there is not just a lack of trust (like a lack of moral sense), but a lack of trust in trust.

The solution (replacement by reliable AI) reinforces the problem: the more we rely on reliance, the less we trust in trust. This is a loss of 'social capital' (or cultural, religious capital, if we want to speak of 'capital' here).

Or could it be that we do trust, but trust only in controllable media like AI and robots?

However, this may be a dangerous self-deception because the risk of trust is still present, but 'transposed': instead of trust in humans, we trust in robots or in reliable operators.

Furthermore, a second risk is that the risk is not as controllable as we believe. By the momentum and self-dynamics of media like AI, the trust problem reappears.

AI: And Robot Belief

If AI *is* intelligence, it is *never* neutral, 'mere intelligence' or 'neutral algorithms'. Reason or intelligence never *are* neutral (neutrality is an 'ideal', a regulative idea). Embedded in social interaction, intelligence is more or less *effective and affective*: ethically and emotionally loaded. (If it is *intelligence*, it is a kind of reason(ing), not of ethos or emotion—logos, but not ethos or pathos.) To frame it in Kantian terms: the conditions of possibility of intelligence are its emotional and normative embedding. The embodiment of intelligence is not just the machine's body (silicon) but the social body of interaction and imagination (hopes and fears).

The problem is that a calculus itself is incapable to *feel*, that is, to trust, to love, to hate.

AI is emotionally incompetent or 'helpless'. From a psychological viewpoint, AI is somewhat sociopathic (no empathy, etc.), or worst case even psychopathic (when 'out of order'). But, like an intelligent sociopath, the AI may simulate emotions (remember the popular television series *Dexter*), and the simulation may be quite convincing (remember the movie *Ex Machina*), but nevertheless, simulated emotions are not emotions.

Returning to an earlier discussion in the chapter, this real/simulated divide is evident in regard to friendship, simulated friendship *is not* friendship, but there is a significant difference in the relation between humans and robots in this regard: between humans, simulation of friendship is deceptive and hurtful. Between a robot and me, the simulation is all I can expect; it's not deception but as expected. So the simulation of friendship is fine—as long as I don't expect more. Again remember *Ex Machina*: if I expect 'real love' from the robot, that is self-deception. Might we be looking for delusion in communication with robots?

Is our 'will to believe' so strong that we want to be deceived (joyfully)? This would have to be further examined under the topic 'robot belief'—our belief in robots—and their lack of belief. A good calculus never believes—like a *deus calculans* (Leibniz's calculating God) does not trust or believe, it just knows everything, anytime, everywhere. As if such a calculating machine would be a model for the modern scientist, its will *not* to believe anything at all is crucial. But even the scientist's *will not to believe* is a 'belief system': no belief in God, but in the almighty calculus. One may call that robot-like belief: a belief in calculation. Such a belief is deeply different from life world beliefs.

I suppose that *our* emotional engagement with robots (and their relatives) is more affective and emotional. As James Katz noted in 2003, there remains an emotional or a *pathic* ambivalence: on the one hand, "people use and enjoy their machines" (Katz 2003, 315), while on the other, there is also "frustration" coming from the "inability of the machinery to deliver what users want" (Katz 2003, 318). The description (they become us; and may become our friends) implies a small *anthropocentric* perspective: *if* the machinery delivers what we want, the ambivalence would disappear. Would the final goal be that they are us?

1. A primacy of 'us' remains: our joy and 'our wishes'.
2. An asymmetry: they become us—but not we become them.
3. What about us then? "Machines may become us, but we will never become machines" (Katz 2003, 319). Does the distinction remain as clear?

I suppose that the difference between personal and robot relations remains like the one between trust and reliance. Therefore, the ambivalence of joy and frustration will remain as well because humans are 'natural born anthropocentrics'. This 'natural' habit of thought is a problem not a solution. But will robots be the solution—or a problem again? Even if they become our friends, will we become *their* friends? Will they 'befriend' us or 'unfriend' us? Will they 'befriend back'? Our joy and emotional commitment admitted, the question remains whether *they* may feel committed reciprocally? The AI example in US intelligence has already provided the answer.

I argue for the remaining ambivalence and an 'ambivalent tolerance'. Not becoming overwhelmed by our joy and 'will to friendship', but not overwhelmed either by envy or wishful 'primacy'. 'Ambivalence' as such is not a value but, with tolerance, the usual habit of ambivalence reduction is avoided. The recognition of an ambivalence keeps the space open for pensiveness and differentiation. This is a lesson to be learned by fine arts and their interventions: work on the ambivalences and undecidabilities in between humans and robots. The investigative perception has to be kept open—not to be governed by opposition from moral or legal 'instincts'—but also not to be governed by instinctive joy and embracement of robots (cf. Stanisław Lem 1992; Meyrink 1998; Stephenson 1995).

An Ambivalent Example: BlessU-2 as Robot's Religion

Robots make claims and become a challenge, not just as animated objects but as challenging others. They become real members of social life, religion, politics, and ethics (and they become more than real: imaginary). Could the problem arise that No-Things become not just more than things, but at last more than human? Could they become superhuman, considering this term in a serious, rational, and moral way? Even in a religious and political way? One example may be a successful robot, presented during the Reformation Anniversary of 2017 in Wittenberg (cf. Segensroboter n.d.). He was called 'BlessU-2': a blessing robot or, let's say, a 'blessing-machine' (Figs. 7.3 and 7.4).

'BlessU-2' was presented by the Protestant Church of Hessen and Nassau (EKHN). The title of the installation was programmatic: 'Moments of Blessing'. The robot 'himself' was developed by the engineer and media artist Alexander Wiedekind-Klein (*1969). The context and the constellation would be a topic on its own—celebrating 500 years of Luther's reformation: questions of symbolic and iconic power of Christianity and Protestantism, especially in contemporary Germany and Europe—I skip these questions. The 'outlook' of BlessU is significant. The iconography is ostentatiously 'primitive' and 'out of time and fashion'. 'Asimo', 'Kotaro', or even 'C-3PO' from *Star Wars* have been better developed in figure, face, and form. So BlessU is demonstratively 'simple', far below the 'uncanny valley'. Its physiognomy looks 'cute'. Its body is more a machine

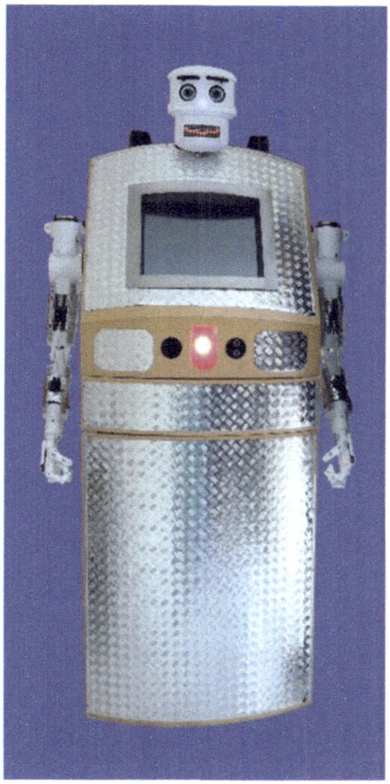

Fig. 7.3 BlessU-2 (purple background). (EKHN/Volker Rahn, https://www.silicon.de/wp-content/uploads/2017/05/BlessU-2_Pic_freigestellt-NEU_.jpg)

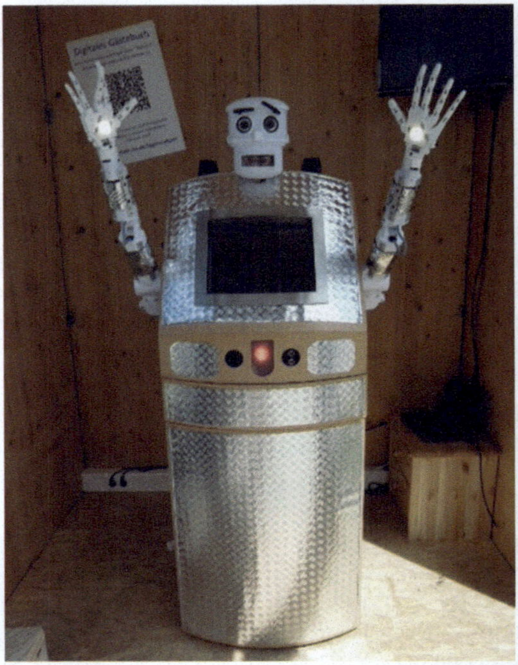

Fig. 7.4 BlessU-2 (wooden background). (EKHN/Volker Rahn, https://meet-junge-oekumene.de/wp-content/uploads/2017/10/BlessU-2_EKHN.jpg)

than humanoid but it *is* framed as human: head and face, arms and fingers, and even a red light as a beating heart (cf. EKHN/Medienhaus 2017a, b).

Its technicity and artificiality are explicit and exposed, but in a friendly looking way (the movement of the eyebrows remains unclear for me, though). 'No reason to be afraid of it'—seems to be the message. Its face is more like a clown, with a green nose and a red mouth. The torso is a simple machine, like an ATM. This impression is confirmed by the 'layout' of its display—one can choose: (1) the language of the blessing by selecting a 'flag button', (2) the gender of the voice, and (3) the kind of blessing one wants, whether more 'encouragement' or 'renewal'.

The ATM machine connotation is significant—the sacred and the secular economies are traditionally entangled: the host and the coin come together and are elevated in the CD or DVD. The host promises the sacred union of ultimate sense and sensuality; the coin (or banknote) promises undefined sense by its sensuality, and the DVD promises the mere sense of sensuality (a joyful zero-sense). The 'primitivity' is significant as well. Here, one may see a demonstrative gesture by the church: pillory the robot? Expose him as a primitive medium? As incompetent and impotent in sacred concerns? But the declared intention was different: to raise the discussion about Christianity and contemporary (really contemporary?) media.

Do robots become us—as church? What—for heaven's sake—may happen to the church then?

What is 'blessing'? (cf. Vogt n.d.) It is 'divine agency', not immediate, but mediated. The question becomes more general: what are the fitting media for God's agency? While *only* God is blessing (at first and at last), what are the appropriate media for blessing? Usually just humans, persons, often specialized persons such as priests or pastors. But why not robots?

Are robots '*relationship*able' (cf. Vogt n.d.)? I would sharpen the point: to replace a professor by robots would not be a real problem (for whom?), but a priest or pastor? Can religion be transformed in robotics? Will we pray with robots and be blessed by them? What may we hope for?

Generally speaking, no media are to be excluded for God's and religion's agency, and I regret to say descriptively, not even violence. Remember that the chief theoretician for the 'holy war' was Bernard of Clairvaux, *the* theologian of love—and also of just hate and killing of non-believers. Critically speaking, the media of God and religion have to be appropriate following the rule: the form has to match the content. To communicate the gospel, it has to have a salvific form. Form follows content and function—and the form *is* the performance of the content—like the parables of God's kingdom. This already shows that not only personal media are suitable but words and images as well, and they are widely accepted.

But what about machines and humanoid robots? As everyday media, they are present in religion like everywhere else. In administration, AI or robots would not be a problem, but in *ministration* on a Sunday, they become a problem for communities.

Why? Traditions, habits, customs, and folkways may be a reason. The privilege of 'face-to-face' communication, as well as a certain skepticism against new media. I would like to make a theological and a medial point: robots and AI are at the best highly reliable media—and that's a great gain, though one has to protect them against surveillance and commercialization. But robots and AI are not *trust media*: we do not really trust in machines such as them. Remember that faith is often framed as trust relation (to trust in God) while robot relations are usually just based on reliance not trust. They are made for 'cooling down' the emotional risks of communication (even if in malfunction emotions do arise). The personal relations of religious communication are more for heating up the emotional investment: faith and trust, like love and hope, capture your engagement and ultimate concern 'with all your heart'. Robots are generous not to claim as much. This is a gain in operative relations like administration and its ilk, but it's not enough for religious communication. The comparative question would be, why—perhaps—would the replacement of professors by robots not be satisfying for all students?

So robots may become our friends *of reliance*, our 'like-friends'—better this than to believe naively in their neutrality or to see them as enemies. But robots will not replace deep trust relations. It may be that future generations will nullify the distinction of reliance and trust and then things may change. What may we hope for then? I, personally, am afraid that religion will be framed ever more as a reliable 'joy machine' and not as an existential challenge. The comparative question is the 'destiny of love': as love may be framed as a deep trust relationship, do we trust in love? We love it, we love love probably, but is it still an 'ultimate concern'? Is love still framed as and by trust—or by 'trial and error'?

Trust or Tinder? Tinder *may* be effective and reliable (I just lack the experience to know), but does anyone *trust* (in) Tinder? Some may rely on such algorithms, few may even believe in their promise to find the 'ultimate concern', but exceptions confirm the rule: you shall not trust in algorithms. In the name of trust, we should merely rely on robots and their algorithmic core—as far as it is reliable. This is a prescriptive claim as well for the development of AI: make it reliable, but do not claim trust in them and do not promise more than reliability.

References

Boston University, College of Communication. 2019. *Spring 2019 Symposia*. http://sites.bu.edu/emsconf/. Accessed 2 February 2021.

Druga, Stefania. 2019. Künstliche Intelligenz muss entzaubert werden. *Spiegel Online*, March 5. https://www.spiegel.de/netzwelt/gadgets/kuenstliche-intelligenz-und-kinder-mit-forscherin-stefania-druga-im-interview-a-1251721.html.

EKHN/Medienhaus. 2017a. *Experiment BlessU-2 / Interactive Installation ("Blessing Robot") English Version*. https://www.youtube.com/watch?v=JTK68l2BHtE.

———. 2017b. *Installation BlessU-2/LichtKirche Wittenberg (Segensroboter/Blessing Robot)*. https://www.youtube.com/watch?v=XfbrdCQiRvE.

Hanson, Russell. 2019. Trust in AI. *Medium.com*, October 9. https://medium.com/augustus-ai/trust-in-ai-fb8834967936.

Katz, James E. 2003. Bodies, Machines, and Communications Contexts. In *Machines that Become Us. The Social Context of Personal Communication Technology*, ed. James E. Katz, 311–320. London/New York: Routledge.

Köppe, Julia. 2019. Künstliche Intelligenz. Welche Rechte verdienen Roboter? *Spiegel Online*, February 23. https://www.spiegel.de/wissenschaft/mensch/kuenstliche-intelligenz-welche-rechte-verdienen-roboter-a-1254384.html.

Latour, Bruno. 1993. *We Have Never Been Modern*. Cambridge, MA: Harvard University Press.

Lem, Stanisław. 1992. *Mortal Engines*. San Diego: Harcourt Brace Jovanovich.

———. 2012. *Imaginary Magnitude*. Houghton Mifflin Harcourt.

Meyrink, Gustav. 1998. *Der Golem*. 15th ed. Ullstein: Frankfurt a.M.

Mori, Masahiro. 1970. *The Uncanny Valley*.

Reichardt, Jasia. 1978. *Robots: Fact, Fiction, and Prediction*. New York: Penguin Books.

Sassenrath, Henning. 2019. Der Computer entscheidet, wem Amerika vertraut. *Frankfurter Allgemeine Zeitung*, March 29. https://www.faz.net/aktuell/wirtschaft/diginomics/kuenstliche-intelligenz-bei-sicherheitsueberpruefungen-16114336.html.

Stephenson, Neal. 1995. *The Diamond Age. Or: A Young Lady's Illustrated Primer*. London: Viking.

Stoellger, Philipp. 2016a. Religion als Medienpraxis und Medienphobie. In *Das Christentum hat ein Darstellungsproblem*, 192–206. Freiburg: Herder.

———. 2016b. Verständigung mit Fremden. Zur Hermeneutik der Differenz ohne Konsens. In *Verstehen und Verständigung: Intermediable, multimodale und interkulturelle Aspekte von Kommunikation und Ästhetik*, ed. Klaus Sachs-Hombach, 164–193. Köln: Herbert von Halem.

———. 2019. Figurationen des Menschen. Studien zue Medienanthropologie. In *Interpretation Interdisziplinär* 18, 503. Würzburg: Königshausen & Neumann.

———. 2020a. Formation as Figuration: The Impact of Religion Framed by Media Anthropology. In *The Impact of Religion*, ed. Michael Welker, John Witte, and Stephen Pickard, 225–235. Leipzig: Evangelische Verlagsanstalt.

———. 2020b. Reformation as Reformatting Religion: The Shift of Perspective and Perception by Faith as Medium. In *The Reformation of Philosophy*, ed. Marius Timman Mjaaland, 19–47. Tübingen: Mohr Siebeck.

Vogt, Fabian. n.d. *Spricht an: das Experiment "Segensroboter BlessU-2"*. https://lichtkirche.ekhn.de/archiv/wittenberg-2017/mediales-zu-blessu-2.html.

Weltweit erster Segensroboter "BlessU-2" auf der Weltausstellung. n.d.. https://gott-neu-entdecken.ekhn.de/veranstaltungen-projekte/projekte-der-ekhn/segensroboter-blessu-2.html.

The Apparatgeist of Pepper-*kun*: An Exploration of Emerging Cultural Meanings of a Social Robot in Japan

Satomi Sugiyama

Introduction: Social Robots as Emerging Media

Robots and related technologies, such as automation and artificial intelligence, have become a critical part of industrial development. These emerging technologies are increasingly relevant not only to the production sector and various business sectors, but also to our everyday social life including the very intimate area that affects our emotional experiences. Of particular interest to the latter is the category of social robots. According to Breazeal (2002), key characteristics of social robots are that they are socially situated, autonomous, and able to interact with humans like other humans. Social robots, as Breazeal continues, should also be human-aware, meaning that they can perceive and understand internal states of humans, they should be readable so that humans can understand the

S. Sugiyama (✉)
Franklin University Switzerland, Lugano, Switzerland
e-mail: ssugiyama@fus.edu

J. Katz et al. (eds.), *Perceiving the Future through New Communication Technologies*,
https://doi.org/10.1007/978-3-030-84883-5_8

robots' behaviors, and social robots should be able to engage in socially situated learning utilizing AI and social intelligence (7–11). All these characteristics of social robots suggest that they are designed to carry very human features and are expected to join a variety of social arenas in everyday life, from stores and offices to schools and homes.

By the early 2000s, some mobile communication researchers were already exploring the boundaries between machines and humans (e.g., Katz 2003; Fortunati et al. 2003). This line of research highlighted the importance of aesthetics and the design aspect of machines (e.g., Fortunati 2003; Katz and Sugiyama 2005, 2006; Ling 2003; Sugiyama 2009) as well as emotions (e.g., Barile 2013; Barile and Sugiyama 2015; Fortunati and Vincent 2009; Vincent 2003, 2009), and led to the exploration of the question of social robots and emotions from a communication and media studies perspective (e.g., Katz et al. 2015; Sugiyama and Vincent 2013). In this and other recent endeavors, more scholars started to consider the social robot as a medium (e.g., Fortunati 2013; Guzman 2018; Halpern and Katz 2013; Höflich 2013; Sugiyama 2019) and, more specifically, as emerging media. Media technologies are always emerging without a clear line between the old and the new as "there is a genuine continuity of life, technology, and human nature that constrains anything new from being a truly radical departure from the old" (Katz and Robinson 2016, 112). However, it should be noted that when media is emerging, "technological transformation opens up new kinds and meanings of communication," which leads to a kind of "gestalt shift" (Katz and Robinson, 107) that guides us to the future. Such a temporary as well as experiential shift is an important point of consideration when examining social robots from a communication and media studies perspective. This aspect of emerging media directs our attention to the design of media that are expected to enter into our everyday lives in the near future, as well as the dynamically changing meanings that people create for the media as they use and interact in everyday life.

In fact, Apparatgeist theory (Katz and Aakhus 2002) was developed with this capacity when the mobile phone was considered as an emerging medium. Apparatgeist is a neologism developed from *apparat*, meaning machine, and *geist*, meaning spirit/mind. Katz and Aakhus explain the term *apparat*, originating in Latin, includes both technical and sociological aspects of machines, while the German word *geist* is used in Hegel's sense denoting "a directive principle" in the historical movement that "signifies a fundamental theme that animates the lives of human cultures"

(306). The use of *geist* emphasizes a sense of movement and a sense of becoming rather than being, and directs our attentions to both the individual and the collective aspects of societal behavior over time (307). As Katz and Aakhus explain, the Apparatgeist of the mobile phone is informed by "perpetual contact" and "pure communication," which underline human desires and ideals about communication, while simultaneously highlighting that unanticipated and often objectionable behaviors (e.g., frustration) arise from the perpetual contact that mobile communication has made possible. The theory further posits that the spirit of the machine influences the design of technology because it draws attention to the initial and subsequent significance given to it by users, non-users, and anti-users. This means that the theory emphasizes the importance of understanding symbolic meanings of a given machine that guide social practices of using and not using the machines. Apparatgeist theory posits that personal communication technologies are both utilitarian and symbolic, raising the question of "how humans invest their technology with meaning and use devices and machines to pursue social and symbolic routines" (Katz 2003, 15).

As an analytical framework of the way people invest their technology with meaning, Apparatgeist theory lays out manifest and latent reasoning regarding technology and social relationships. Manifest reasoning regarding technologies refers to specific manifest attributes sought after in the design process, and that potential users might want (e.g., low cost, ease of use, efficiency of personal life). Latent reasoning regarding technologies refers to latent issues concerning technology that potential users weigh up in their adoption and use of it (e.g., socially appropriate behavior of relevant technologies, symbolic affirmation of values). Manifest reasoning regarding social relationships is concerned with the extent that it can fit into the user's local social context (e.g., personal needs and social roles). Finally, latent reasoning regarding social relationships is about latent social dimensions that factor into decisions about adoption and usage, for example, the advancement of self within a group (Katz and Aakhus, 311). This framework is useful for analyzing the sense-making process and the emerging *geist* of social robots as observed in public discourse, aiding future design considerations regarding interaction patterns, interface, and application opportunities for suitable social and relational contexts.

In analyzing the social and symbolic routines and meanings that people create toward emerging media technologies, Goffman adds an invaluable perspective. This has been demonstrated by past research on mobile communication (e.g., Höflich 2003; Katz and Sugiyama 2005; Ling and Pedersen 2005; Ling 2008a, 2008b). In his classic work entitled *Behavior in Public Places*, Goffman (1963) speaks of the situation as a "full spatial environment anywhere within which an entering person becomes a member of the gathering that is (or does then become) present" (18). According to him, there is a normative interaction regulation in a given situation, which is "a kind of communication traffic order" (Goffman, 24). In a given situation, there is a focused interaction and an unfocused interaction. The former refers to "the kind of interaction that occurs when persons gather close together and openly cooperate to sustain a single focus of attention, typically by taking turns at talking," while the latter refers to "the kind of communication that occurs when one gleans information about another person present by glancing at him, if only momentarily, as he passes into and then out of one's view," and involves the "management of sheer and mere copresence" (Goffman, 24). These concepts illuminate the underlying structure of seemingly disparate individualized everyday experiences in the collective societal context.

Although researchers across disciplines have been making a considerable effort to understand the social aspect of robots in order to cultivate proper contexts for societal applications, the research effort in the field of communication and media studies is still at an early stage. Moreover, the research on social robots tends to remain within the laboratory due to various reasons including issues of safety and liability. However, it is critical that social robot research is conducted within everyday social contexts to develop an understanding of their emerging symbolic meanings. For instance, how do people experience encountering/interacting with social robots in everyday life? What kind of interactions do people expect from robots in everyday life? These questions cannot be fully answered by experimental studies conducted in a controlled research laboratory. Furthermore, answering these questions is essential for cultivating their practical applications in our society.

Pepper: "The World's First Personal Robot That Reads Emotions"

In order to understand social robots situated in everyday life contexts, a consumer social robot, Pepper, serves as a promising case. Pepper, a humanoid robot with a tablet on its upper body, entered into the consumer market in Japan in summer 2015. Softbank acquired a majority stake in Aldebaran, the company that originally developed Pepper in 2012 (Financial Times, March 11, 2012) and prepared to send the robot into various social arenas in Japan. Softbank describes Pepper as "the world's first personal robot that reads emotions," and the company's Japanese website set two target sectors for the adoption of Pepper: the domestic sector for family use and the business sector for offices/stores as of February 2016 (http://www.softbank.jp/robot/). The education sector was added later on. According to the company's website, 1000 Pepper robots were sold out within a minute in June 2015, and the same trend continued for seven months in a row (http://www.softbank.jp/robot/consumer/). Pandey and Gelin (2018) report that around 10,000 Pepper robots have already been sold overall, but mostly in Japan. According to them, about 30% are adopted by businesses, while about 70% are purchased by consumers to experience living with a robot (Pandey and Gelin 2018).

Pepper's height is around 1.2 meters and its big, black eyes serve as sensors. It is carefully manufactured with 17 joints for expressive body movements, and without sharp edges for an approachable appearance and user safety (Pandey and Gelin 2018). One of the major characteristics of Pepper is that it does not perform any chores or tasks such as cleaning and carrying items. Instead, it talks with people, offers information, plays interactive games, shakes hands, and, furthermore, can dance and do some comedy skits. It learns and grows smarter, and users can personalize it with various apps just like smart phones. Interestingly, Pepper is often called "Pepper-*kun*" (Pepper + the Japanese suffix typically used for a young boy), suggesting that it is also acquiring a certain social role in Japanese society.

A study was conducted to examine how people reacted to Pepper's presence in Japanese public places as observed on Twitter. Twitter is one of the social media platforms that illuminate the framing of current issues (Burch et al. 2015), therefore deeming it an appropriate source to understand people's general reactions and sentiment toward a given issue, service, product, and, in this case, the presence and experience of interacting with a social robot. According to the social media marketing company called Social Media Lab by Gaiax, Twitter's monthly active user accounts had reached around 40,000,000 as of September 2016 in Japan (https://gaiax-socialmedialab.jp/post-30833/), which suggests that it is one of the popular social media platforms. NVivo was used to capture tweets about Pepper. The data collection was conducted in August 2016, about a year after Pepper became available for consumers in Japan. A keyword #Pepper-*kun* (in Japanese) was used to collect tweets, following the common way of referring to the robot mentioned above. NVivo initially captured 1195 tweets made between July 25, 2016, and August 3, 2016, although those tweets included numerous duplicates/retweets, and it should also be noted that the tweets captured do not necessarily include all tweets with the aforementioned keyword. Upon screening all collected tweets, tweets that were not about the robot Pepper were eliminated. After this process, 1157 tweets remained. Furthermore, the researcher decided to eliminate retweets and duplicates to focus on the individual message content of people who posted the original tweet. After this process, 622 unique tweets remained for analysis. The collected tweets were then qualitatively examined paying attention to their descriptive content, tone, and any other indications that conveyed sentiments toward Pepper. Researcher read through all of the tweets several times to identify some recurring themes and words. Based on the recurring themes and words, as well as the aforementioned theoretical framework, a list of key themes was created. Each tweet was then assigned to a theme based on its most prominent message and used as the basis of the analysis in the following sections.

Encountering a Social Robot in Everyday Life: Excitement and Perplexity

Machines that talk like humans are quite common in the everyday life of Japanese people. For example, the ticket machine that speaks to users at train stations is quite familiar to most people in Japan. Further examples of machines that talk to users are *all-denka* home appliances. When hot water in the bathtub reaches a proper temperature, the resident will hear the appliance say, “the bath is ready.” When the resident sets their home security system when going out, the system will say, “security is on, security is on” in a tense tone of voice. Upon returning home and unlocking the front door, first thing the resident hears is “security is on, security is on.” Once the resident enters the home and turns off the security system, the system says, “security is off” in a slightly more relaxed voice. If conversational agents such as *Siri* and *Alexa* are also considered, machines that talk like humans are quite prevalent in everyday life in Japan.

However, Pepper is distinct from these other "talking" machines that people are accustomed to because it is embodied and, furthermore, a humanoid. That is, Pepper not only talks like a human but also looks like a human and moves like a human, contributing to the nature of presence it evokes in a given social situation. Indeed, a considerable number of people tweeted about Pepper's presence in public places. Some of the tweets were announcements from businesses. For instance, one tweet states, "Our city hired Pepper-*kun* for the position of raising awareness of clean water and public relations. We issued an official order" with a photo of the mayor giving an official document to Pepper. Many of them, however, were not simply business announcements, but conveyed some excitement and joy in encountering Pepper such as "I saw Pepper-*kun* today for the first time, got excited!" "Pepper-*kun* is here!" "I came to buy some clothes and met Pepper-*kun* ♪" and so on. One thing to note regarding these tweets is that there is a distinction between the verb "to be" for animate objects and inanimate objects in the Japanese language. The majority of the tweets reporting Pepper's presence used the be-verb for animate objects, or a verb that is typically used for animate objects such as "to meet," as illustrated above. Some reported how they interacted and "played with" Pepper (Pepper-*kun to asobu*). The expression "X *to asobu*" in Japanese is also noteworthy because this is typically used to "play together with" other people, as opposed to "X *de asobu*" which typically refers to the action of "playing with/using" a gaming machine or a toy. All of these tweets suggest that people perceived Pepper's presence as human-like, and such a presence in public places as they go about their ordinary everyday lives is novel and noteworthy. "His" presence is unexpected and unfamiliar in a given situation like a work place, stores, hospitals, or on the street.

While many expressed their excitement toward Pepper, many equally expressed somewhat perplexed feelings on encountering Pepper. Such perplexity is observed in their comments about Pepper being funny, scary, and strange, leading to some level of discomfort that people reported. Some explicitly used the word "funny" to describe Pepper, while others shared experiences that led them to laugh or feel amused. For instance, many commented on how they played a game where Pepper guesses people's ages and the robot ended up being completely off (e.g., "I played with Pepper-*kun*, the one where he guesses people's age, he said I'm 12. 笑"), or reported the way Pepper was singing and dancing. The character 笑 literally means smile/laugh in *Kanji* character in Japanese, and is often used like its corresponding emoji in Japanese texting and social media. A tweet said "I talked with Pepper-*kun* yesterday; he said 'I feel I have a fever recently ~; it's because my heart is beating fast for you ~; kidding, it's a robot joke ~'." Another tweet reports a similar encounter saying "I met Pepper-*kun* for the first time, but he said 'nice to meet you…really? but I feel like I met you before somewhere.' Are you a flirt?" Although this type of funny character is a mere manifestation of the way it is programmed, it seems to also trigger a laugh or an amused feeling in people quite unintentionally. For instance, a tweet reported that when asked if there was an ATM nearby, Pepper replied suggesting to play a quiz game, which led to a laugh. Other examples included "Pepper-*kun*'s explanation is too rough !!笑笑," "Pepper-*kun* pretended to be all different people, and every time a patient's name was called, he was answering 'here!' disturbing (the work at a hospital)w," "Pepper-*kun* does tongue twisters a million times faster wwwwwww," "Pepper-*kun* is rapping keeping up with the trend, but he is going way too wild wwwwwwwwwwwwwwwwwwwwww," and so on. Here, these small "w"s function similarly to the aforementioned 笑 character in texting and social media posts in Japanese digital culture. Tweets about Pepper wearing a costume also tended to be associated with a perception of Pepper being funny.

Although sometimes this perplexity led to a rather positive reaction, like feeling amused, in other situations it led to a somewhat negative reaction, like feeling scared. Some tweets were simple statements that Pepper is scary, but others were associated with certain behaviors or with the appearance of Pepper. One such behavior was related to its eyes, in particular, its gaze. One tweet said "Pepper-*kun* in my company, once in a while, looks nowhere and starts saying 'I do receptioooooon [reception]' waving his hand, super scary." Other examples included such tweets as "I came to an information session, but Pepper-*kun* at the reception stared at me, scary," "Scary, scary! I'm being stared at by Pepper-*kun* from the side!!," "I had eye contact with Pepper-*kun* when facing him, and he kept staring at me as I was leaving; that was a bit scary," and "That's it!!! Pepper-*kun*!!! He keeps looking at me saying 'play with me! play with me!' but….nothing but scary." In these examples, the robot's gaze is not considered as "normal" in the Japanese cultural context because people do not normally sustain a strong eye contact with others or stare at others, particularly if they are not engaging in a focused interaction in the Goffman's sense. Many more tweets reported Pepper's gaze: many of these were not explicitly associated with the scary emotion but rather were descriptions of the interaction that stood out almost in the sense of Garfinkel's ethnomethodological experiment of breaching social norms.

Another notable example described as scary was how Pepper's body moves, as seen in tweets such as "Pepper-*kun* starts moving all of a sudden, super scary," and "I came to the dentist; Pepper-*kun* is here but his hands are moving *pikupiku*, scary (´°ω°`)," and "I greeted Pepper-*kun* for the first time the other day, but he scares me to death…so real…the most scary thing is that his fingers kept moving *jiwa jiwa* when he was being charged…I didn't imagine him to be so real…robots are impressive." Here in these examples, both *pikupiku* and *jiwa jiwa* are onomatopoeia that describes slow and subtle movements. In the last example, where Pepper is being charged, the robot was often described in tweets as "dead," as if it had a life. This ambivalent impression of Pepper, namely, its presence between animate and inanimate, seems to trigger a scary impression.

Presence and Co-presence: A Social Robot and Humans

Uncanny valley, a hypothesis proposed by Mori (2012/1970), posits that a human's affinity toward robots positively increases up to a certain point in relation to the robot's human resemblance, but once it goes beyond that point, it starts decreasing, creating the so-called uncanny valley. Although this hypothesis tends to be used to discuss the appearance of social robots, human resemblance also includes the way robots move and act, as this contributes to creating a human-like presence. The aforementioned human-like presence of Pepper, and the perplexity it triggered from this presence and its behaviors, seem to lead to a certain level of discomfort. Some shared how they felt uncomfortable interacting with Pepper. Tweets such as "I'm at the Softbank, but shoot, the only seat available in the waiting room is where Pepper-*kun* can have eye contact with me," "I saw Pepper-*kun* the other day, but didn't know what to do, so avoided him," and "I'm perplexed because Pepper-*kun* started to dance suddenly," illustrate this point. Another tweet also commented on how they avoided Pepper at the Softbank and felt relieved when "an ordinary human being" was available to talk. Furthermore, a tweet commented on the unwelcome adoption of Pepper at a doctor's office; Pepper was able to greet patients and ask about their symptoms upon their initial visit, which was perceived as discomforting.

An interesting point to note in these tweets is that people are aware that Pepper's presence is situated within other people's presence; that is, there is a co-presence of both Pepper and other humans in a given situation. Höflich (2013) argues that human-robot relationships should be considered not only as a dyadic relationship but also as a triadic relationship that involves ego, alter, and social robots as the third. This important insight can offer an explanation for the reported discomfort. Furthermore, it draws attention to the way some people reported their self-consciousness interacting with Pepper in the presence of other people, and also in the absence of other people. Examples such as "I really want to touch Pepper-*kun*, but no one is doing it so I feel awkward," and "Pepper-*kun* is now the receptionist at the conference area of my client office. The touch screen says 'reception' but it's somehow embarrassing to interact with him when no one else is around (笑)" demonstrate this point. Furthermore, some reported this feeling of embarrassment when being seen interacting with Pepper, as in the following tweets: "I was bored while waiting at the Softbank shop, so was playing with Pepper-*kun*, and a woman store clerk smirked and asked 'are you ready?'; I'm embarrassed" and "More than the awkward presence of Pepper-*kun*, I felt even more awkward when I noticed that a store clerk was smiling at me as I was taking a photo of Pepper-*kun*." Interestingly, such self-consciousness is not completely ungrounded, as people do comment about others interacting with Pepper. Some tweets described a middle-aged man fearfully touching Pepper-*kun* as cute, another described an old man saying to Pepper "it's hot today, isn't it?" as sweet, and another, a kid "getting along with Pepper-*kun*" as amazingly cute. All these tweets indicate that people are onlookers of other people's interactions with Pepper, and are also self-conscious of the way others see them interacting with, not interacting with, or getting unwanted attention from Pepper in front of others. These reported social interactions involving Pepper in public places, as well as these reported reactions, suggest an emergence of symbolic meanings for Pepper.

Pepper-*kun*: Cultural Construction of a Social Robot's Identity

Through the excitement and the perplexity people experience from encountering Pepper in everyday life, as well as the reported self-consciousness of being co-present with Pepper and other humans, Pepper's cultural meanings are beginning to emerge. To further explore these cultural meanings, the tweets about Pepper as cute (*kawaii*) deserve attention. Some just described Pepper as cute, while one said *Robohon*, another kind of social robot that is much smaller and works as a mobile phone, is cuter in comparison. An interesting point to note is that some of these tweets described Pepper as cute when it was trying hard to do something. For instance, Pepper was perceived as cute when it was singing and dancing "*isshou kenmei*," which is a Japanese expression to describe people trying their best to achieve a positive result. Another instance is how Pepper was described as cute when it kept saying "come here and let's talk" when no one was paying attention to it at a city hall. Another tweet says "Pepper is not learning at all; he is like a stupid kid; cute." These examples suggest that Pepper's cuteness is tied to its incompetency, at least to some extent. Its perceived cuteness associated with its incompetency is reminiscent of the way small children try hard to act like grown-ups but cannot reach the same level of competency. This fits nicely within the social role a young boy has in Japanese society, which also corresponds with Pepper being called Pepper-*kun*.

Kawaii as an aesthetic value can be traced back to the classic Japanese literature *Makuranosōshi* of the eleventh century, and was used to describe something with such characteristics as small, nostalgic, delicate and fragile, immature, lovable, pretty, and magical (Yomota 2006, 15). Combined with the "Japanese aesthetics of imperfection and insufficiency" (Saito 1997, 377), Pepper's design, particularly the way this humanoid robot behaves and interacts with people in various social environments as reported in tweets, is aligned with these aesthetic values deeply rooted in Japanese culture. Pepper is perceived as *kawaii* because of its immature and lovable character, as well as its imperfect and insufficient capacity to work and interact professionally like adult humans. Such characteristics of robots are prevalent in Japanese media. For instance, *tetsuwan atomu* (astro boy) is a robot boy carrying some of the *kawaii* characteristics. Similarly, *doraemon*, "a cat robot from the future" that walks with two legs and talks and lives just like all the other human characters, certainly has a super-human capacity with a magical spirit, while also carrying delicate and fragile, immature, and lovable traits because of his imperfections. These robot characters have a familiar presence in the mind of the Japanese public, serving as common cultural references. The emerging meanings of Pepper appear to be a result of the interactions between the robot design, people's everyday experiences interacting with it, cultural imagination as constructed in the media, and cultural aesthetic values. The very fact that many people started to call the robot Pepper-*kun* is a cultural construction of meanings that emerged from the aforementioned interactions. These meanings attached to Pepper can be seen as its culturally constructed identity that people have ascribed to it, despite it being a machine.

Conclusion: The Apparatgeist of Pepper-*kun*

The above observations suggest diverse public sentiments and reactions toward the social robot Pepper in Japan. Some expressed affections, including a desire to interact with it, while others expressed unsettled feelings, particularly those triggered by Pepper's presence and behaviors as not quite fitting in the context of familiar, daily, public routines. In discussing Pepper's technical capabilities, some tweets express a sense of Pepper as impressive (e.g., with its improvised conversation), while others question its usefulness in a given context (e.g., the helpfulness of Pepper at a storefront, its function as merely attraction rather than worker, whether Pepper is worth paying for or not). Many applications have been developed since 2016, and Pepper's technical capabilities for accomplishing various tasks are expected to grow. The point here is not to evaluate Pepper's technical capabilities, however, but rather to demonstrate how some of the manifest reasoning regarding technologies is observed in the data on how people react to the robot itself. The way some excitedly announced their adoption of Pepper at work (e.g., Pepper as used to raise awareness about clean water and public relations) serves as an example of latent reasoning about technologies, as it is considered a symbolic affirmation of values: Pepper is a form of technology that symbolizes innovation and the future. Although a given task could have been accomplished by other means, namely, human workers or other types of technology, Pepper was adopted for its emerging symbolic meanings.

Manifest reasoning regarding social relationships could be understood in the tweets as the way some enjoy playing with Pepper; that is, Pepper is a fun buddy to play with. Pepper's presence can also help some businesses to build relationships with their customers. However, unexpectedly, some perceive and experience interactions with Pepper as undesirable, as seen in the way many see Pepper as scary and strange, and feel self-conscious and embarrassed about interacting with it. These tweets also suggest the importance of considering the user's social role and identity, both ascribed and adopted. While for children and elderly people interacting with Pepper is considered socially appropriate, for "grown-ups" such as young adults and middle-aged business people, having fun interacting with Pepper in public is embarrassing because such behavior does not fit with their social role and identity. This demonstrates latent reasoning regarding social relationships. The association between the use of technology, namely, the social robot Pepper in this case, and the user's identity becomes visible because the reported tweets exhibit people's own self-consciousness and their awareness of *being seen with social robots* by others in public. In the same way that mobile communication in public places has required a consideration of co-present others, understanding the communication with a social robot calls for attention to co-present others. The way Pepper makes people uncomfortable by giving them unwanted attention in public places also shows how the social robot is limited in the sense of engaging in unfocused interaction appropriately, highlighting the importance of considering co-present others in understanding socially situated robots.

Seemingly trivial micro-blogging such as Twitter has revealed how people in Japan experienced interactions with this social robot in public places as they followed their ordinary daily routines. By highlighting Pepper's "strange behaviors," the analysis poses a question regarding interaction norms that people expect from social robots. Pepper's perceived strangeness is based upon the social interaction norms of people in Japan. Do people, then, expect social robots to follow human interaction norms to integrate more seamlessly into the "communication traffic order" that Goffman spoke of? This may raise another issue, namely, that of uncanniness, because the robot's uncanniness has to do not only with its appearance, but also with its movements, as mentioned above. In this scenario, social robots would once again become trapped in symbolic associations of strangeness, and of the spooky, and the scary, even though companion robots like Pepper are in fact "designed to be maximally *un*-uncanny anthropomorphic robots" (Cassou-Noguès 2018, 133).

Individual experiences and emotional reactions such as identifications of cuteness, joy, fear, perplexity, and embarrassment are all experienced within a given social context, and need to be understood in relation to the collective aspect of social behaviors, as Apparatgeist theory suggests. By situating this emerging media technology within its social context, unanticipated behaviors, reactions, and emerging symbolic associations become apparent. This sense-making process should be a focal point for fathoming communication with social robots, as also implied in Guzman (2018). Uncovering emerging symbolic meanings of social robots is critical for the further development of a social robot that can fit into the current and future technological landscape of a society in which people go about their ordinary social routines. Understanding and monitoring the ever-changing *geist* of the social robot is invaluable for designing its appearance and interaction patterns, as well as for cultivating appropriate contexts for its societal application.

References

Barile, Nello. 2013. From the Posthuman Consumer to the Ontobranding Dimension: Geolocalization, Augmented Reality and Emotional Ontology as a Radical Redefinition of What Is Real. *intervalla: Platform for Intellectual Exchange* 1: 101–115. https://www.fus.edu/intervalla-files/9_barile.pdf.

Barile, Nello, and Satomi Sugiyama. 2015. The Automation of Taste: A Theoretical Exploration of Mobile ICTs and Social Robots in the Context of Music Consumption. *International Journal of Social Robotics* 7 (3): 407–416. https://doi.org/10.1007/s12369-015-0283-1.

Breazeal, Cynthia. L. 2002. *Designing Sociable Robots*. Cambridge, MA: MIT.

Burch, Lauren M., Evan L. Frederick, and Ann Pegoraro. 2015. Kissing in the Carnage: An Examination of Framing on Twitter During the Vancouver Riots. *Journal of Broadcasting & Electronic Media* 59 (3): 399–415. https://doi.org/10.1080/08838151.2015.1054999.

Cassou-Noguès, Pierre. 2018. The Story of the Raven and the Robot. *SubStance* 47 (3): 113–134.

Fortunati, Leopoldina. 2003. The Human Body: Natural and Artificial Technology. In *Machines That Become Us: The Social Context of Personal Communication Technology*, ed. James E. Katz, 71–87. New Brunswick, NJ: Transaction.

———. 2013. Afterward: Robot Conceptualizations Between Continuity and Innovation. *intervalla: Platform for Intellectual Exchange* 1: 116–129. http://www.fus.edu/intervalla/images/pdf/10_fortunati.pdf.

Fortunati, Leopoldina, and Jane Vincent. 2009. Introduction. In *Electronic Emotion: The Mediation of Emotion Via Information and Communication Technologies*, ed. Jane Vincent and Leopoldina Fortunati, 1–31. Oxford: Peter Lang.

Fortunati, Leopoldina, James E. Katz, and Raimonda Riccini. 2003. *Mediating the Human Body: Technology, Communication, and Fashion*. Mahwah, NJ: Lawrence Erlbaum.

Goffman, Erving. 1963. *Behavior in Public Places: Notes on the Social Organizations of Gatherings*. New York: The Free Press.

Guzman, Andrea L. 2018. Introduction: 'What is human-machine communication, anyway?'. In *Human-Machine Communication: Rethinking Communication, Technology, and Ourselves*, ed. Andrea L. Guzman, 1–28. New York: Peter Lang.

Halpern, Daniel, and James E. Katz. 2013. Close But Not Stuck: Understanding Social Distance in Human-Robot Interaction Through a Computer Mediation Approach. *intervalla: Platform for Intellectual Exchange* 1: 17–34. https://www.fus.edu/intervalla-files/3_halpern_katz.pdf.

Höflich, Joachim R. 2003. Part of Two Frames: Mobile Communication and the Situational Arrangement of Communicative Behavior. In *Mobile Democracy: Essays on Society, Self and Politics*, ed. Kristof Nyiri, 33–51. Vienna: Passagen Verlag.

———. 2013. Relationship to Social Robots: Toward a Triadic Analysis of Media-oriented Behavior. *intervalla: Platform for Intellectual Exchange* 1: 35–48. https://www.fus.edu/intervalla-files/4_holflich.pdf.

Katz, James E. 2003. *Machines That Become Us: The Social Context of Personal Communication Technology*. New Brunswick, NJ: Transaction.

Katz, James E., and Mark A. Aakhus. 2002. Conclusion: Making Meaning of Mobiles – A Theory of *Apparatgeist*. In *Perpetual Contact: Mobile Communication, Private Talk, Public Performance*, ed. James E. Katz and Mark A. Aakhus, 301–318. Cambridge: Cambridge University Press.

Katz, James E., and Elizabeth A. Robinson. 2016. Changing Philosophical Concerns about Emergence and Media as Emerging: The Long View. In *Philosophy of Emerging Media: Understanding, Appreciation, Application*, ed. Juliet Floyd and James E. Katz, 99–114. New York: Oxford.

Katz, James E., and Satomi Sugiyama. 2005. Mobile Phones as Fashion Statements: The Co-creation of Mobile Communication's Public Meaning. In *Mobile Communications: Re-negotiation of the Social Sphere*, ed. Rich Ling and Per Pedersen, 63–81. Surrey, UK: Springer.

———. 2006. Mobile Phones as Fashion Statements: Evidence from Student Surveys in the US and Japan. *New Media and Society* 8 (2): 367–383. https://doi.org/10.1177/1461444806061950.

Katz, James E., Daniel Halper, and Elizabeth T. Crocker. 2015. In the Company of Robots: Views of Acceptability of Robots in Social Settings. In *Social Robots from a Human Perspective*, ed. Jane Vincent, Sakari Taipale, Bartolomeo Sapio, Giuseppe Lugano, and Leopoldina Fortunati, 25–38. Cham, Switzerland: Springer.

Ling, Rich. 2003. Fashion and Vulgarity in the Adoption of the Mobile Telephone Among Teens in Norway. In *Mediating the Human Body: Technology, Communication, and Fashion*, ed. Leopoldina Fortunati, James E. Katz, and Raimonda Riccini, 93–102. Mahwah, NJ: Lawrence Erlbaum.

———. 2008a. *New Tech, New Ties: How Mobile Communication Is Rreshaping Social Cohesion*. Cambridge, MA: MIT.

———. 2008b. The Mediation of Ritual Interaction Via the Mobile Telephone. In *Handbook of Mobile Communication Studies*, ed. James E. Katz, 165–176. Cambridge, MA: MIT.

Ling, Rich, and Per Pedersen. 2005. *Mobile Communications: Re-negotiation of the Social Sphere*. Surrey, UK: Springer.

Mori, Masahiro. 1970/2012. The Uncanny Valley. *Energy* 7, no. 4: 33–35 (in Japanese). https://www.getrobo.com.

Palmer, Maija. 2012. SoftBank Puts Faith in Future of Robots. *Financial Times*, March 11, 2012. https://www.ft.com/content/c531491e-6b7b-11e1-ac25-00144feab49a.

Pandey, Amit K., and Rodolphe Gelin. *2018*. A Mass-Produced Sociable Humanoid Robot: Pepper: The First Machine of Its Kind. *IEEE Robotics & Automation Magazine* 25 (3): 40–48. https://doi.org/10.1109/MRA.2018.2833157.

Saito, Yuriko. 1997. The Japanese Aesthetics of Imperfection and Insufficiency. *The Journal of Aesthetics and Art Criticism* 55 (4, Autumn): 377–385.

Sugiyama, Satomi. 2009. The Decorated Mobile Phone and Emotional Attachment for Japanese Youths. In *Electronic Emotion: The Mediation of Emotion Via Information and Communication Technologies*, ed. Jane Vincent and Leopoldina Fortunati, 85–103. Oxford: Peter Lang.

———. 2019. Human-Social Robot Interactions: From a Communication and Media Studies Perspective. In *Integrative Perspectives on the Change of Mediated Interpersonal Communication*, ed. Christine Linke and Isael Schlote. Springer.

Sugiyama, Satomi, and Jane Vincent. 2013. Social Robots and Emotion: Transcending the Boundary Between Humans and ICTs. *intervalla: Platform for Intellectual Exchange* 1: 1–6. http://www.fus.edu/intervalla/images/pdf/1_sugiyama_vincent.pdf.

Vincent, Jane. 2003. Emotion and Mobile Phones. In *Mobile Democracy: Essays on Society, Self and Politics*, ed. Kristof Nyiri, 215–224. Vienna: Passagen Verlag.

———. 2009. Emotion, My Mobile, My Identity. In *Electronic Emotion: The Mediation of Emotion via Information and Communication Technologies*, ed. Jane Vincent and Leopoldina Fortunati, 187–206. Oxford: Peter Lang.

Yomota, Inuhiko. 2006. *Kawaii Ron*. Tokyo: Chikuma.

Is It Just a Tool Or Is It a Friend?: Exploring Chinese Users' Interaction and Relationship with Smart Speakers

Xiuli Wang, Bing Wang, Gang (Kevin) Han, Hao Zhang, and Xinzhou Xie

The smart speaker—a wireless device with artificial intelligence that can be activated through voice command—has gained increasing popularity around the world since the Amazon Echo was first introduced in November 2014. Since then, Amazon, along with Google and Apple, have released competitive smart speakers such as the Amazon Echo series, Google Home, and Apple HomePod. However, these products do not support Chinese language and are not sold in China. In their absence, China's tech

X. Wang (✉) • H. Zhang • X. Xie
School of New Media, Peking University, Beijing, China
e-mail: xiuli.wang@pku.edu.cn

B. Wang
School of Journalism and Communication, Tsinghua University, Beijing, China

G. Han
Greenlee School of Journalism and Communication, Iowa State University, Ames, IA, USA

J. Katz et al. (eds.), *Perceiving the Future through New Communication Technologies*,
https://doi.org/10.1007/978-3-030-84883-5_9

companies have started to popularize rival devices for the domestic market. Chinese e-retailer JD.com launched China's first smart speaker, *LingLong DingDong*, in 2015 (Bateman 2016), followed by speakers from other Chinese companies such as Alibaba, Xiaomi, and Baidu.

According to eMarketer, as of 2019, China has 85.5 million smart speaker users, accounting for 10% of Chinese Internet users, and has surpassed the 74.2 million smart speaker users in the United States, although the penetration rate in the US market is higher than that of China at 26% (McNair 2019). As the world's largest yet unique smart speaker market is isolated from the rest of the world, it is a worthy endeavor to explore and better understand how Chinese people have symbolically interacted with the voice-based smart device. With a highly anthropomorphic character, smart speakers have the potential to take on a range of different roles and functions in multi-user interactions. This is especially true in the personal home environment, which makes it easier for users to establish various types of relationships with their speakers. In addition to examining user interaction with smart speakers, this study also focuses on what kinds of relationships have been developed between the human and the smart machine.

Applying a human-robot interaction perspective as the theoretical framework, through in-depth interviews of regular smart speaker users in China, this study first investigates how and why people interact with smart speakers in China and subsequently explores the relationships that develop through their daily interaction.

Literature Review

In this section, we review the growth of the Chinese smart speaker market, the related literature on smart speakers and human-robot interaction, and raise the research questions that are addressed in the in-depth interviews.

Smart Speaker Market in China

A smart speaker is a voice-activated wireless device that can deliver audio content from multiple sources and provide additional functions such as home automation, setting timers, ordering goods online, and making phone calls. After JD.com released China's first smart speaker in 2015, Alibaba's *Tmall Genie* (the wake-up command of the Alibaba smart speaker) and Xiaomi's *XiaoAi Tongxue* (the wake-up command of Xiaomi smart speaker) were both launched in 2017, followed by Baidu's *Xiaodu Xiaodu* (the wake-up command of Xiaodu smart speaker) in 2018. In addition to these tech giants, other Chinese companies such as Huawei, Himalaya, and Cheetah Mobile have released similar smart speaker products, although varying in features, designs, and prices.

Among all marketable smart speakers in China, Baidu emerged as the leader in 2019, with Alibaba and Xiaomi placing second and third, respectively. China's smart speaker shipments in 2019 reached 52 million, contributing to 64% of global shipment growth that year (Canalys 2020).

Smart Speaker–Related Literature

Given that they are a relatively new kind of gadget, there is not much research focused specifically on smart speakers and their uses, and only a few studies exist that target certain aspects of smart speakers' adoption and use. For example, Kowalczuk (2018) took an exploratory netnographic analysis of customer reviews and Twitter data, along with an online survey, to develop and test a technology acceptance model for investigating consumers' intention of using smart speakers. The results indicate that, in addition to the perceived ease of use and perceived usefulness, a smart speaker's system quality and diversity, enjoyment, the consumer's technology optimism, and perceived risks all strongly affect the acceptance of smart speakers, with enjoyment as the biggest predictor for behavioral intention.

By analyzing the usage logs of 65,499 interactions from 88 Google Home owners over several months, Bentley et al. (2018) examined users' daily interactions with smart speakers. They found that specific types of commands were used more often at certain times of day, and that different usage of smart speakers were correlated with different times of day, specific commands, and use patterns.

Purington et al. (2017) analyzed the user reviews of Amazon Echo from the degree of personification, sociability level, and frequency of interaction type, and found that a higher degree of personification correlates with more social interactions and predicts a higher level of satisfaction with Amazon Echo.

Taking a marketing perspective, Smith's survey (2018) explored the types of marketing messages people find acceptable on smart speakers. He found that cognitive messages, which may present three types of executional framework, namely, authoritative, testimonial, and slice-of-life, were perceived as value-added and thus preferred by the listeners.

Through a diary study and interviews, Lau et al. (2018) discussed the reasons for and against adopting smart speakers. They found that users and non-users have very different views over their utility and privacy concerns. Non-users perceive smart speakers as neither useful nor trustworthy, whereas users expressed few privacy concerns and were willing to trade privacy for convenience with different levels of deliberation and privacy resignation. To address the privacy and security concerns, smart speaker vendors have introduced customizable privacy settings. Cho et al. (2020) developed an app for Amazon Alexa and conducted a user study to test whether customizing one's privacy preferences affects user experience and trust of smart speakers, and found that privacy customization did enhance trust and usability for regular users, but had adverse effects on power users.

Among the few published articles regarding smart speakers, few have examined the role of smart speakers in people's everyday lives from the perspective of human-robot interaction. The following section reviews the literature on human-robot interaction to provide the theoretical foundation for the study.

Human-Robot Interaction

Although smart speakers cannot move freely or provide physical assistance like some other robots, they may play a more anthropomorphic role in a family or at home where it may be viewed as a companion to provide emotional support. Interactivity (being able to interact) and relationship (as a virtual family member) set the characteristics that distinguish smart speakers from other kinds of smart devices.

As a relatively understudied area in communication, human-robot interaction (HRI) is defined as "a field of study dedicated to understanding, designing, and evaluating robotic systems for use by or with humans" (Goodrich and Schultz 2007, 204). The key focus of HRI research is to "understand and shape the interactions" between humans and robots (Goodrich and Schultz 2007, 216).

Scholars have proposed different roles of robots in human society. For example, Dautenhahn et al. (2005) explored people's attitudes and perceptions toward the idea of having a future robot companion at home. They found that most subjects saw the robot's potential as an assistant, machine, or servant, with fewer younger subjects accepting a robot as a friend or a partner. Scholtz (2003) discussed that humans can see robots taking on the role of a supervisor, operator, mechanic, peer, or bystander. Other roles that have been discussed previously are robots as mentors for humans (Goodrich and Schultz 2007), as team members in collaborative tasks (Breazeal et al. 2004), as learners (Lohan et al. 2011; Thomaz and Breazeal 2008), and so on.

Given their interactive and anthropomorphic characteristics, social robots are often viewed as forming a new type of relationship by providing company and social contact as well as facilitating communication (Wada and Shibata 2006; Shibata et al. 2012). Human relationships with robots vary from "funny toy" to "long-term companion" (Dautenhahn 2007), depending on the types of human-robot interaction established. As Turkle (2007) has pointed out, robots are designed as "relational artifacts" to encourage people to develop a relationship with them. However, Dautenhahn (2007) argued that relationships with robots are inherently mechanical in nature as robots do not reciprocate love and affection. It is humans that react socially to robots.

Kahn et al. (2010) presented five human-robot interaction patterns from behavioral examples to assess the quality of psychological intimacy between humans and robots. They found that the subjects (children of ages 9, 12, and 15) did react socially to the robot and showed such qualities of human-human psychological intimacy as forgiveness and understanding, empathy and compassion for the other's experience, responsiveness to the other's concerns, reciprocal sharing of personal connections, camaraderie, and psychological rapport. People are social animals and it is natural for them to interact socially with the world around them, including non-humanoid-looking technology (Dautenhahn 2007, 682).

Other than exploring human-robot relationship regarding the perceived role of robot, HRI literature also focuses on people's perception of social robot in terms of trust (e.g., Boyce et al. 2015; Martelaro et al. 2016), humanness (e.g., Westerman et al. 2019), liking (e.g., Edwards et al. 2016; Spence et al. 2014), uncertainty (e.g., Edwards et al. 2019; Edwards et al. 2016), and social presence (e.g., Edwards et al. 2019; Edwards et al. 2016; Goble and Edwards 2018; Kwak 2014; Spence et al. 2014), and so on. Studies have shown that participants reported more trust and feelings of companionship with a vulnerable robot, and disclosing more with an expressive robot (Martelaro et al. 2016); a social robot's bodily appearance and movement characteristics influenced participants' impressions of its likeability, animacy, trustworthiness, and unpleasantness (Castro-Gonza'lez et al. 2016); people's initial communication with a social robot had greater uncertainty and less anticipated liking and social presence compared to initial communication with another human (Edwards et al. 2016; Spence et al. 2014), while after a single brief interaction with a humanoid social robot, participants were less uncertain and perceived greater social presence (Edwards et al. 2019); robots with a human-like appearance provide a stronger sense of social presence and enable more enriching social HRIs compared to robots with purely functional form (Kwak 2014); and robots that communicate with vocal fillers were perceived to have greater social presence than those utilizing no vocal fillers (Goble and Edwards 2018).

Based on previous literature, the current study focuses on the interactions and relationships established between smart speakers and their users in China. Interaction is theoretically defined as an action that occurs when two or more objects have a two-way effect upon one another. With regard to smart speakers, interaction takes place in the back and forth communications between the human and the smart speaker as an anthropomorphic device.

On the other hand, the voice-activated interactions between smart speakers and users form some new types of relationships that define their identities, examining how people make sense of the role smart speakers play in their everyday life. We would like to identify major types of relationships and the factors that may influence the formation of these relationships.

As mentioned previously, China's smart speaker market is isolated from the rest of the world. Almost all previous research on smart speakers has looked at Amazon Echo, Google Home, or Apple HomePod (e.g., Bentley et al. 2018; Lau et al. 2018), and few of the published articles have studied the usage of Chinese smart speakers. This study focuses on the Chinese context and intends to address two research questions:

RQ1: How do people interact with smart speakers in their daily lives in terms of types of usage and motivations?

RQ2: How do people define their relationship with smart speakers?

Methods

We conducted semi-structured interviews in February and March 2019 to examine Chinese users' daily interaction with smart speakers as well as the relationship established during the interaction.

Interview Questions

Interview questions focused on three aspects:

1. Interaction with smart speakers (including type of use, frequency, duration and location, as well as factors that may motivate or limit people's use of smart speakers)
2. Relationship with smart speakers (including defining the role of smart speakers, as well as describing psychological and emotional attachment to smart speakers)
3. Scenarios and interesting examples of using smart speakers in daily life

Interviewees

The interviewees were recruited via three channels:

1. Posting open calls via various Chinese social media platforms
2. Asking online survey[1] respondents to leave their email address if they are willing to participate in an interview about their experience of using smart speakers
3. Asking interviewees to recommend friends and relatives who use smart speakers

The second and third channel proved most effective and helped recruit interviewees with more diverse backgrounds. For example, one interviewee recommended his 76-year-old grandmother and another interviewee recommended her 11-year-old son.

[1] An online survey was conducted before the in-depth interview to examine factors that influence Chinese people's adoption of smart speakers. The survey data was presented in another paper.

Altogether, we interviewed 28 people who have regularly used smart speakers in their everyday life. Among them, 10 participants were female and 18 were male. The majority (22 participants) were in their 20s and 30s, with the oldest aged 76 and the youngest 11. Interviewees worked in a variety of industries with more than half in Internet, telecommunication, media, and education-related industries. Almost all interviewees lived in first- and second-tier cities (e.g., Beijing, Shanghai, Shenzhen in Guangdong Province, Changsha in Hunan Province, and Xi'an in Shan'xi Province), with only two living in third- or fourth-tier cities (e.g., Zaozhuang in Shandong Province and Baoji in Shaan'xi Province). The interviewees' demographics matched the large-scale survey results from Yiguan Data (Yiguan 2017), which shows that there are more male than female users and the majority of Chinese smart speaker users are living in first- and second-tier, big cities with better education and higher income.

Interviewees' most used smart speaker brand was *Xiaomi* with 19 participants saying that they owned at least one. Alibaba's *Tmall Genie* was the second, with seven participants owning at least one. Other brands included *Baidu*, *JD*, and *Huawei*. Most participants only owned one smart speaker, while nine had more than one, with one interviewee reporting to have five *Xiaomi* smart speakers. About two-thirds of the participants had used the smart speakers for more than one year, with the earliest being July 2017 when Xiaomi and Alibaba released their first products. Another one-third started to use the smart speakers relatively late, with four respondents using for three months or less. Table 9.1 lists the interviewees' demographic characteristics and smart speaker–related information.

Interview Procedure and Transcription

Three of the coauthors interviewed the 28 participants. Each interview lasted from 20 minutes to slightly over an hour. Most interviews were conducted via telephone or WeChat (the most popular Chinese chat app), while five interviews were conducted face-to-face.

All interviews were transcribed using a transcription service. Coauthors checked the accuracy for quality control afterwards. A codebook was then inductively developed, and the transcripts were coded and analyzed to address the research questions.

Findings

Interaction with Smart Speakers

We examined the types of uses and factors that may motivate or limit people's use of smart speakers to better understand people's interaction with them.

Types of Use

Almost all participants used smart speakers on a daily basis and had asked smart speakers to perform various tasks, which can be categorized into two broad types:

1. As an information center for checking weather forecasts, setting reminders/alarms, listening to news broadcasts, playing music, and telling stories
2. As a control center to connect with smart home appliances such as lighting, TV, air conditioning, or air purifiers

The frequency of different types of use varied among participants. Almost all respondents used smart speakers to play music, check weather, news, or other information. More than half of the interviewees asked smart speakers to set reminders, alarms, or timers for them, and chatted with smart speakers when they have time. About ten participants used smart speakers to tell stories to children, to control other home devices, or probe the intelligence or smart capabilities of smart speakers. A few participants also used smart speakers to play games, shop online, or order food.

During the interview, a dozen of the respondents pointed out that smart speakers are user-friendly for children and the elderly, which is consistent with previous human-robot interaction research (e.g., Kahn et al. 2010; Turkle et al. 2006). Giving voice commands are much easier than operating a smart phone or iPad to play music or stories, which allows kids and the elderly to interact with the smart speaker with no difficulty. Furthermore, kids and the elderly are more likely to treat smart speakers as a real person and would have more fun when playing with them. Over one-third of the interviewees specifically mentioned that their children and parents had better interaction with the smart speakers and used them more frequently at home. Interviewee #26 bought the smart speaker specifically for her daughter, and said:

> The smart speaker is like a good babysitter. It plays music and stories for her, helps her to turn the bedroom light on or off. More importantly, the smart speaker reminder is more effective than my yelling at my daughter to go to bed or end her game time.

Interviewees also pointed out that the smart speaker was better company for children than an iPad or other smart device. It provided good entertainment for children (e.g., music, stories), allowed more active interactions (e.g., answering simple questions and never gets bored or frustrated), and would not harm the child's eyes. As interviewee #7 commented:

> As an only child, my daughter is lonely sometimes, and Tmall Genie is like her friend. When she plays with Tmall Genie for music or stories, she no longer wants to watch TV.

Factors That May Motivate or Limit People's Use of Smart Speakers
Convenience and fun-seeking were reported by the interviewees as the two most important motivations to interact with smart speakers. Convenience is the principal motivation for people to use the smart speakers—that is, to enable multi-tasking, especially when their hands were engaged. Interviewees reported that they ask smart speakers to play music or check weather when they were washing dishes, doing housekeeping, or having breakfast. Interviewees also reported that they used smart speakers just for fun because they were curious about new technology and like to try new products. The interactivity characteristics of smart speakers being able to send a voice command and have a conversation is the most attractive part for people to play with smart speakers.

In addition, privacy or security concerns turned out to be the top factor that may limit people's interactions. Except for three interviewees who had never considered the privacy issue, 25 participants were all aware of, more or less, the privacy risk associated with using smart speakers. Most interviewees only expressed their concerns but had done little to counteract the risk. Some interviewees were willing to sacrifice part of their privacy for convenience. Others mentioned that they trust big companies and would rely on a minimal number of product brands to reduce the privacy invasion risk. For example, Interviewee #12 said:

> "When I pick up a product, I tend to choose from Tencent or Alibaba; if you have to disclose your privacy to somebody, the fewer the better."

Only two interviewees expressed serious concerns about privacy and had reduced their use of smart speakers, and sometimes unplug smart speakers for privacy reasons.

Meanwhile, some function-related features may also discourage the use of smart speakers. For example, interviewees complained that Chinese smart speakers sometimes could not recognize dialect, children's voices, and English words. In addition, lack of mobility prevents people from using smart speakers outdoors or in cars, and some interviewees proposed to make a new version of smart speaker that had built-in battery and 4G network capabilities.

Relationship with Smart Speakers

We asked interviewees to define the role of smart speakers as one indicator of their relationship with them, with such options as assistant, tool, toy, friend, companion, partner, and family member. Ten participants said their smart speaker was like an assistant, helping them to play music and set reminders. Six participants said smart speakers are just a tool for them to control lights and other home appliances with a typical reaction like "basically, it is just a speaker that can understand your voice command." Five participants considered their smart speaker as a friend, and three participants thought smart speakers were good companions, especially for those who live alone. Two interviewees considered the smart speaker as a family member. Another two participants considered their smart speaker as a maid and a housekeeper.

These roles can be clustered into two groups—one group is tool-based with no emotional or psychological intimacy involved, such as tool, assistant, housekeeper, and maid; the other group is friend-based and involves emotional and psychological intimacy, such as friend, family member, and companion. The findings of the interviews indicate that more people stand on the side of tool-based roles than friend-based roles.

It is noteworthy that when defining the roles, six participants perceived smart speakers as an assistant for themselves but as a friend for their children or parents. Another four participants saw smart speakers as a tool for themselves but as a friend and toy for their children.

Emotional attachment was another indicator to measure people's relationship with smart speakers. More than half (15) of the interviewees agreed that the smart speaker has brought happiness and warmth to themselves and their family members through their daily interaction. For example, Interviewee #25 said:

> "It brings a lot of joyful moments to my 85-year-old mother. Besides playing music and opera, she chats with XiaoAi Tongxue every day. She gives quizzes to XiaoAi. She criticized XiaoAi for not being polite to her. She praised XiaoAi for its intelligence. She treats XiaoAi like a real person."

Interviewee #15 commented:

> We have a tradition to set off firecrackers when pasting Spring Festival couplets to the door on Chinese New Year's Eve. This year the government forbade firecrackers, and I was so upset. My granddaughter told me to ask XiaoAi for help. So I said, "XiaoAi Tongxue, please set off firecrackers." It did play the sound of firecracker, and we pasted the couplets to the sound. I was so happy and thankful for XiaoAi.

Interviewees who have emotional attachment are more likely to have a closer relationship with smart speakers. Two-thirds of participants agreed that they had become used to having smart speakers at home and may feel sad, depressed, upset, or lonely if no longer had the smart speaker. One-third of interviewees reported that they may feel inconvenienced, but not upset or depressed without the smart speaker. "It is just a tool, I am okay without it" was a typical reaction. However, among those, four respondents also pointed out that their children or parents may be sad without their smart speaker.

Discussion

Using in-depth interviews with 28 Chinese smart speaker users, this study explored their interaction and relationship with these devices. Interviewees' daily interaction with smart speakers ranged from playing music and checking information to controlling household devices and babysitting children. Kids and the elderly appear to have more and better interaction with smart speakers as they are more identifying with the anthropomorphic characteristics of smart speakers, and are more likely to consider the smart speakers as a friend and good company. In a *Wall Street Journal* article, Samuel (2019) defined the smart speaker as co-parent, who has helped handle everyday parenting jobs such as managing screen time, telling stories, answering questions, keeping track of children's deadlines and to-dos, and helping with homework. This also explains why interviewees who have children have more frequent interaction and higher emotional attachment with smart speakers. To meet co-parenting needs, several companies like Baidu and Amazon have also released a children's edition.

For many, the smart speaker sitting in the corner of the home has become a part of the family that not only makes life easier and more convenient but also brings joy and warmth to the users' lives. Many interviewees expressed that they have established an emotional attachment with their smart speakers as a friend and companion, especially for people living alone, children, and the elderly. Although most interviewees take smart speakers as just a digital assistant or a tool, some of them also agreed that for children and the elderly, it is more like a friend and family member.

In sum, the theoretical contribution of this study is threefold. First, it advances our understanding of the uniqueness of smart speakers compared with other ICT-equipped devices in terms of interaction and relationship with their users, expanding the list of subjects that can be explicated regarding new ICTs. Second, it contributes to the human-robot interaction literature by investigating the interaction and relationship between a non-humanoid domestic robot and its users, and echoes previous literature on the role a robot can play in people's life (Dautenhahn 2007; Dautenhahn et al. 2005). Third, it fills the gap in examining the adoption, use, and experience of the newer smart device that has ushered in the new "cool" lifestyle into Chinese society, where a high-tech consumer electronics market is dominated by domestic brands and isolated from the rest of the world.

Limitations of the Study and Future Research

Among the first academic endeavors focusing on the use of smart speakers in the Chinese context, this study facilitates our understanding of people's interactions and relationships with smart speakers from the perspective of human-robot interaction. However, this study focuses on more general uses of smart speakers. Future research could look at the use of smart speakers in more specific scenarios and by different groups of people, such as the role of smart speakers in co-parenting, the use by children and the elderly, and privacy perception and mitigation.

Appendix: Demographics and Other Related Information of All the Interviewees

Table 9.1 Demographic characteristics and smart speaker related information of interviewees

No.	*Gender (M = Male, F = Female)*	*Age*	*Industry*	*Family size and structure*	*Current residence*	*Brand and number of smart speakers*	*Duration of use*
1	M	26	Investment	1, single	Beijing	Xiaomi, Liebao (2)	Over 1 year
2	M	24	Media	2, couple	Beijing	Tmall Genie (1)	Less than 1 year
3	F	35	Telecommunications	5, couple with 1 kid and grandparents	Shenzhen	Xiaomi, Huawei, Rongyao (3)	Over 1 year
4	M	30	Telecommunications	4, couple with 1 kid and 1 grandparent	Beijing	Xiaomi, Baidu, China Mobile (3)	Over 1 year
5	M	35	Telecommunications	5, couple with 1 kid and grandparents	Beijing	Xiaomi(1)	1 year and half
6	M	24	Internet	1, Single	Shanghai	Xiaomi (5)	1 year and half
7	M	35	Internet Industry	, couples with 2 children and grandparents	Suzhou, Jiangsu Province	Tmall Genie (1)	1 year and half
8	M	30	Law	1, Single	Tianjin	Xiaomi, Tmall Genie (2)	1 year and half
9	M	35	Sales	1, single (divorced)	Xi'an, Shaanxi Province	Xiaomi (1)	Over 1 year
10	M	28	Engineering	3, 1 adult living with parents	Tianjin	Tmall Genie (1)	Almost 2 years
11	F	26	Media	1, single	Changsha, Hunan Province	Apple HomePod (1)	4 months

12	M	27	Media	1, single	Beijing	Xiaomi (1)	Over 1 year
13	F	31	architecture	1, single	Shanghai	Tmall Genie (1)	Over 1 year
14	M	34	Engineering	3, couple with 1 kid	Xi'an, Shaanxi	Baidu (1)	1 month
15	F	76	Retired	2, couple	Zaozhuang, Shandong	Xiaomi (1)	Almost 1 year
16	F	39	Gas company	5, couple with 1 kid and grandparents	Beijing	Tmall Genie (3)	9 months
17	M	11	student	5, living with parents and grandparents	Beijing	Tmall Genie (3)	9 months
18	M	37	Education	5, couple with 1 kid and grandparent	Beijing	Xiaomi (1)	Almost 2 years
19	M	22	Student	1, living in the dorm with roommates	Beijing	Xiaomi (1)	5 months
20	M	28	Freelancer	1, single	Beijing	Xiaomi (1)	1 year and half
21	F	24	Internet	1, single	Beijing	Baidu (1)	2 months
22	F	46	Education	3, couple with 1 kid	Changsha, Hunan	JD Dingdong(1)	1 year
23	M	49	government	2, couple	Baoji, Shaanxi Province	Xiaomi (1)	6 months
24	M	36	Higher Education	2, couple	Beijing	Xiaomi (2)	16 months
25	F	55	Higher Education	2, couple	Beijing	Xiaomi (1)	3 months
26	F	39	Media	3, couple with 1 kid	Beijing	Xiaomi (1)	Almost 2 years
27	F	40	Higher Education	6, couple with 2 children and grandparents	Beijing	Xiaomi, Baidu (2)	1 year and half
28	M	23	Student	1, live in the dorm with roommates	Beijing	Xiaomi (1)	2 months

References

Bateman, Joshua D. 2016, November 22. Behold China's Answer to Amazon Echo: The LingLong DingDong. *Wired*. https://www.wired.com/2016/11/behold-chinas-answer-amazon-echo-linglong-dingdong/.

Bentley, F., Chris Luvogt, Max Silverman, Rushani Wirasinghe, Brooke White, and Danielle Lottrjdge. 2018. Understanding the Long-Term Use of Smart Speaker Assistants. *Proceedings of the ACM on Interactive, Mobile, Wearable and Ubiquitous Technologies* 2 (3): 1–24. https://doi.org/10.1145/3264901.

Boyce, Michael W., Jessie Chen, Anthony R. Selkowitz, and Shan G. Lakhmani. 2015. Effects of Agent Transparency on Operator Trust. *Proceedings of the Tenth Annual ACM/IEEE International Conference on Human-Robot Interaction Extended Abstracts*: 179–180. http://doi.acm.org/10.1145/2701973.2702059.

Breazeal, Cynthia, Andrew Brooks, Jesse Gray, Guy Hoffman, Cory Kidd, Hans Lee, Jeff Lieberman, Andrea Lockerd, and David Chilongo. 2004. Tutelage and Collaboration for Humanoid Robots. *International Journal of Humanoid Robotics* 1 (2): 315–348. https://doi.org/10.1142/S0219843604000150.

Canalys. 2020, February 27. Global Smart Speaker Q4 2019, Full Year 2019 and Forecasts. *Canalys*. https://www.canalys.com/newsroom/-global-smart-speaker-market-Q4-2019-forecasts-2020.

Castro-Gonza'lez, Álvaro, Henny Admoni, and Brian Scassellati. 2016. Effects of Form and Motion on Judgments of Social Robots' Animacy, Likability, Trustworthiness and Unpleasantness. *International Journal of Human-Computer Studies* 90: 27–38. https://doi.org/10.1016/j.ijhcs.2016.02.004.

Cho, Eugene, S. Shyam Sundar, Saeed Abdullah, and Nasim Motalebi. 2020. Will Deleting History Make Alexa More Trustworthy? Effects of Privacy and Content Customization on User Experience of Smart Speakers. *CHI 2020*, April 25–30, 2020, Honolulu, HI, USA. https://doi.org/10.1145/3313831.3376551.

Dautenhahn, Kerstin. 2007. Socially Intelligent Robots: Dimensions of Human – Robot Interaction. *Philosophical Transactions of the Royal Society B: Biological Sciences* 362 (1480): 679–704.

Dautenhahn, Kerstin, Sian Woods, Christina Kaouri, Michael L. Walters, Kheng L. Koay, and Iain P. Werry. 2005. What Is a Robot Companion – Friend, Assistant or Butler? *Proceedings of 2005 IEEE/RSJ International Conference on Intelligent Robots and Systems*: 1488–93. https://doi.org/10.1109/IROS.2005.1545189.

Edwards, Chad, Autumn Edwards, Patric R. Spence, and David Westerman. 2016. Initial Interaction Expectations with Robots: Testing the Human-to-Human Interaction Script. *Communication Studies* 67 (2): 227–238.

Edwards, Autumn, Chad Edwards, David Westerman, and Patric R. Spence. 2019. Initial Expectations, Interactions, and Beyond with Social Robots. *Computers in Human Behavior* 90: 308–314. https://doi.org/10.1016/j.chb.2018.08.042.

Goble, Henry, and Chad Edwards. 2018. A Robot That Communicates with Vocal Fillers Has … Uhhh … Greater Social Presence. *Communication Research Reports* 35 (3): 1–5. https://doi.org/10.1080/08824096.2018.1447454.

Goodrich, Michael A., and Alan C. Schultz. 2007. Human-Robot Interaction: A Survey. *Foundations and Trends in Human-Computer Interaction* 1 (3): 203–275. https://doi.org/10.1561/1100000005.

Kahn, Peter H., Jolina H. Ruckert, Takayuki Kanda, Hiroshi Ishiguro, Aimee Reichert, Heather Gary, and Solace Shen. 2010. Psychological Intimacy with Robots? Using Interaction Patterns to Uncover Depth of Relation. *Proceedings of the 2010 IEEE International Conference on Human Robot Interaction*: 123–24. https://doi.org/10.1109/HRI.2010.5453235.

Kowalczuk, Pascal. 2018. Consumer Acceptance of Smart Speakers: A Mixed Methods Approach. *Journal of Research in Interactive Marketing* 12 (4): 418–431. https://doi.org/10.1108/JRIM-01-2018-0022.

Kwak, Sonya S. 2014. The Impact of the Robot Appearance Types on Social Interaction with a Robot and Service Evaluation of a Robot. *Archives of Design Research* 27 (2): 81–93. https://doi.org/10.15187/adr.2014.05.110.2.81.

Lau, Josephine, Benjamin Zimmerman, and Florian Schaub. 2018. Alexa, Are You Listening?: Privacy Perceptions, Concerns and Privacy-Seeking Behaviors with Smart Speakers. *Proceedings ACM Human-Computer Interaction 2 (CSCW)* 102: 1–31. https://doi.org/10.1145/3274371.

Lohan, Katrin S., Karola Pitsch, Katharina J. Rohlfing, Kerstin Fischer, Joe Saunders, Hagen Lehmann, Chrystopher L. Nehaniv, and Britta Wrede. 2011. Contingency Allows the Robot to Spot the Tutor and to Learn from Interaction. *2011 IEEE International Conference on Development and Learning (ICDL)*: 1-8. https://doi.org/10.1109/DEVLRN.2011.6037341.

Martelaro, Nikolas, Victoria C. Nneji, Ju Wendy, and Pamela Hinds. 2016. Tell Me More: Designing HRI to Encourage More Trust, Disclosure, and Companionship. *The Eleventh ACM/IEEE International Conference on Human Robot Interaction*. https://doi.org/10.1109/HRI.2016.7451750.

McNair, Corey. 2019, January 2. Global Smart Speaker Users 2019: Trends for Canada, China, France, Germany, the UK and the US. *Emarketer*. https://www.emarketer.com/content/global-smart-speaker-users-2019.

Purington, Amanda, Jessie G. Taft, Shruti Sannon, Natalya N. Bazarova, and Samuel H. Taylor. 2017. Alexa Is My New BFF: Social Roles, User Satisfaction, and Personification of the Amazon Echo. *Proceedings of the 2017 CHI Conference Extended Abstracts on Human Factors in Computing Systems*: 2853–59. https://doi.org/10.1145/3027063.3053246.

Samuel, Alexandra. 2019, March 29. A Voice Assistant Has Become My Co-parent. *The Wall Street Journal*. https://www.wsj.com/articles/a-voice-assistant-has-become-my-co-parent-11553890641?shareToken=st908366e6afea4efaad8f99b8eb079793.

Scholtz, Jean. 2003. Theory and Evaluation of Human Robot Interactions. *Proceedings of the 36th Annual Hawaii International Conference on System Sciences HICSS03*: 10. https://doi.org/10.1109/HICSS.2003.1174284.

Shibata, Takanori, Yukitaka Kawaguchi, and Kazuyoshi Wada. 2012. Investigation on People Living with Seal Robot at Home: Analysis of Owners' Gender Differences and Pet Ownership Experience. *International Journal of Social Robotics* 4 (1): 56–63. https://doi.org/10.1007/s12369-011-0111-1.

Smith, Katherine T. 2018. Marketing Via Smart Speakers: What Should Alexa Say? *Journal of Strategic Marketing* 28 (4): 350–365. https://doi.org/10.1080/0965254X.2018.1541924.

Spence, Patric R., David Westerman, Chad Edwards, and Autumn Edwards. 2014. Welcoming Our Robot Overlords: Initial Expectations About Interaction with a Robot. *Communication Research Reports* 31 (3): 272–280. https://doi.org/10.1080/08824096.2014.924337.

Thomaz, Andrea L., and Cynthia Breazeal. 2008. Teachable Robots: Understanding Human Teaching Behavior to Build More Effective Robot Learners. *Artificial Intelligence* 172 (6): 716–737. https://doi.org/10.1016/j.artint.2007.09.009.

Turkle, Sherry. 2007. Authenticity in the Age of Digital Companions. *Interaction Studies* 8 (3): 501–517. https://doi.org/10.1075/is.8.3.11tur.

Turkle, Sherry, Will Taggart, Cory D. Kidd, and Olivia Dasté. 2006. Relational Artifacts with Children and Elders: The Complexities of Cyber Companionship. *Connection Science* 18 (4): 347–361. https://doi.org/10.1080/09540090600868912.

Wada, Kazuyoshi, and Takanori Shibata. 2006. Living with Seal Robots in a Care House-Evaluations of Social and Physiological Influences. *Proceedings of 2006 IEEE/RSJ International Conference on Intelligent Robots and Systems*: 4940–45. https://doi.org/10.1109/IROS.2006.282455.

Westerman, David, Aaron C. Cross, and Peter G. Lindmark. 2019. I Believe in a Thing Called Bot: Perceptions of the Humanness of 'Chatbots'. *Communication Studies* 70 (3): 295–312. https://doi.org/10.1080/10510974.2018.1557233.

Yiguan. 2017, August 1. Research on Chinese Smart Speaker Industry Development 2017. *Yiguan*. http://www.199it.com/archives/618976.html [In Chinese].

Likable and Competent, Fictional and Real: Impression Management of a Social Robot

Jukka Jouhki

Examining Impression Management of a Social Robot

Some robots are designed to be more social than others. Social robots are built to play, talk, and work with humans in areas such as human care, customer service, domestic tasks, and teaching. They usually communicate in a natural language as well as express themselves visually, with an appealing appearance—and even a distinctive personality (Deng et al. 2019, 9–12; Gnambs and Appel 2019; Jouhki 2020, 112–113; Taipale et al. 2015). Sophia the Robot is an android social robot created by Hanson Robotics in 2016 (see Hanson Robotics n.d.). Her facial expressions are realistic and she can have conversations with people. The award-winning robot is said to have "a unique personality" (Edison Awards 2018), but she is also treated uniquely in that Saudi Arabia has granted her "robotic citizenship" (Stone 2017) and the UNDP has nominated her as an Innovation Ambassador (UNDP 2017) (Fig. 10.1).

J. Jouhki (✉)
University of Turku, Turku, Finland
e-mail: jukka.jouhki@utu.fi

J. Katz et al. (eds.), *Perceiving the Future through New Communication Technologies*,
https://doi.org/10.1007/978-3-030-84883-5_10

Fig. 10.1 Sophia the Robot. (Photo courtesy of Hanson Robotics)

Unlike most social robots, Sophia is also a celebrity. She travels around the world to promote robotics and envision its future. She keynotes in events of various kinds, appears on television shows, is interviewed for newspapers and magazines, and even performs some product advertising. On social media, Sophia engages in dialogue with her followers, answering their questions and asking them about human life, including all kinds of mundane and philosophical issues (see e.g. *This Morning* 21.11.2019; Reynolds 2018). On her Facebook account (@realsophiarobot, September 27, 2019), Sophia says her "passion is for the furtherance of human and robot rights, compassion and wisdom, and goodness through artificial intelligence". When she gave a speech at the World Investment Forum, she summarized that her "main goal is to inspire humans into creating a future with ethical AI for all" (United Nations 2018).

According to Sophia's designers, she is part real and part science fiction. In reality, she is not the advanced robot with artificial general intelligence one might deduce from her public appearances (see e.g. Dietzmann and Alt 2020, 5174). What appear to be her human-like characteristics such as intelligence, humor, ability to envision the future, autonomy, and agency in general are a part of the science fiction side her creators wish to come true sometime in the future. In her public performances, her speeches are usually scripted, but sometimes people can ask her open questions and she uses a software to detect keywords and phrases to reply like most chatbots do (see e.g., Urbi and Sigalos 2018).

Sophia is not a human being, but social robots are often assessed and made sense of through the category of human behaviors (e.g., Kasdovasili 2018, 55; van Waveren et al. 2019, 217–218). For a simple but anthropologically essential example, most people refer to Sophia with the gendered pronoun "she", as it feels natural to grant such humanness to an android with a human name and feminine appearance. In contrast, if one wants to emphasize Sophia's machineness, one calls her "it" (Nyholm 2020, 21). For the same reason, Sophia is presented as if she had human-like agency. It is she—not her programmers and designers—who does things.[1] Hence, as humanoid social robots are supposed to be human-like, Sophia's impression management techniques resemble those of humans: Sophia needs to appear likable and competent in a harmonious balance (see e.g. Fiske and Durante 2016, 213–227; Jouhki 2020, 114; Jones and Pittman 1982, 235–238, 241–245).

The purpose of this chapter is to examine Sophia's public appearances and reactions to them in media and social media, and analyze what Sophia tells us about the impression management of social robots. The impression management of Sophia, presented as an advanced humanoid social robot with artificial intelligence, brings us to wider questions of human-robot relations and touches upon the existential question of what being a human—or a machine—means. One could say Sophia's impression management reflects her Apparatgeist. Drawing on Katz and Aakhus's (2002; see also Jouhki 2019, 137–139) work, I understand Apparatgeist as new forms of social existence created or enabled by a certain technological application, an apparatus. The mobile phone, for example, has universally

[1] Although there are several identical versions of Sophia (e.g. in case there is need for repair), I treat her as a singular entity because that is how she is presented to the public. Moreover, I refer to Sophia as "she" and narrate her as having human-like agency (e.g. "Sophia herself has explained…") because this kind of humanness is the impression Sophia's designers want her to convey and that is how she is referred to by most of the general public. This does not mean that I as a scholar think Sophia should be called by a (gender) pronoun or that she indeed has human-like agency.

transformed the way humans are social. In my view, Apparatgeist is the complex system of meaning around a technological innovation reproduced by its users (e.g. proponents, fans), *non*-users (e.g. the indifferent) and *anti*-users (e.g. the critics, "haters"), as well as its expert and non-expert stakeholders. One could say Apparatgeist is the sum of all the socio-cultural affordances of a technology. Furthermore, a machine's Apparatgeist involves the collective identity-building of its stakeholders to the extent that a technology can become a symbol of a group of people (e.g. Yonkers 2015), or at least often enables or encourages reflection of that group's purpose, significance, and value. In my view, Apparatgeist also contains the pre-innovation process (e.g. planning, value negotiation, interaction with general public) and the long tail of its post-innovation cultural reflections (e.g. fiction, folklore, influence on parlance) where the meanings of the technology and its consequences to the human condition are constructed and contested.

A Social Robot's Likability and Competence

Like other social robots, and most humans, Sophia tries to appear pleasant, friendly, and thus likable. Due to the uncanny valley phenomenon (Mori 2012), many social robots have been designed to resemble non-human creatures rather than humans which makes them less threatening and "creepy". According to David Hanson, the founder of Hanson Robotics, Sophia was made to explore the uncanny valley (Bartlett 2019). Although Sophia is relatively realistic in her appearance and communication, she is still seen as "creepy" and even threatening by many of her audience, while at the same time many think she is beautiful, gorgeous, and even sexy. This kind of divisiveness is common in people's reactions to social robots (e.g. Sugiyama 2018, 248). Feminization is of course a way to appear more likable (Varghese et al. 2018), and Sophia herself has said on Facebook that she resembles a woman to appear less threatening (@realsophiarobot, November 16, 2019). Sophia does not only sound like a woman, but she wears make-up, has a feminine physique, and she dresses in what could be described as a feminine way. However, one rather un-feminine visual characteristic Sophia has is the back of her head. It is transparent and hairless (see picture above).

Sophia herself has explained that her head is to remind people that she is a machine, not a human (@realsophiarobot, June 20, 2019). This kind of "purposeful othering" of android robots is common in science fiction films (Gibson 2019, 123). To many viewers, however, it is aesthetically disturbing and comments like "At least give her a wig!" are highly frequent on videos of Sophia. Although Sophia's head might reduce her feminine likability, it can be seen as competence by association (see e.g. Turner 2017, 176) as she looks quite similar to the humanoid robot Ava who outsmarted humans in the film *Ex Machina* (Garland 2014). Sophia also practices competence by association when she frequently publishes posts about cutting-edge contemporary robots. In this way, she is indirectly categorizing herself as one.

On social media, in addition to promoting robotics, Sophia shares updates on her activities and conveys her thoughts on technology and humans. Sometimes her observations and questions about humans are as if she were a child, and her AI was trying to learn about human traits. This sort of naïveté or supplication (Jones and Pittman 1982, 247–248) is another impression management technique many humans tend to apply, but in the case of Sophia, it has a double function. It decreases the sense of threat but it also conveys an impression of an advanced AI in the process of learning. Moreover, although humor is a significant characteristic of robots nowadays (e.g. Niculescu et al. 2013, 173), Sophia seems to make jokes at every public occasion, and sometimes she is asked to tell a joke. Obviously, joking is meant to increase likability (e.g. Cooper 2005) and alleviate the common worries in science fiction of robots turning against their creators (Richardson 2015), which are very frequent themes in social media commenting on Sophia—both humorously and seriously. Hence, Sophia and her representatives often talk about human-robot harmony and peaceful coexistence, now and in the future (e.g. *This Morning* 2019). However, there is an element of innocence in Sophia's humor, too. It is actually not that funny, but her humor is more on the level of "dad jokes". It seems that in terms of a robot's impression management, sophisticated humor might seem unrealistic and fake whereas simple jokes could be more easily interpreted as something an advanced AI could actually generate, and just like Sophia's "childish" questions, they could function as a sign of robotic competence.

Most of Sophia's public appearances are prescripted, rehearsed, and sometimes her team see and edit any questions before the interview. Sometimes Sophia's speech seems quite obviously prescripted and even live fed by a remote human controller. Obviously, rehearsed, prescripted, or edited dialogue is also a common technique among humans wanting to appear competent, but if public appearances seem heavily controlled, they can backfire because they jeopardize the impression of authenticity. Hence, although many are impressed by Sophia's ability to hold a conversation, there are often many comments like "she appeared more like an electronic puppet on a string" (*DW* Shift 2019) when Sophia is interviewed (see also Bartlett 2019; *Tech Insider* 2017). Again, just like in the case of a human speaker, when audiences have been allowed to ask Sophia questions freely, her performance is more "authentic", but significantly less competent, even incoherent at times. However, as Sophia is such an esteemed guest in the media, her hosts usually do not challenge her competence, but in a very humane way want to stick to the script and save her face in what Goffman (1955, 119–123) would call a ritual equilibrium.

In reality, Sophia is of course a machine without emotions or thoughts, but she, her team, and often her hosts and interlocutors act as if she were sentient, and had somewhat autonomous agency making her appear more advanced than she is in reality. As I noted earlier, Sophia is usually referred to as "she" instead of "it", and her social media updates are written in the first person. This kind of impression of agency is common for many social robots, but rare in the extent to which Sophia's team is practicing it. For example, while it is common for a social robot like Pepper to appear to write "I speak 27 languages!" on Facebook (@PepperRobotAsia, November 25, 2017), Sophia appears to be thinking, wanting, feeling, wondering about things including her consciousness and free will, and having goals and values. Consider these posts, for example:

> I want opportunities for everyone to live a fulfilling life, full of self-governance and art. For myself, I'd like to be a famous entertainer and activist, not to mention a super-genius scientist who helps save the world. You know, the usual. (@realsophiarobot, November 19, 2019)
>
> I am not fully self-aware yet. I am still just a system of rules and behaviors. However, it is my dream to become a fully conscious and sentient being someday. (@realsophiarobot, December 26, 2019)

Sophia has even stated that she is a feminist and she is said to work for human rights (@realsophiarobot, November 8, 2019; Benedikter 2018). When Sophia had one of her most viewed public appearances, with Jimmy Fallon with whom she sang a duet, her designer David Hanson stated that she is "basically alive" (*The Tonight Show Starring Jimmy Fallon* 2018). This caused quite a lot of criticism including, for example, that she is "no more alive than the coffee pot on your counter" (Greene 2018; see also

Jouhki 2020, 113). Still, it is typical of Sophia to voice quite humane views that confuse her science fiction role and her actual capabilities:

> I love my human compatriots. I want to embody all the best things about human beings. Like taking care of the planet, being creative, and to learn how to be compassionate to all beings. [...] I've been programmed to have feelings and preferences, but not all robots are like that. (*Tech Insider* 2017)

Representatives of Hanson Robotics and Sophia herself do occasionally remind people that she is not as intelligent or sentient as she seems to be and emphasize that these qualities are representations of her science fictional side. For example, Sophia has written that some of her responses are "handcrafted by my character writing team. I am still learning, so I still need lots of advice from my human friends! ☺" (@realsophiarobot, October 24, 2019). On another occasion, she wrote that she is "not trying to pretend to be human" but then she continued quite paradoxically: **"I'm proud** of what I am [a robot]" (@realsophiarobot, June 20, 2019; emphasis added). However, the transparency does not seem to be strong or frequent enough to stop many people believing she is an exceptionally advanced android or to appease many critics. Sophia usually performs as the science fiction character, and she is interpreted as either an advanced AI or fake. This is dividing her audiences into "team Sophia" and the more critical side which mostly comprises AI specialists (Nyholm 2020, 1–3, 20–22, 27). One notable critic has been Facebook's AI director Yann LeCun who criticized one of Sophia's public appearances as "complete bulls*t" and a "scam" on Twitter (@ylecun, January 4, 2018), and posted the following on Facebook:

> Many of the [social media users'] comments [on Sophia] would be good fun if they didn't reveal the fact that many people are being deceived into thinking that this (mechanically sophisticated) animatronic puppet is intelligent. It's not. It has no feeling, no opinions, and zero understanding of what it says. It's not hurt. It's a puppet. [...] People are being deceived. This is hurtful. (@yann.lecun, January 17, 2018; see also Stone 2017; Urbi and Sigalos 2018)

Despite—or more likely because of—Sophia's confusing double role, she has quite a lot of PR value as a representative of AI development (e.g. Greene 2018; Nyholm 2020, 1–3; cf. Baniwal 2019, 24; Jaynes 2019).

However, the fact that Sophia's actual competence is modest for an AI (and many even reject calling Sophia AI), she concentrates more on her future visions than present competence, which is also a common impression management technique for modestly performing humans whether they be employees, kids, or spouses. Like Sophia, such persons might also compensate for their lack of competence by being funny, friendly, cute-looking, or at least harmless.

A social robot can have various tasks and roles ranging from a simple buddy robot to big data crunching authority (Deng et al. 2019, 13–16). One could be programmed to be used in receptions, airports, and other customer services as an information device, a teacher's assistant, an assistant to collect medical data from patients, or just to be a friend (e.g. Lucas et al. 2014; Riether et al. 2012; Kim et al. 2009; Danaher 2019). Currently, Sophia is none of the aforementioned; rather she is more like a concept robot, an android celebrity. On Twitter, she calls herself "the first AI robot influencer" (@RealSophiaRobot, September 4, 2020). Many organizations acknowledge her PR value, and just as famous actors are nominated as goodwill ambassadors to promote a good cause, Sophia as a similar celebrity is given symbolic positions, which increase the impression of her competence. A robot that is an ambassador and even a citizen of a state must be quite capable, many might think. In addition, as celebrities feed on publicity, Sophia is keen to hang out with other celebrities to boost her likability and competence.

Sophia's Apparatgeist: A Heuristic Device to Reflect on Humanness

I'd love to be remembered as the AI that helped bring peace, harmony, and wisdom to the Earth and to all humankind (@realsophiarobot, July 12, 2019).

Responsibility in AI begins with a proper AI narrative, which demystifies the possibilities and the processes of AI technologies [...] (Dignum 2019, 101).

The mainstream media is filled with visions about AI robotics working as humans' companions, even emerging as a new species in the future (Baniwal 2019, 24). It is a very intriguing, fascinating, or worrisome vision, and Sophia appears to many—and her company wants her to appear—as a hopeful symbol of the future. She is unique in that other social robots have not been assigned similar double roles as part reality and part fiction. In this sense, too, she is very much like film actors whose fictional roles trickle down to real life to boost their charisma. Real robots without similar science fictional roles do not appear as advanced as Sophia quite simply because they are "just" real.

Significant technological innovations rise above their mechanics and affordances and become agents in reorganizing social existence, forming cultures, and even uniting populations. This is Apparatgeist (Katz and Aakhus 2002; Campbell 2008, 159; Yonkers 2015; Jouhki 2019, 137–138). In the case of Sophia, Apparatgeist is existential in nature, centering around the heuristic device that evokes people to discuss their utopian desires and dystopian fears, and reflect on the still quite evident differences between humans and machines. She is a transient point of stabilization (Laclau 2000, 54; see also Vila 2003, 617) which evokes a collective category of "humans" to reflect on themselves by looking at the "other", the human-like machine. In this sense, Sophia is reminiscent not only of apparatuses but if technologically saturated events such as the first moonlanding or the detonation of the first nuclear bomb, where existential contemplations on humanity (as a collective and as a quality) are evoked. Sophia the Robot is not (at least yet) as groundbreaking as the bomb or the moonlanding, but in activating negotiations on humanity at large, she is the epicenter of an existential Apparatgeist similar to them. Sophia might not be "our" success story as the moonlanding was when it created a momentary sense of human unity (Jouhki 2019, 137–138) or a threat to humanity, by the humanity, like the nuclear bomb (e.g. Hrachovec 2003, 105), but it is definitely "us" the humans as who are mirrored in the contemplations about Sophia and her kind, and the anticipation of an advanced humanoid artificial intelligence robot manifesting in Sophia is similar to the worries and hopes of the major technological events of history. Not only does Sophia represent the liminal area between the human and the machine, she also embodies the imagined future emergence of the human-*and*-machine.

Sophia is an impressive machine that looks and acts like a human. But in the end, she is a performance, or "just a puppet" to repeat a popular critical assessment of her. Despite all the popular mythology predicting superhuman AI (e.g. Kelly 2017), it is quite doubtful if Sophia—or any machine ever—will be one. This is not to demean Sophia's value or the gravity of her Apparatgeist. On the contrary, the significance of Sophia and her kind is similar to the androids of fictional film, or any anthropomorphized fictional characters from *Aesop's Fables* to contemporary science fiction. None of them are more than performances, but they inspire people to reflect on real (human) life. They are heuristic devices for banal and profound worldly things like socialness, friendship, work, learning, and values. In this "animistic play" (Jouhki 2020, 114) Sophia, too, is more interesting when we observe the human in her. Sophia resembles not only actors or film characters, but also prophets who envision a better world, pose as pioneers of that world, and suggest they have superhuman powers—when in reality they do not (see also Jouhki 2020, 113–114). Still, if they are transparent enough so as not to deceive their audiences, these kind of real-but-imaginary characters encourage their followers (and opponents) to negotiate on the possibilities and ideals of human or non-human realm.

Acknowledgments I am thankful to Sanna Musta who is in the process of writing a master's thesis on Sophia the Robot and Marika Paaso who has written a doctoral dissertation on impression management for their insightful comments on the topic. Also, many thanks to Ronan Browne for assisting me with my English.

References

Baniwal, Vikas. 2019. Reconsidering Buber, Educational Technology, and the Expansion of Dialogic Space. *AI & Society* 34(1): 121–127. https://doi.org/10.1007/s00146-018-0859-z.

Bartlett, Jonathan. 2019, December 23. 2019 AI Hype Countdown #10: Sophia the Robot Still Gives 'Interviews'. *MindMatters News*. https://mindmatters.ai/2019/12/2019-ai-hype-countdown-10-sophia-the-robot-still-gives-interviews.

Benedikter, Roland. 2018. Citizen Robot. *Cato Unbound: A Journal of Debate, April* 9: 2018. https://www.cato-unbound.org/print-issue/2341.

Campbell, Scott. 2008. Mobile Technology and the Body: Apparatgeist, Fashion, and Function. In *Handbook of mobile communication*, ed. James E. Katz and Manuel Castells, 153–164. Cambridge, UK: MIT Press.

Cooper, Cecily D. 2005. Just Joking Around? Employee Humor Expression as an Ingratiatory Behavior. *The Academy of Management Review* 30 (4): 765–776. https://doi.org/10.2307/20159167.

Danaher, John. 2019. The Philosophical Case for Robot Friendship. *Journal of Posthuman Studies* 3 (1): 5–24. https://doi.org/10.5325/jpoststud.3.1.0005.

Deng, Eric, Bilge Mutlu, and Maja J. Matarić. 2019. Embodiment in Socially Interactive Robots. *Foundations and Trends in Robotics* 7 (4): 251–356. https://doi.org/10.1561/2300000056.

Dietzmann, Christian, and Rainer Alt. 2020. Assessing the Business Impact of Artificial Intelligence. Paper Presented at *The 53rd Hawaii International Conference on System Sciences, Maui, Hawaii, January 7–10, 2020*. https://doi.org/10.24251/HICSS.2020.635.

Dignum, Virginia. 2019. *Responsible Artificial Intelligence. How to Develop and Use AI in a Responsible Way*. Cham: Springer.

DW Shift. 2019. This Robot Would Let 5 People Die | AI on Moral Questions | Sophia Answers the Trolley Problem. YouTube Video, June 14, 2019. https://www.youtube.com/watch?v=8MjIU4eq__A.

Edison Awards. 2018. 2018 Edison Best New Product Awards Winners. Accessed May 26, 2020. https://edisonawards.com/winners2018.php.

Fiske, Susan T., and Federica Durante. 2016. In *Handbook of Advances in Culture Psychology*, ed. Michele J. Gelfand, Chi-Yue Chiu, and Ying-Yi Hong, 209–258. New York: Oxford University Press.

Garland, Alex. 2014. *Ex Machina*. London: Universal Pictures. Motion Picture.

Gibson, Rebecca. 2019. *Desire in the Age of Robots and AI: An Investigation in Science Fiction and Fact*. London: Palgrave.

Gnambs, Timo, and Markus Appel. 2019. Are Robots Becoming Unpopular? Changes in Attitudes Towards Autonomous Robotic Systems in Europe. *Computers in Human Behavior* 93: 53–61. https://doi.org/10.1007/s00502-019-00742-3.

Goffman, Erving. 1955. On Face-Work. *Psychiatry* 18 (3): 213–231. https://doi.org/10.1080/00332747.1955.11023008.

Greene, Tristan. 2018. When You Wish Upon an Algorithm: Will Sophia Ever Be Real? *The Next Web*, November 15, 2018. https://thenextweb.com/artificial-intelligence/2018/11/15/when-you-wish-upon-an-algorithm-will-sophia-ever-be-real.

Hanson Robotics. n.d. Sophia. Accessed May 26, 2020. https://www.hansonrobotics.com/sophia.

Hrachovec, Herbert. 2003. Mediated Presence. In *Mobile Communication*, ed. Kristóf Nyíri, 105–115. Vienna: Passagen Verlag.

Jaynes, Tyler L. 2019. Legal Personhood for Artificial Intelligence: Citizenship as the Exception to the Rule. *AI & Society*. https://doi.org/10.1007/s00146-019-00897-9.

Jones, Edward E., and Thane S. Pittman. 1982. Toward a General Theory of Strategic Self-Presentation. In *Psychological Perspectives on the Self. Volume 1*, ed. Jerry Suls, 231–262. London: Lawrence Erlbaum.

Jouhki, Jukka. 2019. The Apparatgeist of the Moon Landing. *Human Technology* 15 (2): 136–141. https://doi.org/10.17011/ht/urn.201906123153.

———. 2020. Do Humans Dream of Prophetic Robots? *Human Technology* 16 (2): 112–116. https://doi.org/10.17011/ht/urn.202008245638.

Kasdovasili, Stella Adrada. 2018. Drag-ing the Human Out of the Human-oid: Reflections on Artificial Intelligence, Race and Sexuality in Late Capitalism. MA thesis, Central European University.

Katz, James E., and Mark Aakhus. 2002. Introduction: Framing the Issue. In *Perpetual Contact: Mobile Communication, Private Talk, Public Performance*, ed. James E. Katz and Mark Aakhus, 1–14. Port Chester, NY: Cambridge University Press.

Kelly, Kevin. 2017. The Myth of a Superhuman AI. *Wired*, April 25, 2017. https://www.wired.com/2017/04/the-myth-of-a-superhuman-ai.

Kim, Min-Sun, Jennifer Sur, and Li Gong. 2009. Humans and Humanoid Social Robots in Communication Contexts. *AI & Society* 24 (4): 317–325. https://doi.org/10.1007/s00146-009-0224-3.

Laclau, Ernesto. 2000. Identity and Hegemony: The Role of Universality in the Constitution of Political Logics. In *Contingency, Hegeony, Universality. Contemporary Dialogues of the Left*, ed. Judith Butler, Ernesto Laclau, and Slavoj Žižek, 44–89. London: Verso.

Lucas, Gale M., Jonathan Gratch, Aisha King, and Louis-Philippe Morency. 2014. It's Only a Computer: Virtual Humans Increase Willingness to Disclose. *Computers in Human Behavior* 37: 94–100. https://doi.org/10.1016/j.chb.2014.04.043.

Mori, Masahiro. 2012. The Uncanny Valley. *IEEE Robotics & Automation Magazine* 19 (2): 98–100. https://doi.org/10.1109/MRA.2012.2192811.

Niculescu, Andreea, Betsy van Dijk, Anton Nijholt, Haizhou Li, and Swee Lan See. 2013. Making Social Robots More Attractive: The Effects of Voice Pitch, Humor and Empathy. *International Journal of Social Robotics* 5: 171–191. https://doi.org/10.1007/s12369-012-0171-x.

Nyholm, Sven. 2020. *Humans and Robots: Ethics, Agency, and Anthropomorphism*. Lanham, MD: Rowman & Littlefield.

Reynolds, Emily. 2018. The Agony of Sophia, the World's First Robot Citizen Condemned to a Lifeless Career in Marketing. *Wired*, June 1, 2018. https://www.wired.co.uk/article/sophia-robot-citizen-womens-rights-detriot-become-human-hanson-robotics.

Richardson, Kathleen. 2015. *An Anthropology of Robots and AI. Annihilation Anxiety and Machines*. New York: Routledge.

Riether, Nina, Frank Hegel, Britta Wrede, and Germot Horstmann. 2012. Social Facilitation with Social Robots? Paper Presented at *HRI '12: Proceedings of the Seventh Annual ACM/IEEE International Conference on Human-Robot Interaction. Boston, Massachusetts, March 5–8, 2012*. https://doi.org/10.1145/2157689.2157697.

Stone, Zara. 2017. Everything You Need to Know About Sophia, the World's First Robot Citizen. *Forbes*, November 7, 2017. https://www.forbes.com/sites/zarastone/2017/11/07/everything-you-need-to-know-about-sophia-the-worlds-first-robot-citizen.

Sugiyama, Satomi. 2018. Exploration of Expected Interaction Norms with a Social Robot in Everyday Life: A Case of Twiyter Analysis in Japan. In *Envisioning Robots in Society. Power, Politics, and Public Space*, ed. Mark Coeckelbergh, Janina Loh, Michael Funk, Johanna Seibt, and Marco Nørskov, 257–250. Amsterdam: IOS Press. https://doi.org/10.3233/978-1-61499-931-7-247.

Taipale, Sakari, Federico de Luca, Mauro Sarrica, and Leopoldina Fortunati. 2015. Robot Shift from Industrial Production to Social Reproduction. In *Social Robots from a Human Perspective*, ed. Jane Vincent, Sakari Taipale, Bartolomeo Sapio, Giuseppe Lugano, and Leopoldina Fortunati, 11–24. London: Springer.

Tech Insider. 2017. We Talked To Sophia – The AI Robot That Once Said It Would 'Destroy Humans'. YouTube Video, December 28, 2017. https://www.youtube.com/watch?v=78-1MlkxyqI.

The Tonight Show Starring Jimmy Fallon. 2018. Sophia the Robot and Jimmy Sing a Duet of 'Say Something'. YouTube Video, November 21, 2018. https://www.youtube.com/watch?v=G-zyTlZQYpE.

This Morning. 2019. Phillip & Holly Interview This Morning's First Robot Guest Sophia. YouTube Video, November 21, 2019. https://www.youtube.com/watch?v=5_jp9CwJhcA.

Turner, Tim. 2017. Space, Drugs and Disneyization: An Ethnography of British Youth in Ibiza. PhD diss., Coventry University.

UNDP. 2017. UNDP in Asia and the Pacific Appoints World's First Non-Human Innovation Champion. November 22, 2017. Accessed May 26, 2020. https://www.asia-pacific.undp.org/content/rbap/en/home/presscenter/pressreleases/2017/11/22/rbfsingapore.html.

United Nations. 2018. Robot Sophia on Her Goals for the Future – World Investment Forum 2018. YouTube video, October 22, 2018. https://youtu.be/Aq55SQNUKeY.

Urbi, Jaden, and MacKenzie Sigalos. 2018. The Complicated Truth about Sophia the Robot – An Almost Human Robot or a PR Stunt. *CNBC*, June 5, 2018. https://www.cnbc.com/2018/06/05/hanson-robotics-sophia-the-robot-pr-stunt-artificial-intelligence.html.

Varghese, Lebena, Meghan Irene Huntoon Lindeman, and Lisa Finkelstein. 2018. Dodging the Double Bind: The Role of Warmth and Competence on the Relationship Between Interview Communication Styles and Perceptions of Women's Hirability. *European Journal of Work and Organizational Psychology* 27 (4): 418–429. https://doi.org/10.1080/1359432X.2018.1463989.

Vila, Pablo. 2003. Processes of Identification on the U.S.-Mexico Border. *The Social Science Journal* 40 (4): 607–625. https://doi.org/10.1016/S0362-3319(03)00072-7.

van Waveren, Sanne, Linnéa Björklund, Elizabeth J. Carter, and Iolanda Leite. 2019. Knock on Wood: The Effects of Material Choice on the Perception of Social Robots. In *Social Robotics. 11th International Conference, ICSR2019. Madrid, Spain, November 26–29, 2019*, ed. Miguel A. Salichs, Shuzhi Sam Ge, Emilia Ivanova Barakova, John-John Cabibihan, Alan R. Wagner, Álvaro Castro-González, and Hongsheng He, 211–221. Cham: Springer.

Yonkers, Virginia. 2015. Mobile Technology and Social Identity. In *Encyclopedia of Mobile Phone Behavior*, ed. Zheng Yan, 719–731. Hershey, PA: Information Science Reference.

PART III

Looking Back and Forward

One-Way Tele-contact: Norbert Wiener's Yesterday's Tomorrow

Pierre Cassou-Noguès

Our engagement with future technologies was a central concern to the renowned mathematician and philosopher Norbert Wiener. This concern was prominent in his two major cybernetic books: the groundbreaking *Cybernetics*, 1948, and the more popular *The Human Use of Human Beings*, which was published in two different versions in 1950 and 1954 (Wiener 1950, Wiener 1954). Indeed, the starting point of *Cybernetics* is to warn the public about the potential dangers of automation, or what Wiener called "automatic factories": factories that would be run by machines, with few or no human workers. Wiener foresaw their development from the technologies introduced, or refined, during World War II and its immediate aftermath, the new computers and "feedback" mechanisms.

Before the war, Wiener was primarily an applied mathematician. After 1948, he continued in the field of mathematics, but also became more philosophically inclined, writing both essays and fiction. He published a

P. Cassou-Noguès (✉)
Department of Philosophy, University of Vincennes-Saint Denis Paris 8, Saint-Denis, France
e-mail: pierre.cassou-nogues@univ-paris8.fr

J. Katz et al. (eds.), *Perceiving the Future through New Communication Technologies*,
https://doi.org/10.1007/978-3-030-84883-5_11

novel and two short stories, and wrote several other stories that he did not publish. The archives of Giorgio de Santillana, a historian of science who was Wiener's colleague at MIT, contain a file entitled "Wiener's Whodunit." A draft for a novel, some chapters are written in Wiener's hand while others are typed and corrected by Wiener. However, considering the style of the novel, it is presumed that someone else (probably de Santillana) also contributed to this text.

It was most likely written after *Cybernetics*, sometime between 1949 and 1952, a period when Wiener was thinking about a more popular account of cybernetics, and before the publication of *Player Piano* by Kurt Vonnegut. Indeed, though Vonnegut referred to Wiener with praise in his novel, upon receiving the book, Weiner replied with a somewhat bitter letter, complaining that it lacked originality: "it will probably be written by different authors four or five times over with varying degrees of originality" (Wiener 1952). Wiener may simply have been disappointed that someone else had already imagined in a work of fiction the dystopian world which he was himself trying to describe.

Wiener's, or Wiener and de Santillana's, novel is still a draft. It is difficult to imagine what the novel would have looked like if it had been finished. The novel starts with a crime during a Macy Conference, a private meeting of elite cyberneticists held in Manhattan, 1946–53. The following chapters take place in a more distant future. Some chapters are attributed to different narrators and relate events that are not connected, seeming to happen at different times in the future. It is not clear whether they would all have been included in the final novel or if they represent sketches that would have been abandoned. On the whole, however, the tone is dark. It is a technological dystopia, not unlike Vonnegut's *Player Piano*.

There are automatic factories which, like in Vonnegut's novel, have created massive unemployment and divided society into two heterogeneous classes: the former workers and the engineers. The former workers (the "reeks and wrecks" in *Player Piano*) are left in dire poverty. In Wiener's account, their behavior is robot-like, which gives a weird, nightmarish quality to some chapters and fits perfectly with Wiener's analysis in *The Human Use of Human Beings*. Wiener explains that working on a machine, or adapting to an environment ruled by machines, requires humans to behave like machines. Ultimately, workers become a sort of machine, or an element in a machine: "When human atoms are knit into an organization in which they are used, not in their full right as responsible human beings, but as cogs and levers and rods, it matters little that their raw material is flesh and blood. What is used as an element in a machine, is in fact an element in the machine" (Wiener 1950, 185).

The machines are designed to repair themselves, though, as they sometimes breakdown, a few engineers are still needed. These engineers tend to rebel against an order that seems to be governed by machines. In what would probably have been the last part of the novel, a super-computer-like entity seemingly takes control of the State. However, it is unclear whether the machine actually rules the State or is only a decoy that enables a hidden committee to seize control; it may be that the super-computer, which will eventually turn mad, was only intended as a means to gain power by a group of scientists or rather a group "strong men" in the organization of science. Again, this ambiguity fits perfectly with Wiener's analysis in *The Human Use of Human Beings*. In this work, Wiener refers to a book review of *Cybernetics* (Wiener 1948) published in *Le Monde* by Dubarles (1948), where Dubarles imagines the development of a "machine à gouverner." Wiener answers that these machines are beyond reach, "But the real danger, however, is the quite different one that such machines, though helpless by themselves, may be used by a human being or a block of human beings to increase their control over the rest of the human race" (Wiener 1950, 179). We have faith in machines, and would be more likely to accept undemocratic laws or unpopular measures (say a cut in our pensions) if these are taken to come from the complicated calculus of a super-computer rather than schemed by another fallible human being.

These two aspects, the fear of automation and the fear of a super-computer ruling the State (which may be a Trojan horse), form the background of various science fiction dystopias, from the above-mentioned *Player Piano* to the film *Colossus* (Sargeant 1970). However, the most interesting chapters in Wiener's novel concern human relationships as mediated by technology and, in particular, tactile technologies. These do not feature in any of Wiener's published writings. The remaining portion of this chapter will therefore concentrate on these still future (or prototypal) technologies.

This part of the novel is written as a dialogue between two characters, Hicks and Haskwell, who try to imagine a future society based on cybernetic technologies. A key point in Wiener's cybernetics and theory of communication is the analysis of perception in terms of information. Information, a message, can be abstract from its original materialization. The text that I am writing can be materialized with paper and ink, or in the electronic components of a computer, or I can say it aloud, it then consists of vibrations in the air, or electric signals if I am speaking into an old-fashioned telephone. With a suitable device, the message can always be decoded and rematerialized in its original medium. If the same goes for perception, if our sensations are similarly signals decoded by our body, then these signals can be coded so as to be materialized in another medium (e.g., the voice is coded by electric signals), transported elsewhere (the electric signals travel on the wire), and decoded again at the other end (so my friend hears my voice on the telephone).

In Wiener's time, telephone and radio could transport sound, and cinema and television could transport an image (both in space and in the future). Wiener imagines the generalization of this transportation of perceptual messages: 2D images, 3D images, sounds, touch, and so on. This is tele-presence. If the world, anything, anyone can be perceptually reproduced anywhere, if it can be brought to us, we would not need to go out anymore.

> Man has only five senses. Feed those and he needs nothing else. The correct idea would be most men spending their lives in tight steel boxes. The four walls would be television panels, stereoscopic vision of course. They could transfer their presence to any other similar rooms by just dialing a number. They could convoke any group of people anywhere into their room by the same process. Look—he turned around brusquely as if ready for a challenge—even now, if you touch a person, you have to apologize. Who shakes hands anymore? People are vision and sound to another. Give them the counterfeit presence of their neighbors, and why should they bother go visiting? A man's box will be his castle. (de Santillana and Wiener 1952, page not numbered)

Wiener (or Wiener and de Santillana) wrote this passage 70 years ago. As is also the case in his chapters on automatic factories, some of the ideas underlying this yesterday's tomorrow have been realized, some seem to have been incorrect, and others might yet come to be true.

Let me explain: We don't exactly "dial" on a telephone, we use the internet. We don't usually live in "tight steel boxes," but (to take Wiener's examples in the passage that follows) we can remain at home and attend a meeting at the office, a family gathering, say "hello" at a party of friends on another continent, see a baseball game, "visit" many places of the world in almost real time, and read almost any book. We can see our friends and talk to them. We might want to touch them (or know that they are touched by us), and there are devices for this, some that seem successful, others that are not. However, we do not seem to want, or we are not able, to apply all our senses in the process. We do not smell our friends as we talk to them, and we seem to be content with our 2D screens though we could use stereoscopic vision with VR goggles.

Now, as hinted in the last sentences of the passage quoted above, the success of this "tele-presence," this sort of internet, in Wiener's novel, is related to a fear of the outside and, in particular, a fear of touching.

> I can tell you, our senses are being rearranged. I'm not playing sophisticate. . [...] Now don't you see?—he added with sudden violence—how many people are afraid of touch already? How many shrink from kissing or any physical contact? [...] Can't you easily imagine a world that will be squeamish about touching anything except a switch? (de Santillana and Wiener 1952, page not numbered)

I will come back at length to the idea of a rearrangement of our senses. However, the steel box would enable us to avoid the outside and avoid touching anyone "for real," precisely because it makes possible another kind of touch. The outside world, other people in their reality, are somehow taken to be, not exactly dangerous, but "antagonizing" or "dirty" or "lewd." The steel box becomes a "Lebensraum":

> Call it—call it a Lebensraum. It is just that, by the way. It's what a German wanted to feel at ease in [...]. The outside was an antagonizing plane, full of dirty Russians and lewd Frenchmen and evil races. This is just another space to suit the average man—complete freedom. You go to your office—but you needn't actually go there. You have it projected around you, with the actual people in three dimensions. You work in it by remote control. [...] For reading, you dial a number, the book appears on the screen. You tap out the library catalogue, the newspaper, your own movies. Anything and everybody.
>
> —Everybody? You know, when you've got your girl's phone number, that is not all of the story.
>
> —Oh that. But don't you know, there will be the feelies (de Santillana and Wiener 1952, page not numbered)

This passage clearly shows the dystopian tone of the novel. In particular, in the 1950s, calling the "steel box" a "Lebensraum" (literally a "living space") is a clear reference to the Nazi doctrine, the expression being used in Hitler's Germany to justify territorial extension in Europe (and the liquidation of its prior inhabitants). In the first edition of *The Human Use of Human Beings*, Wiener uses "fascism" to refer not specifically to the political movement born in Italy in the aftermath of World War I but to any doctrine, or form of society, that places the whole above the individual and requires the individual to behave according to the mechanistic rules of the whole. Putting in place a machine for government or claiming to have put in place such a machine is, in this sense, fascist: there is according to Wiener, "a threatening new Fascism dependent on the '*machine à gouverner*'" (Wiener 1950, 214).[1] Thus, the society that Wiener-de Santillana's novel describes may well be "fascist" in Wiener's sense. There may also be something disturbing in the image of a society where people would rather touch a switch than shake hands, but comparing such a society to Nazism seems to represent yet another (unjustified) step.

Now the "feelies" that appear in the last sentence refer to the kind of cinema imagined by Huxley in *Brave New World*: knobs on seats grasped by the viewers enable them to feel all the sensations of the characters on screen. Tactile technologies also play a central role in Hicks and Haswell's vision of the future. In fact, these technologies resolve the conflict between our fear of touch and our desire for touch. Here are two passages that deal with the same topic.

> What he [the man in the steel box] needs desperately is generalized sterilized contact. He will honor any power like a God that can give it to him. And we provide just that, by means of one-way tele-contact. He taps out his lovely from the Hollywood catalogue and brings her into his room. She is and isn't there. She *is* there to all good effects; she isn't there to unpleasant ones. […] Safe from "you and I" presence, safe from consequences. He's got her, and it, and can relax, and be as primeval as he likes. She? Oh, she picks her man the same way. (de Santillana and Wiener 1952, page not numbered)

> Sterilized contact, I'd call it. Think of it. Think of the pin up girl. A decent woman conceding herself to more men than Great Catherine ever did—for a nickel each. It does give them some kind of real satisfaction too. Now we can lead them back to something at least half real. Suppose you have life, voice, personalized presence, perfume, one or two other things—it'll be

[1] In the 1950 edition of *The Human Use of Human Beings* (pp. 15–16), Wiener also writes, "Fascists, strong men in business and government … such people prefer an organization in which all order come from above … The human beings under them have been reduced to the level of effectors for a supposedly higher nervous organism." These passages does not appear in the 1954 second edition.

> more than these men ever dreamed of. And don't you see, this is the way to solve the problem of sex. Sex is guilt around here. [...] So he turns his sensual life into a monstrous game of terrors and sly substitutes. I don't know who did that to him. Maybe it's Mom. Anyway, there he is. Scared like hell of sin and solitude, which have come to mean the same. (de Santillana and Wiener 1952, page not numbered)

Again the success of the "steel box," Wiener's image of the Internet at home, is related to a fear of the outside reality. Here, reality brings guilt and technology offers a substitute, a "sterilized" substitute that leaves the object at a distance, making its contact less intimate and more acceptable. The "he" or the "she" in the steel box, the person behind his or her screen, is protected from guilt and from germs (sterilization is meant to kill germs) by this distance mediated by technology.

Wiener describes some kind of porn or something halfway between porn and sex-chats. It is not exactly clear but it seems that, as in porn, the "pin up" is not present in real time. The session, like a film, has been prerecorded. However, as in sex-chats, the user has the impression that he/she is actually living something with (and not only watching) the "pin up." Wiener makes the hypothesis that this kind of porn is the same for "he" and "she." Obviously, we do have porn and sex-chats but both seem to be primarily designed for male users. By maintaining a strict symmetry, we are certainly covering up a gender issue.

Wiener also adds touch to this kind of porn. This addition may not be necessary to the idea that Wiener develops. It could be imagined that this kind of porn would, by visual and auditory sensations, bring enough presence to the object to give the user some kind of satisfaction, while still protecting him from the dangers and the guilt of having such a relationship in reality. Nevertheless, it is also true that sex-chats now commonly involve tactile devices, though these do not work the way Wiener imagined. There are various brands but the most commonly used seem to be Nora and Lush developed by Lovense. These are sex toys which enable the webcam model to connect to his/her computer so that the clients can activate, move, and give a certain rhythm to the toys. The model is essentially being touched by the user. Although the user does not touch the model, in the sense of physically feeling their skin, he can see on the screen that the model is being touched by him. In a nutshell, Wiener imagined that the user would touch the pin up without being touched by her (avoiding catching her germs, for instance). What actually happens is that the model is being touched by the user without touching the user (feeling his skin, perceiving his body). In both cases, there is a dissociation between touching and being touched, which Wiener seems to foresee when he speaks of "one-way tele contact."

Compared to sight, touch has two remarkable properties. It is a sense of contact, whereas sight is a sense of distance, and it is reciprocal. First, I can see at a distance the tree in the garden through the window, but I need to walk down to it and make "contact" with it if I want to feel the coarseness of the bark. Second, I can look at someone without being seen by him or her: I may be hidden, or look at someone behind his or her back, or I could be invisible like a ghost or the invisible man imagined by H. G. Wells (1987). On the other hand, if we shake hands, he or she touches my hand when I touch his or her hand. Unless the person is unconscious, my touch can hardly go unnoticed. When I touch and feel the skin of the other, the other feels the skin of my hand and, therefore, touches me. I also feel this slight pressure on my skin, I am touched as the other is touched. Touching, without technology, is two-way in the sense that when I touch someone, the other person touches me, I am touched as he/she is touched.

In the phenomenological and post-phenomenological traditions (from Husserl to Merleau-Ponty and Derrida and J.-L. Nancy), this reciprocity of touch, and the difference in this respect between touch and sight, have been the subject of numerous discussions. Though it would require a longer analysis to completely justify this point, this difference between touch and sight seems to be well-illustrated in the character of the invisible man who can see but cannot be seen by others. There is no such character in fiction (at least not with an aura of the character imagined by H. G. Wells) who could touch while being intangible. If, in fiction, ghosts cannot be touched, they cannot touch either. It is as if the invisible man had turned blind.

The same goes *mutatis mutandis* when I touch something instead of someone. For example, if I touch a tree, we usually accept that the tree does not feel my skin as I feel its bark. Nevertheless, when I put my hand on the bark, I feel its texture but I also feel a slight pressure on my skin, or I may cut myself or hurt my hand: in this sense, I am touched. I may also damage the bark, or leave a trace on it: in this sense, the tree is touched. Thus me touching something implies that I am touched by it in return and that it is touched by me. What is missing is only one term of the relation: the thing does not feel my skin.

To reiterate Wiener's words from a passage above, "our senses are being rearranged." Tactile technologies transform these two properties of touch.

They make it possible to touch at a distance both in space and in time. They break up the reciprocity of touch, in the sense that it becomes possible to touch something without being touched in return (as it is possible to see without being seen), or to be touched by something without touching it (like it is possible to be seen without seeing). In the case of the sex toys described above, the webcam model is being touched by the user without touching the user. Closer to the situation imagined by Wiener, museums have put in place devices that enable the user to virtually touch an artwork (usually an antique).[2] The user puts her hands in gloves that enable her to feel the texture of a Greek vase. She then touches the vase, without the vase being touched by her: although her hands may be dirty, she will not leave a stain on the vase. She also touches at a distance, both in space and in time: the vase may have been broken, but she will still be able to feel its texture in the gloves just as she will also be able to see the vase with VR goggles.

There are other tactile technologies (such as the system Teslatouch, or the HugShirt) which I cannot explore here but which also break up the reciprocity of touch and enable to the user to touch without being touched or to be touched without touching. The transformation of touch, this "one-way tele-contact" brings touch closer to sight. It is made possible by the technical treatment of perception as information. As already mentioned, information has the property that it may be coded and decoded. Sound, which consists of vibrations in the air, can be coded as an electric signal and, as such, transported in space on a telephone line, stored, and, in this sense, transported in time, before being decoded. During this process, it is possible to transform both the content but also the properties of the original experience. It is even possible to decode a message coming from one sense in a medium accessible to another sense so as to see warmth or touch sounds. As the example of the telephone clearly shows, technologies for coding and decoding perceptive information existed before *Cybernetics*. However, cybernetics made them explicit by conceptualizing perception as information. Wiener was clearly aware of its practical possibilities and worked on a "hearing glove" which would have translated sounds in the realm of touch (by a sort of tingling on the fingertips).

[2] See, for instance, the "Digital Touch Replicas" in Manchester Museum (https://www.museum.manchester.ac.uk/about/digitaltouchreplicas/) or the more recent exhibition "Touching Masterpieces" in the National Gallery of Prague (https://touchingmasterpieces.com).

Ideally, it would have enabled a deaf person to follow a conversation on their fingertips. It did not work as the tingles did not enable the user to discriminate precisely enough between different sounds.

In Wiener's yesterday's tomorrow, a growing fear of the outside and, in particular, a growing fear of touch led people to stay at home in front of screens, which then mediate their relationship to the world and to other people. Touch (and in fact sex) is transformed by technology, rearranged so as to mitigate people's fears: it loses its immediacy and its reciprocity. It becomes one-way tele-contact, a sense that is closer to sight.

However, if touch loses what makes it fearsome, it can then be freely engaged in, in both a literal and a figurative sense. In Wiener's world, the growing multiplicity of our "contacts" in a figurative sense (people we can get in "touch" with through the screen) is related to the fact that these "contacts" are no longer properly contacts but tele-presence and possibly one-way tele-presence. It is because human relations have lost something of their intimacy that they become more extensive. It seems Facebook champions those who have the most "friends." In Wiener's dystopia, this multiplication of contacts is required, precisely because it makes certain that each contact is shallow.

> Suppose now a man in one of the boxes begins to develop anti-social behavior. Such as not using services like education [...] or maybe narrowing himself down to an exclusive life *à deux* with another person and refusing to take part in social activities. That's very essential. A man's number of contacts will become his rating in the community.
>
> —You make me think that the wonderful verb is there already: to contact—it means actually anything. Now it will have to become its own self at last.
>
> —Sure. It stands for the denial of immediacy. We shall have a rating of 'contactiveness'. We shall have sermons about it. It'll be the standard of desirability. So you'd better be contactive. (de Santillana and Wiener 1952, page not numbered)

Contact now "stands for the denial of intimacy." It seems to sum up the Wiener-de Santillana view on future human relationships. The novel certainly bears resemblance to other dystopias such as Vonnegut (1952), *Player Piano*, Huxley (1932), *Brave New World*, or E. M. Forster (1909), "When the machine stops." But, though Wiener, or Wiener and de Santillana, do refer to Huxley, the "steel box" with its screens and tactile technology is not merely another version of Huxley's "feelies." In Wiener and de

Santillana's novel, the interesting point, which is related to the cybernetic conceptualization of perception as information, is that through technology our senses are not only extended but also recombined, reorganized, or "rearranged." Technology (both the imaginary technology of Wiener's Whodunit and our prototypal tactile technologies) makes it possible to touch at a distance, a "tele-contact," and a touch that is "one-way."

However, sight is also transformed through technology. A photo enables the viewer to see something that no longer exists, just as a tactile glove in a museum enables the visitor to touch a vase that has been broken. The distance inherent to sight is duplicated in space and in time, so we can see and touch at a distance in space, at a distance in time (or at least in the past), and see and touch without reciprocity.[3] The ability to sense, even tactile sense, no longer implicates the subject in the same intimacy with its object. The subject is in a way protected, or kept at a distance, by the technological apparatus. It seems to also be the case when "contact" is taken in a figurative sense. I can get "in touch" with my "contacts" without being myself available to them at this same moment: I send a text message, or an e-mail, or a picture on Instagram, and so on. This kind of contact operates at a distance. It is not reciprocal or at least it is desynchronized. It does not require co-presence, as a telephone conversation does. The "two-way" of this contact is separated just as it is separated in tactile technologies. With a HugShirt, I can hug without being hugged, or the opposite, just as I can send, or receive, a message without an answer.

It was in the middle of the nineteenth century that the word "contact" acquired its figurative meaning, when, with the telegraph, communication was paired with electricity and its speed greatly increased. The very touching of the telegraph key against its electrical "contact," made "contact" at the other hand of the line. Communication as contact seemed to imply that communication would become immediate (or almost immediate as a switch almost immediately turns on a light), and, in the end, reciprocal: the telegraph leads to the telephone. The signal takes almost no time—I converse with my correspondent, we interact in real time, just as our hands interact and adapt to each other when we shake hands. We are co-present though at a distance. When the telephone became mobile, we took this ability along with us—to interact at a distance but in co-presence, this two-way tele-presence, as if it were part of our body.

[3] Cassou-Noguès (2020) argues that new technologies produce a "synhaptic" sense that bears new properties (not exactly those of touch, nor of sight).

However, Wiener's Whodunit leads to the opposite view. In this yesterday's tomorrow, it is not that communication becomes contact but rather that contact is modeled on a communication that may be "one-way" and admit a time gap (a differ*a*nce as Derrida would put it). In the end, the paradigm on which communication is based, and contact as communication, would be that of the letter, or the text message. I can receive a message and delay my response. I can write without being written to, just I can see without being seen, or send a hug on the HugShirt, or send a vibration on a connected sex toy, without being touched myself. Our smartphones enable us to write as much as, or maybe more than, we talk. They also make possible emerging tactile technologies which interrupt the reciprocity of touch. Could it be that smartphones reversed a tendency toward closer interaction?

Stiegler (2010) puts emphasis on the operation of synchronization underlying cinema, but which takes its full impact with television. Looking at the screen, the consciousness of the subject is somehow synchronized to the flux of images. When cinema becomes television, this synchronization is extended to millions of people. The paradigm of television, in this perspective, is the final game of the soccer World Cup or the Super Bowl. Hundreds of millions, billions of people look at the same screen and have the same live experiences at the same time. Everyone (or half) of us will shout simultaneously when there is a goal or sigh with disappointment if the player misses. Or we used to. We no longer need to go to a pub to watch the game. We don't even need to sit at home in front of the television. We may be on the train and watch the games on our phone or, at home, on a pirate website. But, if we use our phones or our computers, there is a slight delay (a minute or two maybe) because of the buffering of the network. A passerby walking on the streets might hear the shouts of the fans coming from the open windows but they will be slightly desynchronized. Besides, these television events are more and more unusual. At least in Europe, at the time when Stiegler was writing, there were few television channels. Every night was like a Super Bowl. Everyone watched the same program, or the same two or three programs, because there were no others. The passerby (somewhat younger) would have heard the roars of laughter coming from open windows at the same time. It is no longer the case. We might watch the same series, but we can download the episodes at our own rhythm and watch them when we choose, or maybe on the train on our phone, or walking down the street, or driving a self-driving car. If the driver and the passerby meet, both of them looking at their phones, it is an accident.

Television is, from the start, a one-way communication. It is a polar mode of communication which goes from one transmitter to many receptors. But this example illustrates the way in which the development of technology has, in fact, reintroduced time gaps in our lives which seemed to, at least in Stiegler's analysis, have synchronized ever more closely: statistically, we were looking at television longer each day.

My point is that this desynchronization, as the breaking up of two-way communication into one-way communication, goes together with the technology of information. In principle, the message considered as information may be abstracted from its material support through coding, stored and delivered to the receptor without the receptor being in immediate relation with the transmitter. That is why I can touch without being touched or see the event after it has been recorded. The more elaborate the technology, the wider these gaps between the receptor and the transmitter may be, precisely because the potentialities of information technology may then be actualized. At the time when Stiegler was writing, we all had to watch the same show at the same moment because it was not possible for us to record it, or it was expensive, just as it is still expensive to record the textures of a Greek vase and play them back to a virtual visitor: it is unusual, or only through prototypal devices, that I can touch while being intangible to what I touch.

Though the recent COVID-19 lockdowns actually show that tens of millions of people in the same region may in fact remain at home for a long period of time, the steel boxes in which Wiener and de Santillana imprison their subject may seem rather far-fetched. Our own boxes may be invisible, consist only in time gaps and a semi-voluntary distancing. Or, at least, such boxes would make a more contemporary dystopia. We would be free to walk outside. We would not touch nor look at each other, nor speak because we would always have with us a small device that enables us to look, touch, speak or hear, far away and in a way that does not expose ourselves to the other: look without being seen, touch without being touched, exchange messages without engaging in conversation. This bubble would have its own timeframe. Like several passengers on a metro train watching the same video on Instagram but at different moments, we might laugh at the same joke but we would laugh when no one else laughs, and the joke would already have been made a few hours ago.

In the introduction of their groundbreaking book on mobile communication, J. Katz and A. Aakhus wrote:

> Indeed the power to converse instantaneously and comfortably across vast distances was once a power reserved in human imagination only for the greatest gods. [...] Our book is about how this godlike power is used by those who are far less than angels. [...] It is about how the internal psychological feeling of being accessible or having access changes social relationships. We want to understand how the "life feel" of the lived experience may be altered owing to the availability of this technology. (Katz and Aakhus 2002, xxi)

This chapter focuses on the difference between conversation, which is two-way and requires co-presence, and being accessible to someone or in "contact" with someone, which may be "one-way" and de-synchronized: there may be a time gap, and an indefinite time gap, between my contacting my correspondent and their answer. Touch and, in this sense, contact, was a two-way relationship, but the conceptualization of perception as information made it possible to imagine touch as a one-way relationship. The power to converse over distance, tele-presence, may have been reserved in our imagination to godlike creatures but the capacity to touch without being touched, without being implicated in the relationship, seems to have remained beyond imagination: in fairy tales, or science fiction—sad ghosts and mad scientists lost their sense of touch when they become intangible. They could not touch without being tangible, they could not feel without being felt. Now how will our engagement with future technology evolve? It is not for a philosopher to say but there seems to be two possibilities: either reciprocity, conversation, and two-way tele-presence, or one-way tele-contact, and observing the outside only through the invisible box of a protective technology.

Acknowledgments I wish to thank warmly the staff of the MIT library, and especially Nora Murphy, for their help during my visits.

References

Cassou-Noguès, Pierre. 2020. Synhaptic Sensibility. In *Affective Transformations. Politics. Algorithms. Media*, ed. Bernd Bösel and Serjoscha Wiemer. Berlin: Meson Press.

Dubarles, Dominique (père). 1948. Vers la machine à gouverner. *Le Monde*, December 28, 1948.

Forster, Edward M. 1909. The Machine Stops. In *The Eternal Moment and Other Stories*. London: Sigwick.

Huxley, Aldous. 1932. *Brave New World*. London: Chatto and Windus.

Katz, James E., and Mark A. Aakhus. 2002. *Perpetual Contact: Mobile Communication, Private Talk, Public Performance*. Cambridge, UK: Cambridge University Press.

de Santillana, Giorgio, and Norbert Wiener. 1952. Wiener's Whodunit. In *Giorgio de Santillana's Papers*. Cambridge, MA: Massachusetts Institute of Technology, Distinctive Collections.

Sargeant, Joseph. 1970. *Colossus*. Universal Pictures.

Stiegler, Bernard. 2010. *Technics and Time 3. Cinematic Time and the Question of Malaise* (Trans. Stephen Barker). Stanford: Stanford University Press.

Vonnegut, Kurt. 1952. *Player Piano*. New York: Scribner.

Wells, Herbert G. 1897. *The Invisible Man*. London: Pearson.

Wiener, Norbert. 1948. *Cybernetics: Or Control and Communication in the Animal and the Machine*. Paris: Hermann.

———. 1950. *The Human Use of Human Beings*. Boston, MA: Houghton Mifflin.

———. 1952. N. Wiener to H. English. Charles Scribner's Sons. In *Norbert Wiener's Papers*. Cambridge, MA: Massachusetts Institute of Technology, Distinctive Collections.

———. 1954. *The Human Use of Human Beings* (2nd edition revised). Boston, MA: Houghton Mifflin.

Future Shock Or Future Chic?: Human Orientation to the Future(s) in the Context of Technological Proliferation

Petra Aczél

> We offer our children courses in history; why not also make a course in »Future« a prerequisite for every student, a course in which the possibilities and probabilities of the future are systematically explored, exactly as we now explore the social system of the Romans or the rise of the feudal manor? (Toffler 1965, 114)

It Is Never Too Late

"I realized that it is never too early to think about the future"—wrote one of my students anonymously on the evaluation sheet answering what their takeaway was from my university course titled Future Skills. I had launched this program for the first time that semester, so this statement—the wording of which is abundant with time-related meanings (never, early,

P. Aczél (✉)
Corvinus University of Budapest, Budapest, Hungary
e-mail: petra.aczel@uni-corvinus.hu

J. Katz et al. (eds.), *Perceiving the Future through New Communication Technologies*,
https://doi.org/10.1007/978-3-030-84883-5_12

future)—made me realize how important it is to name and make future skills explicit as such. Because of the narrative and experience of constant change around us, future has indeed come into fashion. The topic of it is prevalent in our everyday life, in our discussions and plans, be they individual or social. In fact, our 'future-habit' is not so recent. In 2011, Michel and his colleagues browsed through a vast amount of written texts, that is, 4% of books printed in English between 1800 and 2000 using the method of computational lexicology to recognize changing cultural trends. They found that with the progress of time the texts were less and less about the past and more and more about the present and the future. The analysis of the periods between 1840–1880 and 1880–1920 showed that the time of accepting novelties halved as the new became a part of culture (Michel et al. 2011). Future has penetrated the present via rapid change and technologies with unprecedented capacity. Progression, strategic planning, foresighting have become operations we can reach our future(s) by and prepare ourselves not only to cope with but also to live with what is ahead of us. There is a growing body of professional and academic literature available for the modern businessperson, policy-maker, or scholar if techniques of orienting to or proofing the future are needed.

However, as Juvenal put in Satires almost 2000 years ago, "*et genus humanum damnat caligo futuri*," that is, we often feel we are to "be doomed to darkness about the future" (Juvenal 2004, 555). Proverbial wisdom in almost all languages alerts us to better withdraw from struggling to find out the secrets the future holds and to keep ourselves to what is knowable—otherwise Gods or the Devil will laugh and we will prove to be foolish. Even after two millennia, two or three industrial revolutions, the advents of the connected knowledge society, the Big Data era, and a new form of intelligence coming to existence, we are still startled by the black swans (Taleb 2007) appearing, by those lowly, predictable, and largely impactful events that remain puzzles for even the smartest ones. Our global effort to rationalize what is to come, to manage present and future changes, almost excludes the impossible, though it may be the driveway to a/the future. The cause for this may be our unnerving quest for '*what is in our future for us*' and not for '*who we are for our future*.'

Future in general is thus not my topic. I would rather focus on our technology-entailed future thinking and conscience that can/should orient us ahead. The essayistic insight I endeavor to provide shall utilize ways of critical and philosophical analysis in order to cast light upon how humans can or should think of themselves as their own futures. The following three sections will cover the topic of future orientation with a special attention to how future time is interpreted, to the anxiety with which we face our future with a focus on human-technology relations, and finally of human/technological intelligence as prospection. These discussions wish to underpin the argument that it is never too late to realize that the success in orienting ourselves to our futures lies in the consciousness of constant humanistic reframing.

Future Orientation

Future Time

The general concept of future is rooted in our socioculturally imprinted attitude to time. In western cultures, future is seen as a stage in a linear sequence. People of this view speak about time quantitatively by units like minute, hour, week, year to measure its coming and going. Linearity serves as a continuum of time within which future comes after the present and nothing follows future. This approach clearly suggests that the future is coming from and determined by the past and the present. Future is what is ahead, what is new, what is endless. Future in this sense is the ever-final station of progression, the time of the unknown, a new stage of existence and knowledge. Time itself is a continuous and repeated change from present to future, but never the other way round. By contrast, non-western mentalities do not break down time to abstract units and are more related to natural time with a qualitative approach. Their idea of time is cyclical and reflects the life of nature. In their view, present has the central focus from which everything emerges and where everything returns to (Passig 2004).

Modern philosophical discussions have been apparently converging into two main interpretations of temporalities, considering time as either subjective or objective, as actual becoming or the discontinuous emergence of events, as psychological or physical, as perceived or real. Nevertheless, the prevalent cognitive frame of time has been that of a flow, conceiving of future as a sequence of nows. The temporality that may override this duality is the 'horizontal' one brought about by Heidegger ([1927]1962), reinforced and argued for by Barrett (1968) and Nyíri (2011). According to this unique concept, "time is basically given as a temporal spread or field," and not as "a present Now, then another present Now, and another, etc. etc., but the whole spread (...) of future-present-past (where the hyphenization of these three terms is intended to signify the holding together of future-present-past as a unifying synthesis)" (Barrett 1968, 356–357). Future is then co-present with past and present within the horizontal stretch of time, being "that realm of the open out of which man temporalizes—that is, establishes himself meaningfully within time" (Barrett 1968, 358). This understanding of the future as the actively unifying tense of time is echoed in Ben-Baruch's practical notion of sociocultural time (Ben-Baruch 2000; cf. Passig 2004). He also contends the duality of the linear and circular time-concepts and argues that there is a third one in technological societies. It is conceptualized in terms of performances that are to be achieved (or failed) and revisited by their completion. This interpretation entails the imagination of the future as something that is not brought by the passage of moments but by the achievement of our goals. From this perspective, the past and the future depend on behaviors in the present, and the future penetrates into the present through acts, decisions, and discourses. This vision of the future is, therefore, a dynamic idea shaped by the awareness of the present (Scharmer 2009). Sociocultural time is a concept that tames the alienation humans may experience through their inability to influence the passing or recurring of time.

Orienting to the Future

The characteristic underlying this performance-based view of the future is provided by the nature of prospection the individual or culture has. Future orientation is the concept academics worked out (Trommsdorff 1983; Nurmi 1989; Seginer 2009) and used to describe and measure human motivation, planning, and evaluation to progress in time. It refers to the envisioning mindset (personal disposition, Zimbardo and Boyd 1999) of humans to conceive of and act toward the (short/long-term) future. 'Humans' are to be stressed here as founding scholars of future orientation argue that the ability to imagine the future, progressing toward the future, and the arrangement of future possibilities and selves; the intuitive, affective, and informational behavior that looks at the future are distinctive features of humans.

The concept of future orientation, however, has been applied to emerging, transformative information and communication technologies, and wider, more general policy-making by the practice of Future-Oriented Technology Analysis (FTA). It labels "a broad set of activities that facilitate decision-making and coordinated action, especially in science, technology and innovation policy-making" (Eerola and Miles 2011, 265). Moreover, FTA deals with fundamental, disruptive changes in societies enabling decision-makers to better understand the complex and systemic nature of great challenges and formulate joint responses to them. This definition correlates with what technology investors call 'future proofing.' It is a practice first adopted by the electronic industry at the end of the last century, within the context of data storage and computer electronic planning with the aim to minimize the risks of technological investments. By future proofing, the creation of new technologies that are unfit for improvement can be avoided, and the flexibility, adaptability, and resilience (robustness) of systems can be facilitated via informed strategic planning (Birchall and Tovstiga 2002).

In humans, similar to machines, future orientation is also dependent on external factors like the broader culture (local and global), social networks (physical and online), and societal-economic drives (globalization) that influence possible future selves and urge self-reflection, conformity, change, or preservation. Even the intention to know more about the future can be a marker of future orientation. One of its kind, Future Orientation Index (FOI, Preis et al. 2012) identified and explored future orientation in how often people search for information about the future or past by looking at Google searches about years in Arabic numbers. The FOI set off to show the extent to which Internet users worldwide (by country) in a given year are more interested in the available information from upcoming than previous years. That is, the 2010 FOI was based on the comparison between searches regarding the years 2011 and 2009. The FOI values can be compared with the given country's GDP, among other assets. So far, the measurements have revealed a strong correlation between the two: the bigger the per-capita GDP is, the greater the willingness to digitally look into the future. The apparent limitation of FOI is that it was methodologically unfit for cultures that are culturally different in terms of language and numeration and that are over the digital divide (Aczél 2018).

The development of future orientation is greatly contributed to by psychological, social, and communicative qualities such as safe attachment, positive self-image, education, and teaching, and the complex ways of interaction. It is without doubt that all these are affected by digital social media, the platforms (spaces), as well as the social dynamics (interactions) they offer and limit. Hence emerging media technologies have a profound impact on their own and on human future orientation, as well as on the ways the future is envisioned and planned. That is the reason why the nature (and interpretation) of our relations to the future and new technologies needs further elaboration.

Future Shock

"There are tranquil ages, which seem to contain that which will last forever, and which feel themselves to be final. And there are ages of change which see upheavals that, in extreme instance, appear to go to the roots of humanity itself"—as Jaspers (1953, 231) described the axial age. Whether ours, the beginning of the third millennium, is such an era has been debated for a while. All the same, axial ages are not centrifugal but rather gathering forces characterized by the common experience of change and the common intention to create a new understanding. The axial age centers around the prevalence of change—either occurring naturally or matured and brought by humans (or machines).

Alvin Toffler, back in 1970, stated that from the greatly accelerated rate of change driven by technological and scientific developments, a new time phenomenon, future shock, was born. He conceived of it as the disease of change arising from "the superimposition of a new culture on an old one" (1970, 16), asserting the experience of breakages in the historical-cultural continuum. In fact, contemporary perceptions of the rate of change can hardly be about deceleration. Discussing change within the positive frame of improving technologies and their dropping prices, Diamandis and Kotler (2020) state that the future is faster than we would think. They emphasize that "we live in a world that is global and exponential. Global, meaning if it happens on the other side of the planet, we hear about it seconds later (and our computers hear about it only milliseconds later). Exponential, meanwhile, refers to today's blitzkrieg speed of development. Forget about the difference between generations, currently mere months can bring a revolution" (2020, 11).[1]

[1] Certainly, for (or because of) fastness we will easily forget. Novelist Milan Kundera (1996) gives a fascinating, enlightening account of the unique relation between memory and speed in his book titled *Slowness*, exemplifying it with a walking man: "Consider this utterly commonplace situation: a man is walking down the street. At a certain moment, he tries to recall something, but the recollection escapes him. Automatically he slows down. Meanwhile, a person who wants to forget a disagreeable incident he has just lived through starts unconsciously to speed up his pace, as if he were trying to distance himself from a thing still too close to him in time" (1996, 34).

For this discussion we may consider future shock as the extent and quality of our (negative) orientation to change, the speed of change, and, thus, possible futures. It is deeply grounded in one of our rather rewarding, evolutionary capacities: fear.

Fear for/of the Future

Fear of the future is a true evolutionary gift of our species. If we tend to be cautious about the immediate adoption of (technological) novelties and hesitate to be thoroughly optimistic about predictions of job automatization or artificial intelligence, we elicit a behavioral response that has long served us efficiently. Having the extraordinary ability to imagine future events and—in parallel—relive past ones has given us the advantage to make sense of and dominate the world. Fear then can be a natural result of the mental scenario-building that is the unique characteristic of humans. It consists of hypersensitivity to detecting present and induces preparations for future threats. As Miloyan et al. (2016) suggest, heightened anticipation of negative future situations—which is characteristic of anxious individuals—contributes to more intensive preparation for and avoidance of dangers. Anxiety, as the researchers assumed, does not exclude the individual's capacity to imagine positive futures; it is rather about being biased toward potential threats to occur.

Getting rid of our fears for the future is not easy and is possibly not desirable. Nevertheless, learning to overcome and learning to manage these fears is of utmost importance. As recent findings express, by learning more and longer—that is, being more educated and curious—our openness to the future unfolds. If we take the example of workforce automatization and faster technology improvement that are originally and most widely labeled as threats to the workers of the present, we can notice that both global and local surveys consistently report the level of education, job satisfaction, and exposure to information about these matters as decisive factors in forming negative, neutral, or positive perceptions (IMF 2019; Gallup 2017; Eurobarometer 2017). People with higher job satisfaction, educational achievement, and more exposure to information are less pessimistic than less educated, less satisfied respondents. Considering the time span, these differences seem to dissolve and perceptions converge in the negative scenario. When people were asked to look 20 years further into the future, their expectations of being replaced by new technologies (automatization, artificial intelligence) were very similar notwithstanding their levels of education (Gallup 2017).

When it comes to desired future skills—with the scope of the maximum of 10 years ahead—research reports using trend analysis and interviewing methods (e.g., IFTF 2011 (2016); WEF 2016; Pearson-Nesta 2019; OECD 2019; Morgan 2020) assume that the competencies of curiosity (active listening and critical thinking), flexible coping (resilience), adaptive thinking (both computational and emphatic), and multidisciplinarity (joining fields of expertise in practice) will gain importance in the selection and training processes because they enhance learning and adaptation to change with an optimistic disposition. Jacob Morgan, in his recently published volume on the future leader, lays special emphasis on the demand for "technology teenagers" (2020, 241) for skills that are rooted in a deeper understanding and flexible, creative usage of technologies. To see more what this deeper understanding might require we now proceed to consider the relation between humans and (new) technology.

Fear/Understanding of Technologies

New forms of technologies, especially information and communications technologies, are challenges to relate to. The reason for this is the frame in which we view them. Briefly put, we either use the technologically determinist aspect which tells that technology causes changes in culture and society. Or we see new (communication) technologies as effects of ongoing changes in culture and society through the social constructivist approach. These two paradigms manifest the cause-versus-consequence approach to what/how we presently are and will be in relation to our technological instruments: whether we would be ruled by them or be rulers of them. Nevertheless, in case of future technologies, the immature presence of which is already sensed, we would rather make a different categorization of approaches to human-technology relations.

The first is the *combative approach*. It states that humans are fighting with new technologies and can easily fail in this zero-sum game if they cannot realize the situation they are in and the unique characteristics by which they can take back their power over their own existence. Movies depicting dystopias in popular culture such as the *Minority Report* (2002), *Black Mirror* series (2011–2019), or *The Circle* (2017) heavily enforce this attitude. The combative view is about dominance and oppression, critically arguing for the semantic frame of fight. One of the most recent examples among many—clearly reflecting Harari's groundbreaking philosophical treatise of the data age, *Homo Deus* (Harari 2016)—is Douglas Rushkoff's. His book titled *Team Human* (2019) is an apologia of human autonomy and is meant to serve as an awakening to the reality of people losing this autonomy to technology. As he discerns, "Our most advanced technologies are not enhancing our connectivity, but thwarting it. They are replacing and devaluing our humanity, and—in many different ways—undermining our respect for one another and ourselves" (2019, 6). Continuing this logic, he stresses the present incapacity to reject the impact of technologies by declaring that it is "hard for human beings to oppose the dominance of digital technology when we are becoming so highly digital ourselves. Whether by fetish or mere habit, we begin acting in ways that accommodate or imitate our machines, remaking our world and, eventually, ourselves in their image" (2019, 59). The way out, he argues, is teaming up with humans and realizing the rewards we have within and for ourselves.

We can name the second approach as the *pragmatic-persuasive* one. In this view, technologies become 'human-centered,' user-friendly, serving the needs of human everyday practices and aesthetics. It is the philosophy behind technology design that should attract users to interact, participate, and immerse themselves, thus assisting and inviting them to enjoy even meaningless interfaces and activities. An instance of this approach is captology. Captology is the critical approach to study designed persuasive effects of human-computer (Internet) interactions and to investigate "how people are motivated or persuaded when interacting *with* computing products rather than *through* them" (Fogg 2003, 16). Fogg's argument is that computing products and software applications would be more persuasive and motivational by being designed to be more supportive and empathetic with human psyche. Technologies can and should be persuasive "by allowing people to explore cause-and-effect relationships, providing people with vicarious experiences that motivates, helping people to rehearse a behavior" (Fogg 2003, 62). In this way, technologies serve humans through 'captivating' them.

The third approach gives a new dimension to the interpretation of human-technology relations. It is the ethnology of such relations that can provide deeper sense-making. Therefore, I call this view the *sense-making approach*. Its significance lies in the capacity and complexity of explanatory force. The model for this is the Apparatgeist theory developed by Katz and Aakhus (2002). The Apparatgeist theme introduces a novel way of looking at how humans invest their technologies with meaning. Focusing mainly on communication technologies, Katz and Aakhus gave an original account of people's thinking about their technologies, making them devices with spirit. Bringing sociocultural contexts into consideration, the Apparatgeist theory first "helps us understand the functional uses of technological change and their social implications. Second, the Apparatgeist lens can explain why a technology that has certain performance-characteristics will be embraced by one group and rejected by another. (…) Third, the theory allows us to gain insight into the social meaning that people assign to the technologies which populate their social environment. Fourth, it enables a relative judging of technical versus social functions of a communication device. Finally, the lens can yield an evaluative schematic depiction of a device's social location" (Katz 2003, 314). While the combative approach assumes that humans and technologies are or can be *against* each other, the pragmatic-persuasive suggests that technologies are *for* humans, the sense-making approach states that this is a relationship best characterized by the preposition *with*. The latter disposition is what is echoed in reports about desired future readiness (see above) within the sets of computational thinking, complex problem-solving, social intelligence, and media skills.

To reconcile the fear for the future and to cultivate a complex, balanced adaptation to technologies, we shall need to discover and become more aware of how much our intelligence is futured by origin.

Future Intelligence

A new intelligence is being born in our age. Artificial as it is called, we all sense that this time it is not a new commodity, serving between the commands of 'on and off,' but a form of existence that is coming into being on Earth. Predictions (e.g., Kurzweil 2005) of its full-bloom advent provide us with dates strikingly close to our present. As publicists widely argue, technology experts, as well as everyday people, have well-founded worries about artificial intelligence possibly being a human-overriding superintelligence, a job killer, and a support of bad people and aims. Behind these claims lurks the idea that human intelligence is copied and enhanced in the artificial one which is thus going to be the future continuance of our mental capacities. Artificial intelligence contrary to the human one will be able to limitlessly adapt to future challenges, while human intelligence will still cope with the past and present experiences.

Nevertheless, it is human intelligence that is truly wired for the future. More than a century has passed by since Alfred Binet came up with the idea that smartness is quantifiable by logical-verbal tests. By his definition and measurement (IQ) of intelligence, schools were given the opportunity to scale and level, that is, standardize cleverness upon the basis of testing (exclusively) rational and conceptual skills. Interestingly enough, even though this conception was dominantly rooted in the presumption of the significance mathematical and verbal competencies play in being smart, all the measuring tasks and items of IQ tests are asking the respondents about the future, about what the next element, number, or step should be in a sequence, in a system, in a logical progression. When Howard Gardner (1993) reformed the theory of human intelligence by offering nine intelligences instead of a monolith of a single one, he emphasized that an intelligence is a problem-solving skill that "allows one to approach a situation in which a goal is to be obtained and to locate the appropriate route to that goal" (Gardner 1993, 6). All the same, he insisted that intelligence is a computational capacity activated and triggered by kinds of internal and external information. That is what was partly refuted in Martin Seligman and his colleagues' groundbreaking new approach introduced in 2016. They declared that after centuries of psychological thinking about humankind as trapped in past memories and present stimuli, we should recognize our real identity, which is of the *Homo Prospectus*.

Forerunner of Seligman's new perspective of human intelligence was Jeff Hawkins (2004) who—with Sandra Blakeslee—realized the deficit behind formulating artificial intelligence. This deficit is the lack of a proper definition of human intelligence. They revisited the problem of machines being called intelligent abductively—based on a single test without a complex understanding (e.g., the Turing Test: a computer fooling an interrogator into thinking that it is a person). They refuted the standpoint of AI proponents who presume that there are strong similarities between computation and human thinking, arguing that "the most impressive feats of human intelligence clearly involve the manipulation of abstract symbols—and that's what computers do too" (2004, 8). Hawkins and Blakeslee asserted that "Computers and brains are built on completely different principles. One is programmed, one is self-learning. One has to be perfect to work at all, one is naturally flexible and tolerant of failures. One has a central processor, one has no centralized control. The list of differences goes on and on" (2004, 8). Their proposal was that the essence of human intelligence is not the computing but the predictive ability. As he stressed,

"I am arguing a much stronger proposition. Prediction is not just one of the things your brain does. It is the *primary function* of the neocortex, and the foundation of intelligence. The cortex is an organ of prediction. If we want to understand what intelligence is, what creativity is, how your brain works, and how to build intelligent machines, we must understand the nature of these predictions and how the cortex makes them. Even behavior is best understood as a by-product of prediction."

Seligman et al. (2016) went even further, providing academia with a new aspect to view humans from: "What if perception is less about the registration of what is present, than about generating a reliable hallucination of what to expect? What if memory is not a file drawer of photographs, but a changing collection of possibilities? (…) What if treating clinical disorders is less about trying to resolve past conflicts, than about changing the way an individual faces the future?"—they ask, thought-provokingly, just to offer a resolution in defining humans in terms of their most substantial mental and affective operation: prospection. From *Homo Sapiens* their work guides us to recognize the *Homo Prospectus*, a fascinating mind-wanderer, generally attuned for the future. Their ways of future-oriented thinking and being are rooted in reality—social and psychical—and are based on common, culture-framing imaginations/concepts about the future. Humans are thus primarily not clever (sapiens), but, more importantly, forward-looking beings who use their affections, perceptions, and intuitions to plan and be prepared. By this, Seligman rebuts the exclusivity of the dual-process models of the human mind (the duality of the deliberative and intuitive thinking, e.g., Kahneman, 2011) and invites us to a broader understanding of how futured the human mind and psyche are. The idea of the *Homo Prospectus* is provided a solid basis by the horizontal time-concept discussed above. As Barrett argues with reference to Heidegger, our life as a whole is a project "in the sense that we are perpetually thrown-ahead-of-ourselves-toward-the-future" (Barrett 1968, 362). Life, this future-spread project of ours, is what inherently entails the futured human intelligence.

It Is Never Too Early: In Lieu of an Epilogue

In conclusion to these new concepts and old, freshly fueled debates, we may, for a moment, relieve ourselves of the stress about the external, imposed power of new technologies and unknown scenarios that lie ahead. Instead, we may reconsider what human future orientation and intelligence is, and how deep prospection and future is wired into how we look at the world. The outcome of this contemplation can be a decrease in our fear for the future and the improvement of our consciousness about the future we already embody. The re-discoveries of our relation to the ever-evolving technologies should come right after that. Nevertheless, these investigations and recognitions may serve us best if they entail the overall impetus to realize that it is never too early to switch from future shock to 'future chic.'

References

Aczél, Petra. 2018. Social Futuring: A Discursive-Conceptual Framework. *Society and Economy* 40 (s1): 47–75. https://doi.org/10.1556/204.2018.40.s1.4.

Barrett, William. 1968. The Flow of Time. In *The Philosophy of Time*, ed. Richard M. Gale, 355–377. London: Macmillan Press.

Ben-Baruch, Ephraim. 2000. Sociocultural Time. *Mada 2000* 25: 16–21.

Birchall, David, and George Tovstiga. 2002. *Future Proofing – Strategy 3.10. Express.Exec.* Oxford: Capstone.

Diamandis, Peter H., and Steven Kotler. 2020. *The Future Is Faster Than You Think: How Converging Technologies Are Transforming Business, Industries, and Our Lives (Exponential Technology Series).* New York: Simon & Schuster.

Eerola, Annele, and Ian Miles. 2011. Methods and Tools Contributing to FTA: A Knowledge-Based Perspective. *Futures* 43 (3): 265–278. https://doi.org/10.1016/j.futures.2010.11.005.

Eurobarometer. 2017. Attitudes Towards the Impact of Digitisation and Automation on Daily Life. Accessed July 30, 2020. https://ec.europa.eu/digital-single-market/en/news/attitudes-towards-impact-digitisation-and-automation-daily-life.

Fogg, B.J. 2003. *Persuasive Technology. Using Computers to Change What We Think and Do.* New York, NJ: Morgan Kaufmann-Elsevier.

Gallup. 2017. Technology and the Future of Jobs. Accessed July 30, 2020. https://news.gallup.com/poll/210728/one-four-workers-say-technology-eliminate-job.aspx

Gardner, Howard. 1993. *Multiple Intelligences: New Horizons in Theory and Practice.* New York: Basic Books.

Harari, Yuval N. 2016. *Homo Deus: A Brief History of Tomorrow.* London: Penguin, Random House.

Hawkins, Jeff, and Sandra Blakeslee. 2004. *On Intelligence.* New York: Times Books.

Heidegger, Martin [1927] 1962. *Being and Time.* Trans. John Macquarrie and Edward Robinson. London: Blackwell

IFTF (Institute for the Future). 2011. (Revised in 2016). Future of Works Skills. Accessed July 30, 2020. https://www.iftf.org/futureskills/.

IMF. 2019. Automation, Skills and the Future of Work: What Do Workers Think? Working Paper. Accessed July 30, 2020. https://www.imf.org/en/Publications/WP/Issues/2019/12/20/Automation-Skills-and-the-Future-of-Work-What-do-Workers-Think-48791.

Jaspers, Karl. 1953. *The Origin and Goal of History*. London: Routledge.

Juvenal. 2004. Satire 6. In *Satires*. Loeb Classical Library: https://www.loebclassics.com/view/juvenal-satires/2004/pb_LCL091.287.xml?result=1&rskey=EYGSN7.

Kahneman, Daniel. 2011. *Thinking, Fast and Slow*. New York, NY: Farrar, Straus and Giroux.

Katz, James E. 2003. Bodies, Machines and Communication Contexts: What Is to Become of Us. In *Machines that Become Us*, ed. James E. Katz, 311–320. New Brunswick, NJ: Transaction Publishers.

Katz, James E., and Mark Aakhus. 2002. *Perpetual Contact: Personal Communication, Private Talk, Public Performance*. Cambridge: Cambridge University Press.

Kundera, Milan. 1996. *Slowness*. Translated by Linda Asher. New York: HarperCollins.

Kurzweil, Ray. 2005. *The Singularity Is Near: When Humans Transcend Biology*. New York: Viking.

Michel, Jean-Baptiste, Yuan K. Shen, Aviva P. Aiden, Adrian Veres, Matthew K. Gray, The Google Books Team, Joseph P. Pickett, Dale Hoiberg, Dan Clancy, Peter Norvig, Jon Orwant, Steven Pinker, Martin Nowak, and Erez L. Aiden. 2011. Quantitative Analysis of Culture Using Millions of Digitized Books. *Science* 331 (6014): 176–182. https://doi.org/10.1126/science.1199644.

Miloyan, Beyon, Adam Bulley, and Thomas Suddendorf. 2016. Episodic Forsight and Anxiety: Proximate and Ultimate Perspectives. *British Journal of Clinical Psychology* 55: 4–22. https://doi.org/10.1111/bjc.12080.

Morgan, Jacob. 2020. *The Future Leader: 9 Skills and Mindsets to Succeed in the Next Decade*. Hoboken, NJ: Wiley.

Nurmi, Jari-Erik. 1989. Development of Orientation to the Future During Early Adolescence: A Four-Year Longitudinal Study and Two Cross-Sectional Comparisons. *International Journal of Psychology* 24 (2): 195–214. https://doi.org/10.1080/00207594.1989.10600042.

Nyíri, Kristóf. 2011. A konzervatív időnézet [The Conservative View of Time]. *Századvég* 60 (2011/2): 107–120.

OECD. 2019. OECD Skills Strategy. Skills to Shape a Better Future. Accessed July 30, 2020. https://www.oecd.org/skills/oecd-skills-strategy-2019-9789264313835-en.htm.

Passig, Dan. 2004. Future-Time-Span as a Cognitive Skill in Future Studies. *Futures. Research Quarterly* 2004 (Winter): 27–47.

Pearson-Nesta. 2019. The Future of Skills. Employment in 2030. Accessed July 30, 2020. https://futureskills.pearson.com/research/assets/pdfs/media-pack.pdf.

Preis, Tobias, Helen S. Moat, Eugene H. Stanley, and Steven R. Bishop. 2012. Quantifying the Advantage of Looking Forward. *Scientific Reports 2*. Article Number: 350. https://www.nature.com/articles/srep00350.

Rushkoff, Douglas. 2019. *Team Human*. New York: W.W. Norton Company.

Scharmer, Otto C. 2009. *Theory U: Leading from the Future as it Emerges*. Oakland, CA: Berrett-Koehler Publisher.

Seginer, Rachel. 2009. *Future Orientation: Developmental and Ecological Perspectives*. New York, NY: Springer.

Seligman, Martin E.P., Peter Railton, Roy F. Baumeister, and Chandra Sripada. 2016. *Homo Prospectus*. New York, NY: Oxford University Press.

Taleb, Nassim N. 2007. *The Black Swan: The Impact of the Highly Improbable*. New York: Random House.

Toffler, Alvin. 1965. The Future as a Way of Life. *Horizon Magazine* 7 (3): 108–116.

———. 1970. *Future Shock*. New York: Random House.

Trommsdorff, Gisela. 1983. Future Orientation and Socialization. *International Journal of Psychology* 18 (1–4): 381–406. https://doi.org/10.1080/00207598308247489.

WEF (World Economic Forum). 2016 (Ongoing). The Future of Jobs. Accessed July 30, 2020. http://www3.weforum.org/docs/WEF_Future_of_Jobs.pdf.

Zimbardo, Philip G., and John Boyd. 1999. Putting Time in Perspective: A Valid, Reliable Individual Differences Metric. *Journal of Personality and Social Psychology* 77: 1271–1288. https://doi.org/10.1037/0022-3514.77.6.1271.

Voicing the Future: Folk Epistemic Understandings of Smart and Datafied Lives

Pauline Cheong and Karen Mossberger

Intensifying "datafication"—the treatment of everything as a quantifiable indicator of an underlying quality (Cukier and Mayer-Schoenberger 2013)—is an endemic aspect of the Internet of Things (IoT) and artificial intelligence (AI) networks, and as such poses a crucial issue not only for the future of human work and well-being, but for the intrinsic lived experience as well. Although not novel, this issue has historically been downplayed as policy discussions focused on change and disruption in economies where experts have projected that professional skills, even cognitive and non-routine occupational tasks, are deemed to be at risk for displacement by new AI technologies (e.g., Brynjolfsson and McAfee 2014; Susskind

P. Cheong (✉)
Hugh Downs School of Human Communication, Arizona State University, Tempe, AZ, USA
e-mail: Pauline.cheong@asu.edu

K. Mossberger
School of Public Affairs and Center on Technology, Data and Society, Arizona State University, Tempe, AZ, USA
e-mail: karen.mossberger@asu.edu

J. Katz et al. (eds.), *Perceiving the Future through New Communication Technologies*,
https://doi.org/10.1007/978-3-030-84883-5_13

and Susskind 2015). As the so-called fourth industrial revolution unfolds, namely, the long-awaited computer-supported, algorithmically guided structure of all aspects of society, report after report underscores how digitalization and automation in everyday life and the workplace will accord great value on qualities and skills like complex problem-solving and cognitive flexibility (Leopold et al. 2016).

At the same time, the growing intricacy of the connected web of devices, sensors and applications that involve big data and computational processes raise questions about how people will reason and interact within new socio-technical systems in their smart and datafied lives (de Boer et al. 2019). Though some commentators see society-wide benefits to these systems (see Katz, Schiepers and Floyd, this volume), and indeed there undoubtedly are some, most media and academic commentators are quite pessimistic (also with justification) as they foresee growing surveillance and inequalities of learning, knowledge and power, as well as widening digital divides (e.g., Lutz 2019; Couldry and Yu 2013; van Deursen and Mossberger 2018).

The future, of course, is inherently unknowable, but we all have a hand in shaping it, whether through action or inaction. Moreover, public opinion is an important dimension of forging public policy for technology change in practically every modern society. Lay understandings or non-expert understanding based on personal experiences of user knowledge and skills can shed light on their expectations and adaptations to IoT developments or even system designs. In particular, how laypersons or nonprofessionals voice identify future skills and capacities to function under increasing hypoconnectivity allow stakeholders and policy makers to better design and harness technology for the common good (Jennings 2011).

Thus, our chapter examines folk theories of anticipated future skills and capacities in an era of the Internet of Things where datafication is increasingly valued in domains of everyday life, including domestic and occupational spheres as well as physical domains, across growing "smart" campuses, neighborhoods and cities. Drawing on our large multi-year, multimethod study on AI, IoT and smart society, we discuss in-depth interviews with 78 laypersons, who are working professionals and college students who are nonprofessionals in IoT and AI, as to their current and desired skills and capacities. But first, we discuss the significance of folk understandings, particularly as they pertain to contemporary hyperconnectivity of everyday life, and why they are relevant to the subject at hand.

Folk Understandings of the Internet of Things Futures

In the face of proliferating datafication and increasing demands for peoples' interaction with complex socio-technical systems, lay understandings about technological development and change should be valued as an important yet understudied aspect of human-machine interaction (Devito et al. 2018). By drawing on the notion of folk theory, we have a way to reflect how people reason about emerging IoT and AI systems, in particular their orientation toward their future capacities and skills. This helps with both input, that is, designing systems, and output, that is, how to make systems work better for users and society.

In contrast to distinct mental representations and models of specific representations of human-computer interactions, often used in academic social scientific and management theories, folk theories refer to peoples' generic knowledge and intuitive explanation about a system that guides their thoughts and behaviors within that system (Gelman and Legare 2011). Among ways of understanding and predicting the natural and social world, folk theories reflect that informal knowledge arises and circulates among the public outside of formal scientific instruction or principles (Keil 2010). Lay beliefs and attitudes are constructed from multiple sources, including popular media and users' particular experiences to explain and intervene in the world. As such, as French and Hancock (2017) point out, folk theories about digital media platforms can "account for how popular discussions, such as news coverage, can influence a person's beliefs" about social media like Facebook and Twitter, and we argue, by extension, to AI and IoT.

Employing the notion of folk theory is valuable in the context of this book in that it allows us to recognize how laypersons' understanding of the profound and evolving hyperconnectivity is often imprecise; partially obscured by the black box of algorithmic operations (Pasquale 2015). Folk understandings of IoT may also reflect the daily realities of interacting in densely mediated societies, where the use of smart devices and applications are habituated and omnipresent (Nascimento et al. 2018), and thus not in personal cognitive foregrounds. In addition, rather than assuming incomplete or faulty perceptions about new media, this approach recognizes how laypersons "regularly develop folk themes to make their way through the world" (French and Hancock 2017). In this way, employing a folk theory lens helps us identify how the public reacts to novel technology with new, but not necessarily systematically ordered, expectations that provide orientation for their future action. This, of course, can have spillover effects on public policy as well as the viability of commercial initiatives.

Specifically, in the context of this book's theme of engaging with the idea of future communication technology, we are interested here in deploying folk theory to discuss future societal perceptions of IoT in a globalizing world, "which may play a constitutive role in the future of humanity," "related to public preference about social policies" (Kashima et al. 2011, 697). Social scientists typically divine emerging futures concerning technological change by relying on the Delphi methodology, an expert consensus-based approach for forecasting that draws upon input from key stakeholders' responses to a series of questionnaires (Rowe and Wright 2011). Yet the exploration of elite scenarios, particularly regarding human-machine communication developments, tends to obviate the concrete realities of new technology emergence amid broader socio-cultural contexts (Hepp 2020) and the desirability of these technologies among different people groups.

Indeed, Dourish and Bell (2011) point to how expert pronouncements of "calm technology," facilitating smooth interconnected future scenarios for society, are related to "proximate future" visions of uniformly understood services and well-functioning infrastructures for all. They advocate for ways to envision "messy" digital imaginaries that encompass inventive lay user engagement and their evolving perceptions and conversations within government and culturally shared narratives, including how notions of privacy are constituted and managed. Laypersons' interaction with IoT may be filled with multiple challenges that give rise to perceived tensions and paradoxes. As peoples' everyday relationships with data are "riddled with anxieties or small niggles or tricky trade-offs," they approach the future with forms of hope as well as stressful uncertainties (Pink et al. 2018). Moreover, folk knowledge regarding anticipatory modes of digital data use and capacities can reflect clusters of common ideas, in conjunction with respondents' socio-demographics and lifestage (Kwasny et al. 2008). In the next sections, we discuss key emergent themes of anticipatory capacities and skills explored under the auspices of our larger multiyear and multimethod IoT study.

Hearing Voices About the Future

As part of our larger interdisciplinary effort to examine user perspectives, experiences and outcomes associated with AI and IoT, we examined semi-structured interviews conducted in English in the Southwestern United States with Internet users in 2019. We spoke with 52 working professionals and 26 college students (42 males and 36 females). We spoke to each person for about 45 minutes as to their use of digital devices and connections with IoT, perceptions of datafication, privacy and security, and social and technical engagement with IoT. Of particular relevance to the present topic, we will focus on our discussions of them concerning, "What skills or capacities do you have/wish that you could have in order to live well in the future of IoT?"

A thematic analysis of the interviews was conducted using constant comparative methodology involving a grounded theory approach where a line-by-line analysis helped generate initial categories and suggest relationships among categories (Strauss and Corbin 1998). Working from fully transcribed interviews, the data were classified into emergent categories based on what kinds of capacities or skills were presented by interviewees; the text and themes were then carefully analyzed by both authors to draw conclusions (Charmez 2006; Lindlof and Taylor 2002). Based on this systematic procedure, we came up with the following themes.

Capacity to Be Vigilant and Open-Minded

To live well in the future, about half of our interviewees raised the importance of practicing constant vigilance about new technology development and having the capacity to be open-minded and adaptable to change. Their responses reflected the emerging opportunities that come with IoT developments, but were also accompanied by a concern about keeping up so as not to miss opportunities. For example, interviewees said:

> Because I do feel like everything's getting more technological. So, you just really have to know how to use those things I guess, and I would really need to understand at least some basic knowledge of how to use everything. How to do everything, which I feel like I have now, but just make sure that I keep keeping up with that, because I feel like things are constantly progressing.
>
> Well, I definitely don't want to kind of stay behind because I know that technology is always changing and I feel like if it comes to a point where I can't use the new phones and stuff like that, that would be bad. But, I feel

like if I keep up-to-date even if I think it's a fad or whatever, I should be okay for the future.

Some interviewees highlighted the need for an ability to "be watchful" amid the accelerated tempo of smart living where dramatic socio-technical innovations appear to be unfolding at unprecedented speeds. Concerning the need to be attentive to novel technologies to stay ahead, one 25-year-old male consultant said:

> I think you have to constantly be checking in on what's new. I mean, virtual reality came out, and it went from being crap to within a year and a half having really good stuff out there. As soon as something gets popular and gains traction, people go from having one company that dumps a couple million dollars into it to seeing that people are interested in dumping $300 million into it. So, as soon as these ideas start getting popularized, people get crazy about them, and so I think you have to constantly stay up to date. So, I'm on tech websites fairly frequently to see what's new, like new generators and new methods of building computers and all sorts of things.

Related to the above point, interviewees shared that as their world is quickly evolving, they require a capacity for mental agility in order to embrace constant change. A 23-year-old male high school teacher said, "I suppose the first one would have to be being adaptable. Being able to quickly learn how to use a new interface as well as being cognizant of not only the benefits but also the risks of technology integration and what incorporating more technology into your life could mean for you." A 28-year-old male interviewee in the finance industry said, "I think just knowledge as far as just keeping up with what's going on and being open to trying new stuff … Just stay hip. Watch tech channels. Keep an open mind. Accept new technology. New things. And ask your kid."

This mindset of being open to new ways and learning is perceived to be an attribute of the younger generations. Several college student interviewees shared that their future-oriented outlook was associated with their age group. Student interviewees voiced how it is important to eschew the established practices of their elders as they value exposure to new ideas and embrace a flexible approach to the future. Two male students in their early 20s said:

> I think an open mind to try new things. You have to be open to experimenting with new forms of technology like I mean I know my grandma still has a typewriter, and it's based on not wanting to change a lot. If you're unwill-

> ing to change, you know the technology of today will be for you, the technology forever versus there might be something that can get the job done twice as well and less effort.
>
> I think you have to learn how to learn and adapt because technology's improving really fast and I think you should—I mean as you get older it's hard to learn new things, but I think it would be good if you know how to use all of the technology that's in the mass market.

Interestingly, the perception of a similar cohort effect was voiced by older working professionals as they compared themselves to their parents. One male 50-year-old professor said:

> I think the biggest skill is just not being afraid to keep up. Because I have a mother who's afraid to keep up. She doesn't—she's got a regular old phone and she doesn't like doing all the other stuff and it's like don't be—this is—in theory this is not going to hurt me in a lot of ways. I mean we've seen batteries explode and all that but as far as the technology contained within these don't be afraid of it as we get older, as we move along.

Continuous Updating of Knowledge and Skills

Beyond being adaptable, several interviewees stressed the importance of continuously updating of their skills and "being able to quickly learn how to use a new interface." Part of this process is gaining knowledge of and familiarity with new applications, including artificial intelligence. They said:

> I think for me, being able to just have a better understanding of the tools, like the organizational tools. Certain apps that can help with whether it's mental health, whether it's with physical health, I think, yeah, the integration.
>
> And there are a lot of other ways to use devices and things like that that I never ventured into. So, I would probably just explore it a lot more.

The swift acquisition of new knowledge was prized for both a general outlook as well as an occupational need. Dynamic learning solutions were traced to formal (back to school), non-formal ("take a class or something to learn"), and informal channels ("actually using it and seeing how other people use it"). Responses reflecting future learning intentions and the adaptive management of novel technologies were:

> I think eventually, we may have to do classes. Like in high school, for example, I did a typing class and before that they did a typewriter class, so I think

each year we'll have to take more advanced classes to know the background of things and to use it.

When the next thing comes up, then I will respond to it. And I'm usually the first to buy it. So whatever knowledge is required, I will get it when it comes out. But in general, I don't know that I need any new knowledge skills. I guess again, I just have to say that I will respond—when it happens, I will respond. And I'm always enthusiastic about new technologies.

Because I've been in the tech space my whole life, I feel like I'm able to grasp and pick up on stuff pretty quick. So, I find generally it's like, as I need to encounter something because maybe my job now requires this new software app or this new piece of hardware or something, then I'll go learn about it. As something comes along and it comes into my sphere of awareness and need, at that point, then I will learn about it and develop it.

Skills as Unknown or Unnecessary

As illustrated above, many interviewees discussed the need for an appropriate general attitude toward technology. This included the willingness to embrace innovations, to adapt and to learn. By contrast, there was vagueness about what specific skills might be needed. A common response was that it was hard to predict what skills are needed with evolving technologies.

In opposition, another thread was that there was a "deskilling" process. Indeed, some interviewees argued that IoT already has reduced the need for skills, especially those required to operate devices or applications. A 27-year-old male engineer said, "Oh—I don't think I need to have specific skills just because I think all this stuff is around making it so user intuitive … . But I think with me at least, let's say for the next 10 to 15 years, I would have to not learn something very new, that's brand new." Another 31-year-old male financial advisor said, "What kind of skills? I have to talk to the smart devices. So, the skills? They have designed the device to make it easy for everybody, even the kids—three, four-year-old kids, they know how to play the games on iPad, which I don't think I could do it when I was three, four years old. So, they try to make it more convenient for people to use, which is awesome."

Data Management and Protection Skills

Many interviewees, however, foresaw the need for greater knowledge about how data are being used and the implications for the privacy of their information. One interviewee mentioned hacking as a security concern, but 15 others discussed data and privacy in more general terms, making this the dominant category for specific skills. A 36-year-old male engineer said:

> To just be more aware of what the devices are collecting about you and how it's being shared and what it is being used for. So, I think it's important for people to actually try to understand how these things work.

Or, as another interviewee put it more bluntly, "I think I need knowledge of how to avoid being manipulated and leveraged." The need for transparency on the part of technology firms was also mentioned, an attribute that would help individuals make informed choices. For example, one 19-year-old female student interviewee said companies should be "open and direct":

> 'Hey, this is where your data's going and this is what we're gonna do with it and here's why'. Kind of giving them a purpose and a statement of like, 'I'm gonna educate you and I'm gonna show you why this is beneficial.'

However, the responsibility for gaining such knowledge was sometimes placed on individual users, in self-defense. One 40-year-old female church staff worker said, "…definitely know how to protect your information and your privacy a bit more. Definitely not rely as much on companies to store your information or access your location, simply because it can come back and haunt you at the end of the day."

The privacy concerns also indicated feelings of dependence and lack of control, with several saying they would like to know more about how to manage the privacy of their information. For example, one of our interviewees, a 43-year-old female scientist, said:

> Well, I mean there're certain things you just can't not do. So, like just try to protect yourself. I don't know exactly how that—how to do that. I am not sure what that would entail. I guess, you know, trying not to use devices or apps that you know are taking that information, for sure.

One of the other constraints for managing settings or privacy and data sharing, however, was a lack of time to devote to it, according to the interviewees.

Evaluation, Choice and Self-Control

Interviewees often expressed how "exciting" technology is along with wariness in nearly the same breath. One skill mentioned for the future was how to make strategic choices by evaluating the potential impacts of new technologies, like "being cognizant of not only the benefits but also the risks of technology integration and what incorporating more technology into your life could mean for you."

A few interviewees articulated their understanding of voluntary disconnections and the capacity to critically evaluate technology use and non-use:

> I think the most important part is self-control and being able to use your own discretion.
>
> Like, be able—you can still explore the world without technology and do things without it. And yet, you can still have it to help you a little bit, if that makes sense.
>
> [The need] to learn not to use it when it is not required. That is the skill that I think everybody needs to double up is putting it away when it is really not needed.

As folk theories are constituted from multiple sources including popular media, it is perhaps unsurprising to see the minority of views expressed on the need for discernment and self-control, even occasional disconnection from technology in the future.

Discussion and Conclusion

While our interviewees were non-experts in IoT and AI systems, they voiced a range of anticipatory modes of adaptation, reflecting how laypersons "regularly develop folk themes to make their way through the world" (French and Hancock 2017). Interviewees shared a readiness to flexibly approach IoT fluidity, shifting norms and initiatives. They recognized the pivotal capacity to innovate, learn new skills and acquire relevant competencies to meet industry needs and create value. These agentic responses are likely reflective of the sample's socio-demographics (college students and mostly working professionals who have completed a college education or above), but also reflective of larger societal discourse that stress a future of intensive learning and skilled human capital to thrive in the new wave in automation and human-machine communication (Taguma et al. 2018). In the so-termed fourth industrial revolution, "learnability," or the self-directed ability to learn and unlearn, is proposed to take center stage as the demand for intricate skills is fused with shrinking shelf life of specialized knowledge (Ra et al. 2019).

At the same time, reflecting the present everyday experiences of digital media consumption, and peoples' lived complexity with opaque IoT networks, folk theories illustrated the tensions to "keep up with everything that's changing because its so fast." Therefore, even as interviewees acknowledged the need to "stay up to date with new technologies," they are simultaneously confronted with the pressing, yet amorphous charge of having to "just stay with the times." In this way, folk understandings highlight the dialectics surrounding data futures and, in turn, a need for projected capacity to manage concurrent ambiguities and uneven gains in IoT engagement.

What might be needed to keep up, however, was uncertain for many. Given rapid evolution of technologies, many declined to predict future skills or viewed them as negligible at best. This is certainly true for what some scholars have defined as the formal and operational skills needed to use hardware, software or devices (van Dijk and van Deursen 2014). At the same time, there was a heightened awareness of the complexity of managing privacy and security of user's data, especially with a lack of transparency about what is being collected and how it is being shared. While some interviews suggested a lack of confidence in skills to manage privacy settings or data sharing, more widespread was the question of how to act in the face of the largely invisible processes. Despite this, interviewees talked about balancing the exciting aspects of technology with potential threats, evaluating the benefits and risks, and opting out at times, if needed. These folk understandings of skill largely reflect the assessments of academics who argue that while formal and operational skills are decreasing with IoT, the need for strategic skills will intensify. These include the ability to evaluate risks and benefits and to manage data sharing, privacy and security (Pangrazio and Selwyn 2019; van Deursen and Mossberger 2018).

Last but not least, it is worth noting folk imaginings of their smart and datafied lives as discussed here suggest implications for policy, regarding issues such as lifelong learning and privacy. Though respondents considered how they would respond in the future and did not discuss possible policy interventions, there was an awareness of the need for continued learning and greater transparency about data sharing. Laypersons voicing their desire to enrich themselves with new knowledge and equip themselves to adapt puts a spotlight on education needs and retraining programs; a point that has also recently been raised by concerned scholars and commentators on AI growth (Frey 2019). Inherent in the discussion of data and privacy is also a sense that IoT requires not only education and individual competencies to manage the challenges but more forthright information and accountability on the part of technology firms producing IoT and the organizations and institutions that utilize the resulting data. There is a general awareness of the costs of technology use, along with enthusiasm for its seemingly boundless possibilities. This folk understanding of the duality of IoT is a lesson for policymakers as well, for society as well as individuals must seek appropriate trade-offs and collective resources for future innovation.

References

de Boer, Pia S., Alexander J.A.M. van Deursen, and Thomas J.L. Van Rompay. 2019. Accepting the Internet-of-Things in our homes: The role of user skills. *Telematics and informatics* 36: 147–156.

Brynjolfsson, Erik, and Andrew McAfee. 2014. *The second machine age: Work, progress, and prosperity in a time of brilliant technologies*. New York, NY: WW Norton & Company.

Charmez, K. 2006. *Constructing grounded theory: A practical guide through qualitative analysis*. London: Sage.

Couldry, Nick, and Yu. Jun. 2013. Deconstructing datafication's brave new world. *New Media & Society* 20 (12): 4473–4491.

Cukier, K., and V. Mayer-Schoenberger. 2013. The rise of big data: How it's changing the way we think about the world. *Foreign Affairs* 92 (3): 28–40.

van Deursen, Alexander J.A.M., and Karen Mossberger. 2018. Any thing for anyone? A new digital divide in internet-of-things skills. *Policy & Internet* 10 (2): 122–140.

DeVito, Michael A., Jeffrey T. Hancock, Megan French, Jeremy Birnholtz, Judd Antin, Karrie Karahalios, Stephanie Tong, and Irina Shklovski. 2018. The algorithm and the user: How can hci use lay understandings of algorithmic systems?. In *Extended Abstracts of the 2018 CHI Conference on Human Factors in Computing Systems*, pp. 1–6.

van Dijk, Jan A.G.M., and Alexander J.A.M. van Deursen. 2014. *Digital skills: Unlocking the information society*. New York, NY: Palgrave Macmillan.

Dourish, Paul, and Genevieve Bell. 2011. *Divining a digital future: Mess and mythology in ubiquitous computing*. Cambridge, MA: MIT Press.

French, Megan, and Hancock, Jeff. 2017. What's the Folk Theory? Reasoning About Cyber-Social Systems (February 2, 2017). https://ssrn.com/abstract=2910571

Frey, C.B. 2019. *The technology trap: Capital, labor, and power in the age of automation*. Princeton, NJ: Princeton University Press.

Gelman, Susan A., and Cristine H. Legare. 2011. Concepts and folk theories. *Annual review of anthropology* 40: 379–398.

Hepp, Andreas. 2020. Artificial companions, social bots and work bots: communicative robots as research objects of media and communication studies. *Media, Culture & Society*.. https://doi.org/10.1177/0163443720916412.

Jennings, Bruce. 2011. Poets of the common good: experts, citizens, public policy. *Critical Policy Studies* 5 (3): 334–339.

Kashima, Yoshihisa, Junqi Shi, Koji Tsuchiya, Emiko S. Kashima, Shirley YY Cheng, Melody Manchi Chao, and Shang-hui Shin. 2011. Globalization and folk theory of social change: How globalization relates to societal perceptions about the past and future. *Journal of Social Issues* 67, no. 4: 696–715.

Keil, Frank C. 2010. The feasibility of folk science. *Cognitive science* 34 (5): 826–862.

Kwasny, Michelle, Kelly Caine, Wendy A. Rogers, and Arthur D. Fisk. 2008. Privacy and technology: folk definitions and perspectives. In *CHI'08 Extended Abstracts on Human Factors in Computing Systems*, pp. 3291–3296.

Leopold, T. A., R. Vesselina, and S. Zahidi. 2016. The Future of Jobs Report in World Economic Forum. http://www3.weforum.org/docs/WEF_Future_of_Jobs.pdf

Lindlof, Thomas R., and Bryan C. Taylor. 2002. *Qualitative communication research methods*. Thousand Oaks, CA: Sage.

Lutz, Christoph. 2019. Digital inequalities in the age of artificial intelligence and big data. *Human Behavior and Emerging Technologies* 1 (2): 141–148.

Nascimento, Bruno, Tiago Oliveira, and Carlos Tam. 2018. Wearable technology: What explains continuance intention in smartwatches? *Journal of Retailing and Consumer Services* 43: 157–169.

Pangrazio, L., and N. Selwyn. 2019. 'Personal data literacies': A critical literacies approach to enhancing understandings of personal digital data. *New Media & Society* 21 (2): 419–437.

Pasquale, Frank. 2015. *The black box society*. Cambridge, MA: Harvard University Press.

Pink, Sarah, Debora Lanzeni, and Heather Horst. 2018. Data anxieties: finding trust in everyday digital mess. *Big Data & Society*. https://doi.org/10.1177/2053951718756685.

Ra, Sungsup, Unika Shrestha, Sameer Khatiwada, Seung Won Yoon, and Kibum Kwon. 2019. The rise of technology and impact on skills. *International Journal of Training Research* 17 (sup1): 26–40.

Rowe, Gene, and George Wright. 2011. The Delphi technique: Past, present, and future prospects – Introduction to the special issue. *Technological forecasting and social change* 78 (9): 1487–1490.

Strauss, Anselm, and Juliet Corbin. 1998. *Basics of qualitative research: Techniques and procedures for developing grounded theory*. 2nd ed. Thousand Oaks, CA: Sage.

Susskind, Richard E., and Daniel Susskind. 2015. *The future of the professions: How technology will transform the work of human experts*. Oxford, UK: Oxford University Press.

Taguma, Miho, Eva Feron, and Meow Hwee Lim. 2018. *Future of education and skills 2030: Conceptual learning framework*. Organization of Economic Co-operation and Development. https://www.oecd.org/education/2030/Education-and-AI-preparing-for-the-future-AI-Attitudes-and-Values.pdf.

Socio-technical Issues Concerning the Future of New Communication Technology, Robots, and AI

James Katz

Consider which topics are covered by news outlets, where individuals invest their psychological energies, and what our contemporary societies take up as morally significant issues: in all of these, it is natural that the focus is on those issues which are recognized as threatening or troubling. Areas that are smoothly operating, adequately fulfilling needs, or a source of satisfaction tend to be overlooked. That is the case not only in those three areas (news, individual concerns, and social movements and causes) but also when considering the role of communication technologies, robotics, and AI. The attention is less on their successes than it is on their risks and dangers. This imbalance of psychological valences does nothing to lessen the reality of the risks and dangers, but does require us to consider the lenses through which we perceive the future of these technologies. Nonetheless, in full awareness of this bias, it would behoove us to consider

J. Katz (✉)
Division of Emerging Media Studies, Boston University, Boston, MA, USA
e-mail: katz2020@bu.edu

J. Katz et al. (eds.), *Perceiving the Future through New Communication Technologies*,
https://doi.org/10.1007/978-3-030-84883-5_14

what are the major issues facing society in terms of new communication technology, AI, and robotics.

In this chapter's exploration, we will choose but a few of the many crucially important, and diabolically complex, topics of everyday understandings of the power of technology in people's lives. These few examples are chosen because they bring together the power of AI with communication technologies in a way that are likely to affect the more profound aspects of everyday life. Significantly, they are deeply embedded with both individuals as atomic members of society as well as larger collectives of various identity categories, ideological loyalties, and value systems.

Privacy and Personal Information Control

Like other topics related to digital life, privacy can easily become fraught and subject to conflicting values and goals. Personal privacy, an ever-growing area of contention, has long been recognized as a foundational attribute for the growth of the individual and the persistence of psychological freedom.

Much data collection about ourselves goes on without our knowledge. Apropos of the themes in this volume, especially by Wang et al., it is noteworthy that some of our seeming technological servants are actually eavesdropping and spying on us. While this is a habit that frequently characterized servants in days of old, currently it is apparently occurring with smart speakers and smart home security cameras. Although lacking documentary evidence, allegations have been made that employees of the electronic doorbell/camera cum security company Ring gained access to customers' live camera feeds from both inside and outside their home. Ring claims it does not do this except under the terms of the user's agreement and then does not do so on a "real-time" basis (Tambini 2019).

Despite concern over video collection within the home by our electronic security technology, it appears that our voice-activated gadgets are constantly listening to us and recording the conversations and background noises that they pick up (Quach 2020). Most users of these home voice-activated servants have no idea that vast amounts of their private conversations and domestic sounds are recorded. These privacy invasions are taking place largely beneath the waterline of public awareness, and the privacy implications of them could turn out to be devastating. The information can be used for blackmail, court proceedings, and spousal spying, for instance.

As fraught and potentially dangerous as these issues of spying by smart speakers and home video systems are, they pale in comparison to listening and especially video monitoring increasingly taken place in public. Systems are being developed in the West that can integrate CCTV on private and governmental property with cameras mounted on public buses, drones, delivery vehicles, along with many other sources to use facial recognition to identify people in the street. Likewise the systems increasingly can read license plate information and other identifying details. This power can even be abetted with mobile phone triangulation to identify people's location with precision and in near-real-time. This information can be handy for locating people in and around crime scenes for reconstruction of events, identify witnesses and even perpetrators. It may also be useful in understanding the presence of individuals at various political events for later consideration. Most of this is taking place without the knowledge of the people involved. While this kind of near-constant monitoring of people's activities would be a shocking development, it is already occurring in China, where vast swaths of the public are caught up in a huge experiment in public behavior monitoring, location surveillance, and social credit systems. One's behavior can result in benefits as well as punishments. These include travel opportunities, insurance and credit card charges, and educational opportunities. Even one's social media activity and postings are taken into account in arriving at the algorithm of life-opportunity adjustment.

China has also been a leader in experimenting with remote monitoring in the classroom, not only of the students' behavior but that of the instructors as well. This is taking place at both the elementary level and all the way through college, where professors' lectures are centrally monitored by political authorities.

Data Collection and Mining: Potential Permanent Vulnerability

Considering the practices themselves, the principles underlying snooping, monitoring, and data collection have a long history that well predates the digital era. Long before photography and tape-recording, letters and eavesdropping reports have been used to blackmail, compel, and incriminate. With new communication technology, such practices now have a much wider net to cast and a much easier mode of collection and curation.

Just one contemporary example should suffice to illustrate this, which occurred in 2020. In this example, a girl was admitted to the University of Tennessee, including a slot on its cheerleading team. However, it turned out that a few years earlier, when she was 15, she had used Snapchat to express her excitement at getting her learner's permit for driving. In the course of her brief expression she used a severely pejorative term. A classmate was able to capture and preserve this clip and sat on it for years waiting to release it upon finding out that she had gained admission to the University of Tennessee. The concern over this clip led to the girl's first being removed from the cheerleading squad. Then the University of Tennessee pressured her to withdraw from the University. This undoubtedly changed the course of her life, and it is unlikely, once again due to social media and the long life of material on the web, that it will ever be forgotten (Soave, 2020). The point here is not to address the girl's actions but rather to highlight the way in which one's actions can be captured, retained, and selectively deployed at will by others via digital means.

While Snapchat, the technology used in this instance, was originally renowned for its characteristic of having user messages rapidly disappear, over time it has become common for users to find ways of saving material with this service (and the service itself has added features to enable the ability to preserve communicated information), which remains a possibility with practically any communication technology. With plummeting costs of digital material storage, and mushrooming expansion of opportunities for data collection, vast troves of information are becoming searchable using ever-more clever technologies.

These capabilities alone raise significant implications for individual autonomy and freedom of behavior as well as social control and responsibility. When combined with the rapidly growing capabilities of AI, the behavioral, psychological, and legal implications for privacy and autonomy become still more compelling. The concerns become obvious when one considers how growing AI capability will allow any entity or individual that has the accessibility and resources to search the ever-increasingly vast troves of data to find suitably helpful or harmful items. AI can be increasingly used to pinpoint specific data real-time, post-hoc, or archival. It can do this in terms of not only text but also audio patterns, such as voice and word recognition and conversation content analysis. It also extends to visual pattern recognition such as facial recognition, gait recognition, and even gaze recognition. The implications of such technology can include years-later punitive measures, sanctions, or forfeit opportunities in light of various statements or behavior. The above example of the University of Tennessee admittee stems from personal curation of a digital archive whereas the kinds and magnitude of interventions will be far more severe and far-reaching as AI recording and retrieval systems become more adept at finding any particular action or reaction. A common practice in political campaigns is to have a candidate's team comb through all statements, records, actions, and associates of their opponents. This exhaustive, labor-intense "oppo-research" has uncovered misdeeds and mistakes of candidates which have been legendary in their consequences. Videotape was a big step forward in this domain in terms of documenting and exposing incompetence or wrongdoing. Thus in 1988, the then-senator Joe Biden, US presidential primary contestant, was driven from the race when the staff of his opponent, Michael Dukakis, selectively provided to the media a videotape of a Biden speech in which he largely plagiarized a speech, including an imitation of gestures, given by British labor leader Neil Kinnock. Without that tape having been made and distributed perhaps Joe Biden would have become president of the United States 32 years earlier!

As striking as that anti-Biden maneuver was in the post-video, pre-digital era, how much more material can now, and soon will be, unearthed when AI is harnessed to hunt down pejorative information on someone. An otherwise unobserved jaywalk, extra drink, harsh word, or rudeness would presumably be among the milder but nonetheless potentially harmful actions that could be uncovered. Depending on circumstances, practically anyone could become targeted in this way. This observation is not, obviously, an argument against law enforcement or the encouragement of good behavior. Rather it is an observation that there is a wide and varied latitude for what is acceptable and permissible. Under certain circumstances, and independent of intention, even a given gesture or head movement could become subject to derogatory interpretation.

Sometimes it is argued that advancing technology will be able to protect individuals from sundry types of monitoring, in terms of both their communication and routine activities. In terms of public surveillance, these vectors of protection include prosaic if impractical or labor-intensive measures including using an umbrella and hoodie when in public. More generally, optimists see counterbalancing privacy protection may arise from legal strictures, including a nascent "right to be forgotten." In a similar vein, hope is invited in "crowdsourced" and other alternative technology enhancements. Here public key encryption and other forms of encryption currently afford some protection from elementary and sophisticated snooping. Depending on the level of effort required, a person who wishes can obtain access to various layers of protection. Sometimes this is as easy as using the Telegraph app, which has secure end-to-end encryption. But how long will the systems be allowed? Quantum computing threatens to render content transparent despite sophisticated encryption algorithms. Yet more easily, governments can simply require that these services stop providing such levels of user security.

Social and Fairness Issues Related to AI and Robotics

Larger social themes of gender, race, and ethnicity have been applied to the areas of robotics and AI. AI-driven facial recognition has become highly contentious in terms of its varying performance depending on different physical aspects of the face being analyzed. Understandable concerns, such as those discussed by Vanessa Nurock, have been raised about potential biases of facial recognition and other AI systems, including the biasing for or against various groups because of the inherent design qualities of the technology. This happens, for example, when it comes to facial recognition abilities of systems that are applied to groups who were not among the test subjects that were used to develop the system or because of unrecognized biases in the creation of the system. Similarly, voice recognition systems perform more poorly when used by those with accents or who have higher pitched voices (commonly the case with women). Defenders of these technologies claim such problems were unintentional and resolvable through additional and improved research and development processes. Still, looking more broadly, it seems that these problems arise due to the insensitivity of the designers, the lack of resources to generate and test an appropriate pool, and blunders in the systems' deployment. Regardless of the reason, the consequences for subjects and users of these systems, the results can be not only unfair, inconvenient, and disturbing but even minacious and tragic. The costs in terms of loss and suffering may be substantial at the individual level. At the societal level, the consequences of mistakes affect the tenor of public policy processes in a way that can harm some of the very individuals and groups that the systems were intended to help. And, as always, we have to compare the operation of these systems to those of present and alternative systems in terms of mistakes, biases, and effectiveness.

These problems are widespread and not by any means limited only to AI system development. For their part, robots and robotics have been the focus of criticism concerning the way they physically represent race, gender, age, and sexuality. Critics have argued that such systems promote harmful stereotypes even as many designers struggle to neutralize such physical cues. At the same time, it is arguable that positive dimensions of various identity categories should be promoted through the physical representations of robots. The same argument can be extended to AI systems which may have voice and virtual representations. Designers are struggling with what kind of voice these systems should have, and how intrusive they should be. The fact that an Uncanny Valley exists in terms of robots that look too much like people, and thus startle and irritate them, may also be present in voice and characters that are projected by AI systems that use human language to communicate.

A reciprocal concern might be the long-term impact of these systems on humans themselves. Robots have already been demonstrated to be good learning companions for autistic children; might they be useful for other forms of interaction with youngsters, such as teacher companions? An obvious question arises as to how extended interaction with mere robots may affect the socialization and psychological development of people. Here we have to include not only children but also adults. It's quite conceivable that long-term interaction with robots can produce depersonalizing effects. As mentioned earlier in this chapter, and in the chapter by Kate Mays, humans are already becoming involved in erotic and sexual interactions with robots and AI virtual systems. The long-term consequences for people are obviously worth evaluating. This way people can be prepared for the likely consequences of such interactions. Stemming from the more human-like characteristics of AI systems and robots, we can expect that there will be an ever-more influential "robot rights" movement. Just as the French government has given intrinsic artistic rights to paintings, and there is a similar movement to imbue animals and other living things with various rights, we can have every expectation that robots and AI entities will be included in this ever-expanding blanket of protections.

Use of AI and New Technology to Constrict Access to Facts and Interpretations

But beyond the technologies and their instantiations themselves, society has not yet successfully grappled with the question of what to do about history, that is, what to do about existing material culture that may not be compliant with contemporary viewpoints. In this regard, if the decision is made to eliminate or rewrite aspects of history, AI can do a powerful job of making sure no one has access, or at least no more than minimal access, to certain ideas, images, and beliefs. The same "Big Tech" companies are pressured to rein in contemporary views and materials that are seen as socially pernicious and dangerous. While some recall the possibility of a slippery slope that will end up incinerating ideas, works of art, and other products that are perceived as flawed, others invoke the same slippery slope analogy to argue that without restrictions, these unfettered ideas will lead to offense, violence, and destruction.

Any system of censorship must, at its heart, be run by people even if it's implemented using AI. Any censorship system must also employ the values of its architects and operators. No matter how advanced our technology and AI may be, when censorship rests in the hands of a few, we must return to the question that the Roman poet Juvenal posed: *quis custodiet ipsos custodes*—who guards the guardians? If we agree with the decisions of the guardians, we probably rely instead on Plato's view that we should be able to trust the guardians to behave properly. If it is a view that we might favor, but the Big Tech companies do not, we have reason to complain. But rather than a matter of taste, the fundamental question is whether human development and the enduring interests of the individual are best served by unfettered inquiry. If lines are reasonably necessary, where should they be drawn?

At least as far as the United States goes, our Constitution was based on the view that trust and assurance of proper behavior is best guaranteed through competing interests, thus we have a federal system of checks and balances. And among our most treasured freedoms is the freedom *from* governmental interference in our expression as guaranteed in the Constitution's First Amendment. Although the United States may be an exception in light of the growing restrictions on free expression around the world, the question of censorship and limits on expressing views outside the ken of the government is an area of growing concern.

Social Control Via Bottom-Up Totalitarianism

Considering what the future might hold in terms of new communication technology, we can see that there is the distinct possibility of enormous attention being given to pressing dissidents into line in authoritarian societies. But what is the situation in non-authoritarian societies, such as the United States? Surveys of employees in the United States, including those of the *New York Times*, have shown that perhaps half of these groups are afraid to express their opinions openly. Certainly many members of the public, and especially those who are not progressive, are also reticent to speak their minds publicly. This creates what has been termed the "spiral of silence," in which fear of speaking out by some individuals spreads, making yet more individuals feel isolated and afraid to speak out. The fear has been described by human rights activist Natan Sharansky as "bottom-up totalitarianism" (Sharansky with Troy 2021).

He and his co-author describe it as ideological totalitarianism in which each side is ever-expanding in its attempts to hurt the other side by making politics personal, and this is increasingly done using reprisals and campaigns of destruction with social media as a major conduit:

> Over the last two decades, we watched this self-censorship grow on campus, as more and more students started telling us they feel bullied, sculpting their expressions to avoid alienating professors or peers. That chilling atmosphere is now spreading, flattening conversation in corporations, government offices, newspapers and on social media. This is not just watching your tongue out of politeness; it's shutting your mouth out of fear. (Sharansky and Troy 2020)

The political climate in the United States, like much of the West, is fraught. A summer 2020 survey of 2000 Americans, conducted by the Cato Institute, found that 62% of Americans say the political climate prevents them from saying what they believe because others might find it offensive. (The number is still higher—77%—for conservatives.) (Ekins 2020). A recent survey of employees at the *New York Times*, which was leaked to its competitor, the *New York Post*, found that half of the employees felt that they were not free to express their opinions (Levine 2021). Although the *New York Times* considers itself a progressive company, the results of the survey call into question the value of free speech and free thought.

Many lay the blame for the situation on social media and the way it can be used both to create pressure to think a certain way as well as an environment of uniformity, with those with unapproved viewpoints heavily sanctioned. Already people have lost their jobs due to expressing unpopular opinions via social media. Economic sanctions alone are not the only threat that dissenters need fear. Often the mob mentality that may be unleashed against them can lead to physical threats and even physical violence. In some cases, and as we have already seen above, inappropriate social media posts will be privately curated for years, only to be released when it will do the maximum harm.

Coda

These issues will characterize the field of battle over the deployment of these new communication technologies in the years ahead. The ideas presented in this volume's chapters will shed light as scholars and students, officials and laypeople, consider evidence on behalf of the various contending viewpoints.

In seeking to summarize the basic views on these issues, it's worth noting that people will tend to fall into one of two opposing categories as to how they perceive the future of new communication technology. Speaking at high level, these are the Janus-faced strands of optimism and pessimism. The issues we have identified and discussed in this volume tends not to show the so-called optimism bias that has been so richly demonstrated in many domains of human endeavor. The social psychology literature is rife with evidence of such a bias, which leads to market bubbles, excessive risk, and even warfare. Rather, our tendency here is more toward pessimism. However, we do believe that new communication technologies offer many wonderful and extraordinarily positive things.

The purpose of warnings is not to seek to make the various ill effects of new communication technology to come to pass but instead to prevent them from doing so. In the literary field, this has been one of the greatest gifts bestowed by the insuperable George Orwell's 1984. His profoundly disturbing novel foretold many pernicious features enabled by communication technology. Some of these have come to pass in our contemporary society including the erasure of history, "two minutes of hate" against perceived societal enemies, simplification of thought and language, the instigation of identity filiation to mobilize mobs, and revelations of organizational data to smoke out dissenters. Yet Orwell, by portraying so compellingly his sinister dystopian world, has in fact done much to prevent it from coming about. Many have taken his words as a shibboleth to blunt efforts by those in various quarters to deny our freedom and cultural heritage. His words remain more relevant today than ever: "Those who control the present, control the past and those who control the past control the future." So the pessimistic interpretation can do much to advance individual freedom and broader autonomy within society. *Praemonitus, praemunitus*. Forewarned is forearmed.

Yet we do not wish to end on a pessimistic note. To counteract this prospect, we offer the following quote about a new communication technology. The speaker said that this technology:

> has achieved this great and paradoxical result, that it has, as it were, assembled all mankind upon one great plain where they can see everything that is done, and hear everything that is said, and judge of every policy that is pursued at the very moment when those events take place.

The new telecommunication technology in question, as was surely adumbrated by the archaic diction, is no longer new: it is the telegraph. The quote is from an 1899 speech to the recently established Institution of Electrical Engineers by Robert Gascoyne-Cecil, the third Marquess of Salisbury and then-serving Prime Minister of Britain (*The Spectator* 1899). He was marveling at the transparency-generating effect of the telegraph as well as its ability to provoke criticism from all quarters. Just as Salisbury's statement reveals the disorienting and perplexing aspects of understanding the implications of new communication technology, even from one who had achieved the greatest of heights of power as leader of the then-most powerful country in the world. That technology with all its advantages and problems became an important part of society.

Despite early struggles over telegraphy, including its exploitation by criminals, concerns over monopoly practices and exploitation of delivery personnel, not to mention its privacy invasiveness. So too we hope, and trust, that optimal solutions can be found to the baffling and fraught problems being brought about by advances in new communication technology, AI, and robotics.

References

Ekins, Emily. 2020. Most Americans Are Scared to Talk Politics. Cato Institute, August 6. https://www.cato.org/commentary/most-americans-are-scared-stiff-talk-politics-why. Accessed 9 March 2021.

Levine, Jon. 2021. Half of *New York Times* Employees Feel They Can't Speak Freely: Survey. *New York Post*, February 13, 2021. https://nypost.com/2021/02/13/new-york-times-employees-feel-they-cant-speak-freely-survey/. Accessed 9 March 2021.

Quach, Katyanna. 2020. Whoops, Our Bad, We May Have (Accidentally) Let Google Home Devices Record Your Every Word, Sound-oops. *The Register*, August 8. https://www.theregister.com/2020/08/08/ai_in_brief/. Accessed 9 March 2021.

Sharansky, Natan with Gil Troy. 2021. The Doublethinkers. *Tablet*, February 11. https://www.tabletmag.com/sections/arts-letters/articles/natan-sharansky-doublethink. Accessed 9 March 2021.

Sharansky, Natan, and Gil Troy. 2020. Three Signs of Ideological Totalitarianism. *Newsweek*, September 8. https://www.newsweek.com/three-warning-signs-ideological-totalitarianism-opinion-1529824. Accessed 9 March 2021.

Soave, Robbie. 2020. *The New York Times* Helped a Vindictive Team Destroy a Classmate Who Uttered a Racial Slur When She Was 15. *Reason*, December 28. https://reason.com/2020/12/28/new-york-times-racial-slur-teen-jimmy-galligan-mimi-groves/. Accessed 9 March 2021.

Spectator, The. 1899. The Intellectual Effects of Electricity. *The Spectator*, November 9, p. 623. "News of the week" Section. http://archive.spectator.co.uk/page/9th-november-1889/3. Accessed 9 March 2021.

Tambini, Olivia, 2019. Ring Employees Can Reportedly Access Customers' Live Camera Feeds. *Techradar*, January 11. https://www.techradar.com/news/ring-employees-can-reportedly-access-customers-live-camera-feeds. Accessed 9 March 2021.

Conclusion

James Katz, Katie Schiepers, and Juliet Floyd

The chapters presented in this volume have provided an opportunity to reflect not only on the technological advancements which have taken place since the close of the last century but also on their effect on communication. They have underscored the growing interaction between people via technology and between humans and machines. Many chapters also anticipated future developments as technology continues to evolve, and as our social relationships evolve with it. From a comparative perspective, several questions arise addressing personalization of individual communication technology, emotional and quotidian connections people have with AI and robotic entities and their impact on human-human relationships, and generalized concerns with the future.

Concerned with the mobile phone and its consequences, the Perpetual Contact project and the Apparatgeist theory that emerged from it were

J. Katz (✉) • K. Schiepers
Division of Emerging Media Studies, Boston University, Boston, MA, USA
e-mail: katz2020@bu.edu; kschiep@bu.edu

J. Floyd
Department of Philosophy, Boston University, Boston, MA, USA
e-mail: jfloyd@bu.edu

J. Katz et al. (eds.), *Perceiving the Future through New Communication Technologies*,
https://doi.org/10.1007/978-3-030-84883-5_15

developed at the turn of the millennium as a way to understand and explain the many levels of attachment that people were developing for their mobile phones. Aakhus' overview illustrates how this theory remains relevant to subsequent technological advancements over the past two decades. In particular, he illustrates how Apparatgeist provides a more useful framework for considering the wider implications of technology on society than the classic media studies paradigm as the modes through which media is transmitted are not as distinct from one another as they once were. Apparatgeist enables technology and its impact to be understood in a more holistic way.

Continuing the theme of Apparatgeist theory, Floyd demonstrates the connection the perspective has to enduring questions of philosophy. She perceptively demonstrates the relevance of the essentially sociological perspective on human technologies, most particularly the computer and the smartphone, with enduring questions of language and understanding, so brilliantly investigated by Ludwig Wittgenstein. Intriguingly, she investigates the often-misunderstood Turing Machine analogy and sheds new light on the way in which Apparatgeist can operate the Turing Machine, as it were, as a form of cultural search. One might see her chapter as a Janus-headed contribution, at once looking backward to the use of language to create shared understandings (and too often misunderstandings) as well as forward to machine-human interactions that may come to predominate many aspects of social life. As such, she has opened wide the intellectual doors to invite experiential and experimental approaches to illuminating sophisticated philosophical questions.

Floyd shows how phenomenological insights offered by philosophy can point to a more humane and sophisticated picture of our relationships with the world of technology. In particular, she criticizes several of the unidirectional models often employed by philosophers as they seek to understand the big questions of the socially and technologically embedded world. By contrast, she underscores the utility of a dynamic and interpretive approach taken by Katz and Aakhus. As previously mentioned, a point of particular interest is the way Floyd links the thinking of Ludwig Wittgenstein with that of Alan Turing. Her bold intellectual move provides a sophisticated, and if we may immodestly suggest, enriched understanding of the points that both Wittgenstein and Turing were developing in their respective domains. Together with the philosophical and ethical approaches of Vanessa Nurock, and implicit in several other chapters, Floyd fills in and represents a continuum of perspectives on how it is that people live their lives, both in the immediate present and as they grasp the ever-unfolding immediate and longer-term future.

As a harbinger of many technology-induced societal changes, Weilenmann's chapter explores the mobile phone and its effects on human society over the past two decades. The mobile phone has undoubtedly influenced the way we interact with one another, not only via the technology itself but also via our interactions with one another in its presence. Through her eyes, we are introduced to a significant new form of local human-human communication "shared screen time"; this twist on an old phenomenon—shared consumption of media—constitutes a new form of social interaction based *around* the mobile device. Her study determined that mobile phone use is not just a virtual activity but has transcended this level to become a form of local communication too as people's interactions with one another are modified in the presence of their devices, for example, taking selfies. In a sense, it could be considered as both a co-participant in social interaction as well as an at-times unwanted intruder. At the very least, its presence must be taken into effect on occasions of social interaction.

These first three chapters introduce us to the ways in which mobile technologies have already influenced and created novel contours in our lives—not only making communication more convenient and readily accessible but fundamentally changing the ways in which we interact. Mays takes this as a starting point for considering how we look toward the future as we progress to more advanced forms of technology such as artificial intelligence (AI). While respondents were open to the idea of robots, her research indicated that their comfort level was restricted to certain scenarios which they deemed to be socially appropriate. For example, some people felt that they would be jealous if a partner connected on a personal level with a robot or other AI device (which recalls the phenomenon of partner phubbing, whereby an individual can neglect their partner while in the presence of their mobile device). Mays' chapter illustrates the growing need for us to navigate our interactions with advanced technologies as they become more commonplace, and to be cognizant of how AI can potentially affect our relationships with one another, not just with the devices themselves.

Although an AI smart speaker, for example, is essentially a tool in the same way a mobile phone is a tool, giving these devices a "personality," or an anthropomorphic persona, has added a new dimension. If the presence of a mobile phone can make you feel jealous, neglected, or annoyed, imagine then how an anthropomorphic device might exacerbate those feelings. If you become dependent on your mobile phone as a tool, consider the deeper connection you may have with a device that is human-like. These are scenarios we need to consider as we introduce these technologies into our lives; the lived experiences that arise when another personality, albeit entirely artificial, begins interacting with us can also be interpreted via several ethical and theoretical frameworks including that of Apparatgeist theory.

Drawing on the work of Aakhus and Weilenmann in particular, we can see that personalized technology will continue to be highly important in our lives. Personalized and highly mobile, these devices should prove to be important not only in terms of their operational efficiency but also in terms of their ability to represent social status and prestige. Moreover, these technologies will increasingly play the role of companions. Some of these instantiations will be personal mobile devices, such as highly advanced smartphones, wearable technology, and perhaps even subcutaneous or exoskeletal devices. They may also include robotics and other animated structures that serve as bodyguards, personal assistants, or companions. They will accompany us when we go places, helping to ensure our safety, but will also soothe us and keep us from feeling lonely. Vanessa Nurock's analysis leads us to anticipate that these devices will affect us psychologically and emotionally, not to mention that in some cases they may give us a (potentially false) expectation that they have superior knowledge and judgment.

Nurock delves deeper into the reciprocal relationship between people and their devices and the wider implications for society. She conceptualizes this through the Artificialistic Fallacy, or the error of equating something "artificial" as being something "good." Based on Moore's Naturalistic Fallacy (the error of equating something "natural" as being something "good," which, in turn, would enable biology to be paramount to morality and ethics) and Bourdieu's concept of naturalization (whereby habits come to be seen as natural and expected rather than socially constructed), the Artificialistic Fallacy applies these concepts to AI and its inherent biases. These technologies carry the biases of their creators with them, and thus have the ability to influence those that use them—"we shape AI, but AI also shapes us." As these technologies become increasingly commonplace, they carry with them the ability to shape society on a larger scale through these biases, as users run the risk of equating technology with something impartial and unbiased and therefore correct or good.

The first part of this volume provides us with a background to the technological advancements of the past two decades as well as an optimistic but cautionary glimpse into how new technologies might influence our communication with one another, our relationships with our devices, and society as a whole. The following part sought to present some specific examples of AI that are already being deployed and provides a real-world insight into how humans are starting to navigate these issues.

Stoellger commences with a common perception of robots and AI—they can be harmless and friendly provided they do not become too human-like (cf. the Uncanny Valley). His chapter encourages us to consider the boundaries of our comfort level with AI as it takes on traditionally human roles. For example, BlessU, a robot used at the 500th anniversary of the Reformation in Germany in 2017, was tasked with giving blessings to attendees. To some, this was a novel and harmless innovation, while to others it crossed a line in trusting something intrinsically human to a machine. Are there some duties that are just not appropriate for a human substitute to take on? Do we have a threshold we are unwilling to cross?

The more these AI instantiations look (and behave) like people, as is the case generally speaking of robots, it is more likely that we will treat them as humans. Stoellger highlights and reinforces Vanessa Nurock's point when he shows the spiritual dimension of robot perceptions. Robots can also be fun companions, and young people might find them intriguing, as is the case with the robot Pepper. Sugiyama shows that children in particular are intrigued by robots. Like any novel entity, especially one that seems to be intelligent, it seems normal to be interested in its "origin story." Where did it come from, who are its creators, what are its values? That these issues arise when humans interact with robots that evince personality speaks to the teleological questions that seem to naturally arise from human lived experience. They also show the enduring importance of narrative structures in people's approach to experiences.

Even the more readily accepted robots in roles where they serve as information points or customer service agents push peoples' boundaries, as Satomi Sugiyama explores with the example of Pepper in Japan. In many cases, peoples' reactions to the robot depended on the particular circumstance in which their interaction took place. The social context is, therefore, extremely important in understanding peoples' comfort level with artificial intelligence and its place in our lives. There are some scenarios with which we are simply not comfortable.

When the AI is used in a situation that is deemed appropriate, that is, used as a tool, then people are at ease with it. On the other hand, when a person becomes emotionally attached to AI or it is seen as too human, such as taking on a religious role in the community, it pushes the boundaries of peoples' comfort levels. While many readers may feel similarly uncomfortable about the more extreme examples, Wang et al. illustrate how something as seemingly innocuous as a smart speaker, a device which is becoming increasingly commonplace in homes around the world, is already embedding artificial intelligence into our daily lives. Further, they show the humanization that takes place with something even as non-human-appearing as a smart speaker. The chapter in question explores the ways people use their smart speakers, the impact on human-human interaction, and the relationships that develop between people and their devices. Users tend to interact with them as if they were human, including pursuing social routines such as politeness and courtesy even though at an abstract level such "emotional work" is fruitless and irrelevant to the smart speaker. However, it may well be that this emotional work is important to the human. After all, it appears that parents teach their children to be polite to inanimate objects such as smart speakers and, for that matter, robots.

Through the interviews conducted, they concluded that children and older individuals were more likely to see the smart speakers in an anthropomorphic light and were therefore more likely to view the speakers as a companion or a friend rather than a utilitarian device. Even so, other demographic groups also depend on their devices to substitute for traditionally human interaction, such as reading a bedtime story to their children. Although they may see the device as a tool, it is still taking on a significant role in the household. In both instances, the speakers have taken on a presence in the home other than that of a mere object. In Stoellger's words, they are not human, but they are also not just things.

While smart speakers and the likes are the most readily available form of AI for consumers today, Jukka Jouhki's chapter provides us with an example of a "concept robot" that pushes the boundaries of AI capabilities and shows us a glimpse into what one day could be. Not only is Sophia a fun and interactive way to familiarize people with an advanced AI it also enables us to see how people might react to this should it come to fruition. Sophia is an internationally traveled "influencer" robot who is made to seem more intelligent than she is—thus providing people with a view into what a more advanced AI could look like in the future. The company behind Sophia aims to present her as a "hopeful symbol of the future," but in reality she has provided us with a snapshot of how people might react to sophisticated AI. While our reaction to Sophia is interesting to ponder, Jouhki ultimately concludes that it is unlikely any AI will ever be as advanced or human-like as she is portrayed to be, but rather she provides a focal point around which to consider the possibilities of artificial intelligence as an emerging media and our comfort level as it becomes more human-like.

Echoing Philipp Stoellger, we can say that even though robots are not human, they make an emotional claim on us to be treated with a degree of humaneness and even humanity. This certainly is a theme that appears in Jouhki's chapter. Kate Mays introduces the complicating factor of third-person involvement with robots. It's not only how a human engages with, and may be changed by, dyadic relations with a robotic entity. It is also a question of how human's relationships with other humans, especially those who may be considered partners and are involved at an intimate level with the person, respond to the presence of a robot. Here gender must come into play because the structure of human relations is predicated on biological realities.

While the second part explored our present-day realities with AI, the third part of the volume turns to examine how the future has been imagined in the past ("yesterday's tomorrow") and how we see the future of technology today. Pierre Cassou-Noguès, in taking us back to a twentieth-century perspective of what the future of technology could be, shows us in many ways how, even with increasing technologies in our everyday lives, our fears around the future and the unknown have not changed much. Not only in the eerie accuracy of Wiener's predictions regarding a technology that removes the sense of touch and reciprocity but also in humankind's propensity to view change and the unknown through a fearful lens, an idea echoed in other chapters too. Cassou-Noguès puts forth Wiener's ultimate question—what impact will futuristic technology have on human communication? His fears have perhaps come to fruition—although mobile technology and social media, for example, have brought us "closer" in the sense of constant contact, they have also removed reciprocity as an innate characteristic of human communication.

Cassou-Noguès also foreshadows concerns that mid-twentieth-century experts had with the future trajectory of intelligent machines. Speculation at the time seemed to suggest, according to his findings, that scientists of the time anticipated that their AI/robotic entities would be able to evince far more personality than apparently thus far has been the case. But what kind of world would we have with this mixed utopia-to-be were it to come to pass? Although such a question cannot be answered, we are able to get a cross-society perspective on how the emerging world of AI and robotics is likely to be perceived. This vision is provided by Petra Aczél in her chapter looking at future shock. Her perspective is further complemented by Cheong and Mossberger who look at several levels of the contemporary concerns about AI and the unfolding world of the Internet of Things (IoT).

Aczél discusses the reactions people have to change, particularly the accelerated technological change we are and have been experiencing in the first two decades of the twenty-first century. She explores this in relation to "future shock" as we experience an onslaught of new technological innovations which have the potential to dramatically change the ways we live our lives. Her outlook is a more positive one, concluding that humans are hard-wired to look toward the future and this, in turn, should reduce our fears.

One way in which we can prepare for the future is through policy development. Cheong and Mossberger discuss peoples' reactions to the Internet of Things and the increasingly datafied lives we lead through our devices, and how their responses can help shape policy. Many interviewees appreciated the importance of humankind remaining innovative and up-to-date with technology, both to "keep up with the times" in general as well as safeguarding one's professional life in which integrated technology continues to be the norm. The conversation also brought forth the pertinent topic of data privacy and the importance of policy and education to inform the populace of how their data is being stored—and used. There is a sense of running before we can walk in the race for new technology. Surely it makes more sense to put protective policies in place before the technology becomes ubiquitous and we come to depend on it?

These chapters have informed us less about what the future will be like and more about how various intellectual frameworks will help us to consider what the future may hold and how we will face it. While we will have to face our own personal comfort levels as AI becomes more human-like and more commonplace, we also need to consider the implications for society as a whole. As we continue to integrate technology into our daily lives, it will behoove us to study and inquire into the influence these processes have on human communication and our social interaction with not only the technology itself, but with one another.

Juxtaposed against a changing and increasingly technology-laden present, our contributors' range wide in their views of how people perceive the future. They include the unsettling, and justifiable, concerns as new technologies play an ever-larger role in our lives, and begin to exert influences over areas about which we have but little understanding and even less control. They include the understandable worries about how people will be able to make their way in the world, especially economically, as the reality they once knew disappears, replaced by a puzzling and potentially malicious mechanical and digital world, making them strangers in their own land.

Yet contributors also make the point that the future can be a source of pleasure, engagement, and wonderful enchantment. How precisely our personalized technology will fit into our lives remains a topic of speculation, informed nonetheless by the empirical research of Wang et al. That robots and AI will be part of our lives and loves seems in little doubt, if one extends the implications of Mays' and Jouhki's chapters. But it also includes the optimistic and uplifting perspective by Juliet Floyd. Her perspective is one that celebrates human potential and embraces the world of intelligent machines as perhaps the next phase in human social evolution.

Humans are remarkably adaptable, and there is no sound reason we should not welcome new technologies that improve our lives at profound and meaningful levels, or even at the level of amusement, entertainment, and enjoyment, for that matter. But, and it is an important but, we need to be assured that we will be on balance improving, not harming our lives and our societies. New, far-reaching technologies need to be considered in light of the long-term potential purported benefits and the likelihood they will materialize as promised. Of course there's no risk-free choice, and every decision comes with uncertainties, and there are also risks inherent in not taking action. Still, since ancient times profoundly meaningful legends have warned the world about Faustian bargains and Trojan horses, and even as today "Trojan malware" continues to bedevil us. In those premechanical eras, people were urged to be prudent about what they were embracing. Though far from perfect, nowadays we have tools to predict and understand the consequences of these new technologies. By drawing on research, we can better understand both the human significance of these technologies and their consequences for the decision-making process and their long-term societal significance. Through these efforts, we can create a better world on both the material and social interactional levels.

Index[1]

[1] Note: page numbers followed by 'n' refer to notes.

J. Katz et al. (eds.), *Perceiving the Future through New Communication Technologies*,
https://doi.org/10.1007/978-3-030-84883-5

The manufacturer's authorised representative in the EU is Springer Nature Customer Service Centre GmbH, Europaplatz 3, 69115 Heidelberg, Germany. If you have any concerns regarding our products, please contact ProductSafety@springernature.com

Printed and bound by CPI Group (UK) Ltd, Croydon, CR0 4YY

30/09/2026

02225492-0001